# COUNSELING
# AMERICAN INDIANS

## Laurence Armand French

**University Press of America, Inc.**
**Lanham • New York • London**

Copyright © 1997 by
**University Press of America,® Inc.**
4720 Boston Way
Lanham, Maryland 20706

12 Hid's Copse Rd.
Cummor Hill, Oxford OX2 9JJ

**Library of Congress Cataloging-in-Publication Data**

French, Laurence.
Counseling American Indians / Laurence Armand French.
p.   cm.
Includes bibliographical references and Index..
1. Indians of North America--Mental health services. 2. Indians of
North America--Mental health. 3. Indians of North America--
Counseling of. I. Title.
RC451.5.I5F73   1997   362.2'04256'08997--dc21   96-39394 CIP

ISBN 0-7618-0635-0 ( cloth: alk. ppr.)
ISBN 0-7618-0636-9 ( pbk: alk. ppr.)

# Contents

# Chapter 1

# Indians and Substance Abuse: The Major Clinical Issue

## Introduction

American Indians and Alaskan Natives have the highest rates of alcoholism and alcohol problems in the United States. Since World War II, when reliable data began to be collected, alcoholism has registered as the single most serious health problem among American Indians accounting for the four leading causes of death among members of this group: accidents; cirrhosis of the liver; suicide; and homicide. Other substances abused by American Indians include inhalants and tobacco (cigarettes and smokeless tobaccos) as well as other substances such as marijuana, stimulants, tranquilizers, hallucinogens and cocaine. Of all these substances, alcohol is the most widely abused followed by tobacco and inhalants (notably gasoline). Recently, the American Medical Association, the Department of Health and Human Services' Indian Health Service, and the U. S. Public Health Service have attempted to gauge the exact nature of this problem so that viable preventive and treatment programs could be designed and implemented. Large foundations such as Ford and Robert Wood Johnson have dedicated substantial proportions of their available grants to American Indian health and education. The Ford Foundation has established a grant for the

Navajo to eventually educate and certify 4,000 Indian teachers while the Robert Wood Johnson foundation has dedicated its grants since the late 1980s to Indian prevention projects relevant to health issues (mainly diabetes, alcoholism, tuberculosis control, alcohol and drug abuse, and injury. Thus, while substance abuse, notably alcoholism, is seen as the single most critical issue facing American Indians today, this has not always been the case. In this section we look at the nature of the problem from pre-Columbian times (aboriginal traditional cultural-ways) to the present. We will analyze the situation using P. Clayton Rivers' sociocultural thesis. Next we look at the phenomenon of fetal alcoholism (Fetal Alcohol Syndrome) and its role in the "cycle-of-abuse." Lastly, we present the case of an Indian FAS birth following his life from his adoption to the present.

In aboriginal times alcohol and other mind-altering agents were used in prescribed rituals. Even tobacco was controlled by prescription for socially-acceptable use along with proscriptions against abuse. Furst (1974) linked the use of natural elements in pre-Columbian (aboriginal) American Indian rituals in his book, *Flesh of the Gods.* Here, he noted that the ritualistic use of mushrooms, peyote, morning-glories and tobacco was for hallucinogenic communication with the spiritual world. Accordingly, the use of these mind-altering agents was mainly restricted to spiritual leaders within the tribe. Perhaps this proscription against common unsanctioned use is best illustrated with the aboriginal use of coca among the Incas. It is commonly believed that the Inca, the leader of the Incas, controlled the use of this agent -- Erythroxylon coca. Fermented corn beer was also popular among aboriginal Indian groups. Again, it seems that its use was strongly regulated and limited to socially-sanctioned events. Certain of these events allowed licentious drinking and behaviors as a form of sanctioned tension release much as Mardi Gras precedes Lent within Catholic societies. In what is now Mexico and the southwestern United States, pulque, a fermented alcoholic brew derived from the agave cactus, was probably even more popular than corn beer. Traditional Indian groups in North America maintain the use of many of these rituals while the movement back to traditionalism among other Indian groups is reintroducing these substances as prescribed rituals within their culture.

Many wonder how such a disparity between aboriginal and contemporary use of substances could exist. Perhaps this mystery is best explained by Rivers' thesis (1994) concerning sociocultural bases of substance use. (Although he applies his thesis to alcohol use and abuse, one can see its application to other substances as well.) Briefly stated, Rivers posits that within cultures and religious groups where substances are used with few social and health problems, the group ascribes to the following social norms:

1. There is a gradual socialization of children in the use of alcoholic beverages.
2. There is relatively low social pressure to drink.
3. The group has well established, negative sanctions against excessive drinking.
4.There are positive, accepting attitudes toward moderate, nondestructive drinking.
5. There is a well-established consensus on the customs of drinking.
6. There is freedom from ambivalence in the drinking situation. By the same token, cultures and religious groups where high-risk for substance abuse is likely share the following social attributes.
1. There is a high social pressure to drink.
2. There are inconsistent or nonexistent social sanctions against drunkenness.
3. The goals of drinking are utilitarian or convivial.
4. There are ambivalent attitudes and feelings toward moderate drinking.
5. There is a total prohibition against drinking.

From this analysis we can see how aboriginal, traditionalism provided for socially acceptable prescriptions (ritualistic use) along with strong proscriptions against illicit use. Rivers applied his thesis to the larger U.S. society stating that drinking was the norm during the colonial period where rum, beer, wine and cider was served in lieu of contaminated surface water. Rivers noted that the American Puritans had a reputation for excessive devotion to drink but that social problems and alcoholism were not prevalent due to the proscriptions against public drunkenness. The social prescriptions allowed children to drink along with adults but no one was allowed more than a half pint of brew at a time and and no one was allowed to drink in a tavern for longer that a half hour. Moreover, no drinking was allowed after 9:00 P.M.

Abusive drinking in America was linked to its economic exploitation. Along with this came a relaxation of both the social prescriptions for drinking and the proscriptions against abuse. Rivers links this abuse to both the slave trade and barter with American Indians for furs. Another factor that was introduced during this period was that of distilled whiskey. Now we have greatly increased the potency of alcohol along with reducing sanctions regarding its use. Once alcohol was introduced to American Indians in substantial amounts and uncontrolled circumstances the traditional norms regulating substance use were abandoned making existing tribal folkways more difficult to enforce. Tribes soon felt the need to request outside help from the very society that posed this problem. During the late 1700s and early 1800s, Tribes appealed to the federal governmnent for intervention stating that whites were violating treaties and trading liquor illegally within Indian Country.

A number of responses followed. The Trade and Intercourse Act of March 30, 1802 was the first such endeavor. This replaced the temporary trade and intercourse acts passed in 1790, 1796 and 1799 and remained in effect until it was replaced by a new code in 1834. Its basic function was to establish the boundaries of Indian country and levy fines for whites who trespassed as well as criminal sanctions for whites who committed criminal offenses on tribal lands. An important element of this Act was the prohibition of alcohol as a medium of trade between white traders and Indians (U.S. Statutes at Large, 1802). This set the stage for the most stringent form of temperance in U.S. history -- the Trade and Intercourse Act of 1834. This Act enforced federal prohibition in Indian Country for one hundred and nineteen years (1834-1953).

This Act addressed civil and legal issues much like its predecessor but went further in addressing the issue of alcohol. Section 20 stipulated: "That if any person shall sell, exchange, or give, barter, or dispose of, any spirituous liquor or wine to an

Indian in Indian country, such person shall forfeit and pay the sum of five hundred dollars...," Section 21 made it illegal for any person to run a distillery in Indian country. Indeed, the only alcohol allowed in Indian country was that designated for the white administrators and for non-Indian military personnel (U.S. Statutes at Large, 1834).

During this time, a number of other federal actions served to disrupt aboriginal traditionalism. Among them was the forced removal during the 1830s of most Indian groups east of the Mississippi River to Indian Territory (Oklahoma) and Texas. During the 1860s, plains tribes were also removed from their traditional lands to Oklahoma. Removal was followed by Allotment. Here, Indian Territory (Oklahoma) was opened to white settlers (allotted land grants) with the attempt at dissolving tribal recognition. Initiated in 1887 and ending with Oklahoma statehood in 1907, General Allotment was a blatant attempt at cultural genocide -- an attempt to destroy any semblance of Indian traditionalism that survived removal (U.S. Statutes at Large, 1887; 1891; 1893; 1898).

Indian citizenship came in 1924, nearly sixty years after blacks were granted this right. Citizenship was followed with an attempt to again protect tribal lands and establish Indian country as a federal protectorate. This was done through Reorganization, better known as the Wheeler-Howard Act of 1934. Indian Reorganization was augmented with the Johnson-O'Malley Act which promoted federal support for the public education of Indian children and youth (U.S. Statutes at Large, 1934a; 1934b).

This progressive era ended less than two decades later with the combined devastation of Termination and Relocation. During the Eisenhower administration, attempts were made to terminate Indian country reverting the land to the states and treating tribal resources as exploitable property. Relocation, on the other hand, was the effort to get young Indians off the reservations, away from their traditional language and culture, and to place them in urban ghettos. The former was a dire failure and was itself officially terminated in 1973 with the Menominee Restoration Act while the former resulted in the establishment of Urban Indian Centers regulated by a separate federal agency --

Administration of Native Americans (U.S. Statutes at Large, 1953a; 1953b; 1973). Ruport Costo and Jeannette Henry, of the Indian Historical Society, viewed termination and relocation as the crassest example of government ignorance of the Indian situation: "The 'Indian problem' did not go away. It worsened. The policies of the Eisenhower administration, which espoused the termination of federal-Indian relationship, was shown to be a failure, a gross injustice added to a history of injustice" (Costo & Henry, 1977:42).

This brings us to the end of Indian prohibition in 1953. The U.S. Congress now determined that American Indians could drink legally off-reservation and that now tribal governments could decide whether alcohol would be legal on their particular reservation. Clearly, the repeal of Indian prohibition was part and parcel of termination. The idea was that if state, and not federal, control was to be the norm, then this control had to be extended to the legal use of alcohol. When it became evident that termination was doomed to failure, the federal government put pressure on tribes to vote against legalizing alcohol in Indian country. Indeed, only a few tribes have elected to do so and this has occurred only recently. The new impetus to legalizing drinking on the reservation is closely linked to gaming in Indian county. The most common scenario since repeal of Indian prohibition has been the emergence of "drunk towns" immediately off the reservation. White Clay and Valentine, Nebraska and Gallup, New Mexico are examples of off-reservation drunk towns where Indians migrate for binge drinking. The Nebraska towns serve the "dry" Pine Ridge and Rosebud Sioux reservations while Gallup serves the "dry" Navajo Nation and Zuni Pueblo.

These and other federal policies, including prohibition in Indian country, were basically designed to destroy Indian traditionalism and, at best, replace it with Christianity. This is known as "cultural genocide." In competition with cultural genocide was the more devastating policy of "physical genocide" better known by the statement -- "the only good Indian is a dead Indian." Physical genocide ended as an official policy in the late 1890s with the Wounded Knee massacre and the murder, while in captivity, of Crazy Horse and Sitting Bull. For the survivors in Indian country, the twentieth century has been a long, rough road where they have been forced to walk in two worlds without belonging fully to either. This is the most devastating element of cultural genocide. It produces Indian marginality for many Indians, mainly those who do have access to their language and traditional customs. Erik Erikson studied this phenomenon in the late 1930s and early 1940s. He termed this process "identity confusion." Identity confusion, according to Erikson, is due to the sense of uprootedness from one's traditional Indian culture which then results in a lack of a clear self-image or identity (Schultz, 1990). Accordingly, "marginality" in this book is defined as cultural and personal ambiguity resulting in identity confusion (a poor sense of one's Indianism). This will be discussed throughout the book.

When applying Rivers' thesis to the contemporary American Indian situation we see that the traditional prescriptions for meaningful use of substances has been greatly eroded. Moreover, over a century of proscriptions against alcohol has created an environment conducive to high-risk abuse. Part of this problem is the marked differences which exist between the western norms governing the larger dominant U.S. society, those based upon the tenets of the Protestant Ethic, and the values of aboriginal traditionalism, those based on the Harmony Ethos. The western values, which the U.S. has long tried to impose on American Indians values individual culpability and responsibility as well as competition and materialism. The Harmony Ethos departs from this world-view in that traditional Indians believe in cooperation and living in harmony with nature. The aboriginal Harmony Ethos is comprised of a complex social code whereby individual freedom was checked by tribal folkways. These folkways, in turn, were designed to provide balance and purpose within the group. Within the Harmony Ethos, Mother Earth is seen as the source of all life while Father Sky is viewed as the source that sustains life (fire, rain, wind). Respect for, and cooperation with, nature is a critical element of this belief system. In order to accomplish this balance with nature and within the group certain behavioral traits emerged common to North American Indians.

   1. The avoidance of overt hostilities regarding interpersonal matters and an emphasis on nonaggressiveness in intrafamilial/clan/tribal interactions.
   2. The use of a neutral third person, or intermediary, for

resolving personal altercations (avoidance of direct confrontations).
3. A high value placed on independence (personal freedom to act as long as one conforms to tribal folkways and avoids taboos).
4. A resentment of authority (leaders commanded respect as against demanding submission).
5. A hesitancy to command others.
6. Caution in interactions with other persons (culturally based shyness with strangers).
7. A reluctance to refuse favors and an emphasis on generosity (the "give away" best illustrates this behavioral attribute).
8. A reluctance to voice opinions publicly.
9. Avoidance of eye and body contact (handshakes, back slapping, and the like) when interacting with others.
10. Emphasis placed on group cooperation and not on individual competition (the individual excels via the group and not alone).
11. Deference to elders: "old equals good equals honor."
12. Challenging life in the raw (exploring life first hand for the sake of the experience aka "counting coup").
(French & Hornbuckle, 1981).

This value system strongly supported the traditional prescriptions for ritualistic use of substances while providing sufficient proscriptions against their abuse. Once prescribed customs were outlawed by the federal government there existed few proscriptions other than prohibition which was imposed on them by an alien culture. Add identity confusion to this formula and we have the ingredients for high-risk substance abuse. Ruben Snake, a respected Indian elder, expressed this phenomenon among his people in testimony to the American Indian Policy Review Commission:

> The American Indian and Alaska native are caught in a world wherein they are trying to find out who they are and where they are, and where they fit. The land which was once their 'mother,' giving them food and clothing was taken. Their spiritual strengths were decried as pagan, and familial ties were broken.

...The Indian people of today are proud of their heritage and are fighting to maxim its influence upon their lives in a dominant white world. Many have not. ...(The) destructive use of alcohol and drugs ...is inextricably interwoven into all aspects of their lives and any effort to alleviate the problem must be comprehensive in scope and with the full commitment of the Indian people (Snake, 1976:13).

Alcohol abuse within the U.S. remains highest among American Indian and Native Alaskan groups. The data indicate that the Navajo (Dine'), the single largest tribe in the U.S., have lower rates than the total U.S. population but those who do drink are quite visible in that they migrate to Gallup, New Mexico, nationally known as "Drunk Town, USA." Hence, we can see how the "drunken Indian stereotype" emerges even when this image is not representative of the majority of tribal members. On the other hand, the Utes, Ojibwas and Sioux have very high drinking and alcoholism rates. In addition to alcohol American Indians are disproportionately represented in the use and abuse of inhalants (mainly gasoline sniffing), snuff, and marijuana. It is estimated that many American Indian youth use these "gateway" drugs prior to alcohol. Once alcohol is introduced on a regular basis it becomes the prime substance of choice while still being augmented with these other substances, notably snuff. Gasoline is reserved for times when alcohol is not available. It is the "cheap drunk" and causes the most damage in terms of physical health. Marijuana use tends to drop off with adulthood. (Beauvais, et. al., 1989; Berlin, 1987; May, 1982; Medicine, 1982; Young, 1988).

## Fetal Alcoholism

Fetal alcoholism is termed the most preventable serious birth disorder. The term, not the syndrome, is relatively new being coined in 1973 by D. W. Smith and K. L. Jones to describe the cluster of defects associated with alcohol abuse during pregnancy. We now realize that these births, prior to this classification, were often listed as "unknown" or "unspecified" etiologies. Fetal Alcohol Syndrome is currently listed in both the *Classification in Mental Retardation*, the medical/clinical standard for the American Association on Mental Deficiency, and in the *Diagnostic and Statistical Manual*, the standard for psychiatry, psychology, counseling, nursing, and social work (Grossman, 1983; APA, 1994).  The basic features of FAS include facial anomalies, heart defects, low birth weight, behavioral problems and even mental retardation.  Other physical problems may include the following:

1. Hearing problems.
2. Clumsiness and poor fine and gross motor coordination.
3. Short stature and small size.
4. Malformed or misaligned teeth.
5. Spinal deformity (scoliosis).
6. Sensory awareness problems (hypersensitive or hyposensitive).
7. Small head (microcephaly).
8. Altered palm crease patterns.
9. Poor visual-motor coordination.
10. Seizures

These physical symptoms impact upon educational, behavioral and social functioning:

1. Inability to structure time in school and at home.
2. Perservation, distractibility; poor attention span.
3. Poor memory; difficulty learning from past experiences.
4. Impaired rate of learning, especially arithmetic.
5. Low motivation; low tolerance to stress; poor problem- solving skills.
6. Learning disabled--some mentally retarded.
7. Behaviorally disorganized; poor social judgment, impulsive; easily influenced; social immaturity.
8. Hyperactivity; self-stimulation.
9. Speech delays; over-talkative; stuttering and stammering; articulation difficulties.
10. Problems with interpersonal interactions; attachment to strangers; difficulty getting along with caretakers and peers.

Some of the best and earliest research on the effects of fetal alcoholism is being conducted at the Boston University School of Medicine. Their research indicates that the effect of alcohol on the fetus is not equal for all women. In fact, it is dose related according to a number of bio-cultural factors. The critical factors appear to be: (1) gestational stage at time of exposure; (2) fetal susceptibility to alcohol; (3) maternal nutrition; and (4) chronicity of the mother's alcohol abuse, and the prevalence of stress and anxiety in the mother's life. Accordingly, the risk of having a child with FAS may increase with the addition of each mediating factor (Weiner, Morse, & Garrido, 1989).

Norma Finklestein (1990) noted a number of stress factors associated with substance-abusing women. These include:

1. A poor self-image, especially their sexual image (whore or lush).
2. Feelings of powerlessness and learned helplessness.
3. Stormy relationships with men, including violence and abuse.
4. Labile (anger, depression, guilt, shame, stigma, dependence).

Women who drink within social environments with these factors present have a high FAS probability (up to 85%). On the other hand, women who drink (moderately), with the absence of these factors, the probability is very low (less than 2%). The implication here is that well nourished, mentally and physically healthy women who drink moderately have only a slight chance of having a FAS birth (Weiner, Morse, & Garrido, 1989).

What accounts for the dramatic jump from 2% to 85%? We now feel that PTSD (the Post-traumatic Stress Disorder) plays a critical role in this cycle-of-abuse. The symbiosis of a culture of poverty, marginality and alcoholism appears to account for the high rate of FAS/PTSD among American Indians and Native Alaskans. This relationship between FAS and PTSD is based on the contention that a FAS birth is a traumatic birth. The birth trauma and PTSD relationship is a relatively new approach within the clinical field in that FAS was recognized in 1973 while PTSD became part of the clinical literature in 1980 with the *Diagnostic and Statistical Manual, Third Edition* (APA, 1980). PTSD is defined as a recognizable stressor that would bring stress to anyone suffering from this situation. Associated features include:

1. A markedly diminished interest in one or more
significant activities.
2. Feelings of detachment or estrangement from others.
3. Constricted affect.
4. Hyperalertness and an overexaggerated startle
response.
5. Sleep disturbance.
6. Memory impairment or trouble concentrating.
7. An intensification of symptoms when exposed to an
event that symbolized or resemble the traumatic event.
(In this case, alcohol abuse by those traumatized by a
FAS birth -- maintaining the cycle-of-abuse).

Reviewing both the FAS list of symptoms and those of PTSD we
can see the close similarities between these clinical disorders.

This relationship between FAS and PTSD came to light in the
1980s when clinicians, treating violent (aggressive/suicidal)
adolescents for substance abuse, found that a substantial
number of these youth were victims of early-life trauma (prenatal,
neonatal, infancy, and early childhood stages) and that drinking,
or other forms of self-medication (substance abuse), appeared to
be an associated clinical feature of this unresolved trauma.
Within this relationship, substance abuse is seen as an attempt to
cope with the unresolved anxiety surrounding the unknown or
unrecognizable early trauma.  Fetal alcoholism is clearly one of
the most significant, in both frequency and intensity, of these
unrecognizable early traumas.  The FAS/PTSD relationship helps
explain the cycle-of-abuse which surrounds these forms of early
traumas.  Those who were abused as children abuse their own
children; those who were born under the influence of alcohol
give birth to their own children under the influence.

The FAS problem among American Indians and Native Alaskans
was cited in the 1986 Congressional Hearing on "Native
American Children, Youth, and Families," presented before the
U.S. House of Representatives', Select Committee on Children,
Youth, and Families.  Part of this document was a study on
"Epidemiology of Fetal Alcohol Syndrome among American
Indians of the Southwest."  The findings indicated that the
mothers of FAS children led highly disruptive and chaotic lives
and were frequently isolated from mainstream social activities.
Indian Health Service indicates that the Plains Indians have the

highest FAS rate of any Indian group in the U.S. Of the Plains Indians, the Aberdeen Area has some of the highest FAS and substance abuse problems, not only among American Indians but in the entire nation. The Aberdeen Area is comprised of sixteen tribes (most Siouan groups) in a four-state area: North and South Dakota, Nebraska, and Iowa. Within the district, it is estimated that nearly all children, adolescent and young adults are at high risk for mental health problems setting the stage for a continued need for self-medication and a continuation of the FAS/PTSD cycle-of-abuse.

Finally, in 1992, the respected Journal of the American Medical Association (JAMA) confirmed the suspected FAS/PTSD link, relating it to American Indian/Alaskan Native youth. In this article, the authors noted the following: "American Indian-Alaska Native adolescents reported high rates of health-compromising behaviors and risk factors related to unintentional injury, substance use, poor self-assessed health status, emotional distress, and suicide." These are clear indicators of the Post-traumatic Stress Disorder. The JAMA article went on: "Interventions must be culturally sensitive, acknowledge the heterogeneity of Indian populations, be grounded in cultural traditions that promote health, and be developed with full participation of the involved communities (tribes) (Blum, et. al., 1992: 1637-1644)."

Another illustration of FAS and PTSD was that of Michael Dorris' award winning (1989 National Book Critic's Circle Award) book, *The Broken Cord*, about his adopted Indian son, Reynold Abel Dorris. A Dartmouth College professor and part Indian (Modoc), Professor Dorris unwittingly adopted his son as an FAS infant. This was when FAS was first being recognized as a serious syndrome. Yet, it is quite likely that federal agencies, such as Indian Health Service (IHS) and the Bureau of Indian Affairs (BIA), knew that many of these adoptees were seriously impaired. Dorris details the difficulties his son suffered as well as the trials and tribulations he and his ex- and current wife suffered over the years (Dorris, 1989). Clearly, this is a case study in a FAS engendered Post-traumatic Stress Disorder. Ironically, his son was killed by a car two years later on September 22, 1992 as he walked along a road in Hanover, New Hampshire. He was twenty-three. In a similar vein, we present a FAS/PTSD case of an

Indian male who, like Reynold Dorris, was adopted shortly after birth and brought up in New Hampshire.

## Little Hawk

Little Hawk was born on December 4, 1969 in Indian Country in Alaska. He is a full-blooded Athapaskan Indian (kin to the Navajo and Apache). He was adopted at age 4 months by an upper-middle-class mixed-race couple. This was a federally-sanctioned adoption. Both of his new parents were in their late twenties. The mother is an anglo whose father was a physician. Little Hawk's new father came from Japan, the son of a wealthy family. He eventually became a U.S. citizen. Little Hawk's new parents met while his father attended Yale University and his mother was a student at what was then Southern Connecticut State College (since absorbed into the state university system). The couple shared the liberal sentiments of the time and opted to adopt difficult to place children. Both of their children were adopted. The first was a Japanese/anglo girl. Then they adopted Little Hawk. The girl, other than being short of stature, was a normal infant and grew up to be a healthy teen and adult.

Little Hawk, on the other hand, was a different story. The new parents were told that Little Hawk had "some health" problems. These health problems included a low birth weight (4 pounds, 4 ounces) despite a full-term delivery. He had a hairy, small head (microcephalic), seizures, excessive hair growth (hirsutism), and defective bladder and kidneys. He also suffered from childhood hyperactivity which he finally outgrew at puberty. His mother and the schools noted a host of other problems. These included inappropriate friendliness to strangers, impulsivity, learning disabilities and problems with organizational skills. His educational progress apparently peaked in middle school and his seizures continued into adulthood. He is naive and can not handle a checkbook, money or finances. He has been caught shoplifting. He harbors inappropriate expectations for independence, schooling, and a profession. He repeats past mistakes. Regarding the latter, his mother noted that he seeks a geographic solution to problems (move someplace else and start over). Having known Little Hawk his entire life, I can verify these attributes. As is readily evident, these attributes clearly fit the FAS/PTSD classifications.

Little Hawk (his Indian name) went through school with a confused identity in that his parents gave him an Hispanic first name to go with his Japanese last name. Many of his peers thought that he was either Hispanic or Asian. Later, Little Hawk's parents divorced but remained involved with both adopted children. At nineteen, we attempted to find out more about his tribal affiliation. The Bureau of Indian Affairs responded, notifying him of his blood degree (4/4), his tribal identification (enrollment number), and his Village Corporation (Ahtna, Inc.). They also stated that his parents were alive and that they had more children after him. The implication was that Little Hawk was the only child placed into adoption. They also provided him with his birth name and the names of his parents and bother and sisters. Obviously, this was a traumatic revelation. It seemed that he needed to connect with traditional Indians from a culture similar to his as soon as possible. New Hampshire was a poor place for this to happen. First, the state has no recognized (state or federal) Indian groups residing within its borders. Secondly, the so-called "Indians" in New Hampshire are mainly "wanna-bees" -- pseudo-Indians or those who are part-Indian but have no tribal or language linkage to any viable Indian group.

Immediately following these disclosures about his biological family, I left to take a position in southwestern New Mexico. I invited Little Hawk to come and stay with me for a while. His mother was supportive of this effort especially since she was beside herself in attempting to deal with him basically singlehandedly since he was 9 (that was when she and her husband divorced). She never remarried. It is only fair to say that she did as much as possible to deal with Little Hawk's problems. She supported my effort to get him off Dilantin and on Tegretol for his seizures especially since the former tended to dull one's cognitive capacity while the latter did not. She felt that she did what she could and now hoped for a miraculous transformation from a troubled childhood and teen years into an autonomous, and hopefully self-sufficient, adulthood.

Little Hawk drove cross country with a friend who dropped him off and quickly left with fifty dollars of his. He arrived just in time for the State's first "Indian week" (proclaimed by the Governor to be recognized March 18 - 24). Being the faculty advisor for the Indian Club at Western New Mexico University, the club had a week of events planned, including lectures by prominent Indian leaders and a pow wow. This was Little Hawk's first exposure to real Indian activities outside of what he read about. He quickly became absorbed in the activities, interacting and asking numerous questions. He was well liked and readily adopted into the Indian Club. The high point of this experience was when one of the Indian leaders took him into the hills for a coming out ritual (a vision quest of sorts). It was at this time that Little Hawk made the transformation from a child to a man. This is when he received his first exposure to his "Indianism." This is when he became "Little Hawk."

This would make an excellent ending to this story -- if in fact Little Hawk became a viable member of the Navajo or Apache, but this was not to be. Unable to get BIA funding for school, Little Hawk was soon frustrated and again left the area. This time he went back to New Hampshire for a short time and then went to live with family friends in Florida. During his eight-month stay in Florida, his mental health deteriorated and he was compelled to return to New Hampshire suffering from a serious psychotic break that required immediate hospitalization. Part of this problem seems to be related to the fact that Little Hawk took it upon himself to discontinue his seizure medications. The initial stage of his Involuntary Emergency Hospitalization (IEH) was for a three-week period in the psychiatric ward at a community hospital. The hospital stated that: "This has been the first psychiatric hospitalization for this 21-year-old single male, who had developed bizarre behavior after returning from an 8-month stay in Florida, where he had been residing with friends. Prior to admission he had been listless and uncommunicative, had displayed impaired sleep, crying spells, and appeared preoccupied with matters that he would not openly discuss. ...Even with medication, the patient continued to appear extremely depressed, preoccupied, and psychotic. He was clearly preoccupied with matters that he would not openly discuss, and appeared to be having auditory hallucinations. Concentration was grossly impaired, short term memory was impaired, and abstract thinking ability was also impaired."

Having been held as long as he could at this facility, he was transferred to the State Hospital, again as an involuntary emergency admission. The condition on Discharge was unimproved and the prognosis was guarded. He was on Tegretol (anticonvulsant), Prozac (antidepressive), Trilafon (antipsychotic) and Cogentin (anticholinergic). His stay was for two weeks (he attempted an unauthorized leave during this time). Again the symptoms include blank stare, flat affect, soft voice, speech latency with tangentiality and paucity of content, depressed mood (without suicide ideations), preoccupation with feelings of guilt for past transgressions, paucity of movement, low energy level, apathetic, poor concentration, decreased attention span, impaired short-term memory, poor insight, periods of confusion, sleep disturbance, appetite loss, crying spells, periods of unresponsiveness, and bizarre responses. Little Hawk's diagnosis at Discharge from the State Hospital was as follows:

DSM-III-R Diagnosis
Axis I:   Rule out Major Depression, Single Episode with
          psychotic symptoms, mood congruent.
          Rule out Schizophreniform Disorder.
Axis II:  Deferred (Learning disability by history)
Axis III: History of kidney malfunction.

Little Hawk was now transferred to one of the regional community mental health facilities for out-patient care. His medications remained as prescribed at his first hospitalization. This was the fall of 1991 when Little Hawk was 21 years old. He was described as being homeless and unemployed. Initially he was placed in a shelter administered by the community mental health facility. Here his treatment plan included:

1. Community resource needs: housing with case management.
2. Medications, supportive psychotherapy, support group.
3. Family involvement in treatment.

An interesting error across all mental health facilities was the classification of Little Hawk as being "white" despite the obvious fact that he is a full-blooded American Indian and looks like a full-blooded Indian.

Little Hawk and I met each spring and summer while I was in the area. During this past visit (1993), we had an opportunity to tape an interview.  Also, during this time, he finally received his social security supplementary income and was assigned to a private home in the same city serviced by the community mental health facility.  He had only been there a few months when he announced that the landlady had told him that she "loved" him.  This was Little Hawk's first intimate relationship and he pursued it despite over twenty years difference in age, not to mention inexperience (his new love has a son Little Hawk's age), between him and his new girlfriend.  Little Hawk brought his new girlfriend with him to the state's only Indian center -- the Abenaki Indian Center.  On the surface, this would seem like a poor mix but eight months later they are still together, Little Hawk is off all his medications and SSI, and he has held a job longer than ever in the past. (He works with his girlfriend as an unskilled laborer.)  Perhaps the best indicator of Little Hawk's degree of marginality and the continued impact of his FAS birth, is the interview I had with him in June, 1993.  I am 'LF' and Little Hawk is 'LH'.

## Interview with Little Hawk

LF:     Little Hawk, we've known each other for....
LH:     Twenty-three years.
LF:     Yeah, all your life.
LF:     One of the most interesting things during this time was when we were trying to find out about your family, you know, who you were prior to your adoption.  How do you feel about that?
LH:     It was important to know about my heritage in general.  It wasn't important to know the specifics of it.  I mean, I don't have a real desire right now to meet my original parents, but it's always in the back of my mind.
LF:     Well, you knew that you were an American Indian and adopted.
        What did you think were the circumstances of you being adopted?
LH:     I'm not really sure.  I guess my parents, my original parents, couldn't or felt they couldn't provide for me so they gave me up for adoption.
LF:     But it was only four years ago that you found out that

your mother and father are still alive and that you have brothers and sisters.

LH: Yeah, I have two sisters and one brother.

LF: And they're all older than you, right?

LH: The brother is younger, I believe.

LF: Before that you didn't know if your parents were alive or dead.

LH: Right.

LF: After that you came to New Mexico. This was the closest you got to Indian Country since your birth.

LH: Right. That was at Western New Mexico University. I met the Indian students and one of them took me out to the mountains.

LH: I don't remember his name.

LF: Peter Garcia. He's Hopi.

LH: He and I sat on a large rock and smoked a pipe and he explained the significance of the ceremony that we'd undergone.

LF: Right. And that was your rite-of-passage. That was your Indian rite-of-passage.

LH: He said there was an introduction from me to the Creator. Now the Creator knows of my presence upon the earth.

LF: And that was important to you.

LH: Very important.

LF: Before that all you had was the piece of bear meat that I saved for you.

LH: Yeah.

LF: It was from an adolescent bear. And it was like you, an adolescent male. You got to eat some of that meat. That's the way it's supposed to be in the Indian culture; you don't destroy anything without giving something back.

LH: I've never done a Sweat or a Vision Quest. I might do it this summer.

LH: I remember you and I talking about the Vision Quest.

LF: Right. I also stated that the purification Sweat comes first.

LF: I take it that these things are important aspects of life since going to New Mexico and getting in touch with your brothers and sisters.

LH:     Yeah, it's very important to me to have a sense of
        belonging to my people.

LF:     And then we went up north and met that Micmac family,
        Fawn, her father, and her Navajo boyfriend, Leon Haskel.
        That was another link between Arizona, New Mexico and
        New Hampshire. Remember, Fawn and Leon went to
        Navajo Community College.

LH:     Yeah. Do you know anything about a medicine school
        out west?

LF:     Well, for what? Medicine Men?

LH:     Uh huh. Cause I've read in a book called *Profiles in
        Wisdom* that there is a school out west somewhere
        where you can go to train to be a medicine man.

LF:     Well, my understanding is that you are selected
        internally, from your people, and that somebody who
        already knows the medicine takes you under his
        supervision and you go through an apprenticeship. That
        is how tribal medicine is usually conveyed from one
        generation to the next. Now, while you are an
        Athapaskan and the Navajo are Athapaskan, and the
        Apache are Athapaskan, you would have to be adopted
        into one of these groups prior to even being considered
        for such an apprenticeship. I not aware of any school
        where you learn how to be a medicine man.

LH:     Uh huh.

LF:     Am I correct in understanding that you would like to go
        back to Indian country?

LH:     Are you talking about Alaska or New Mexico?

LF:     New Mexico.

LH:     Yeah. I plan to go back. Maybe to the Navajo Community
        College.

LF:     That's good. If you went to the main campus, it's close to
        Canyon de Chelley, Tse'yi', and there's a lot of medicine
        in that area. I understand that the canyon is supposed to
        be a very strong healing place.

LH:     Cause that's something that would interest me.

LF:     And you'd like to relate that to the human services that
        you're interested right now?

LH:     Uh huh. I plan to be a... a clinical psychologist.

LF:     Uh huh.

LH:     Part of the trouble of growing up in the "white man's
        world"   is I was often mistaken by my... my race was
        often mistaken  for another.  I was often thought to be
        Japanese or Chinese or Hawaiian or Filipino or Mexican.
        It wasn't until I went out west with you that people could
        see that I was Indian, and they'd know it instantly. They
        would look at me and say: "You're an Indian.  How could
        you be anything else?"  They recognized the features.
        When I was growing up, there was nobody around to
        recognize the features.  And it was a shame, really.

LF:     You're right.  I remember how you were welcomed when
        we had our special Indian week at Western.

LH:     Yeah, and you were having the pow wow the day I
        arrived.  There was a lot of dancing going on when I was
        there.

LF:     Right.  You came at an ideal time.  And you're right;
        people  noticed you right away.  And there was no
        question about it, who you were, and it's like you were
        family.  I noticed that. Everybody just accepted you.  It
        must have been a very unique experience.

LH:     Yeah, it was the most peace I'd felt in a while.

LF:     How do you contrast that with what happening to you
        now?

LH:     Right now I'm having a bit of an identity crisis.  I've been
        going to the Abenaki Indian Center in Manchester and
        when I go there I hear of all the Indians talking about the
        troubles that the Indians are having now with their land
        rights and their blood degrees, and I've heard how some
        of the Indians who are Indians... when they were born, as
        a favor to their family, the people in the records would
        write down that they were white because it wasn't... it just
        wasn't fashionable to be an Indian at this time, and being
        an Indian would be a disadvantage.  So they often
        thought that they'd be doing the Indians a favor by
        putting down on the birth certificate that they were
        actually white.  And when I go to these socials, I realize
        how out of touch I am with the Indian people, and it
        bothers me.

LF:     There is no question about your blood degree.  Maybe
        it's because you came from Alaska and your tribal group

may have been more insulated, but it is clearly stated that
you're full blooded.  They stated it as four fourths
because they have always used fractions to
describe blood degrees.

LH:     Uh huh.

LF:     And of course the Navajo, Apache and many other Indian
groups kept pretty good records.

How does it feel going to the Abenaki Indian Center?

LH:     I feel... I feel a lot of love from the people that are there.  I
feel very at peace when I'm there.  I've often thought of
just giving up this Portsmouth life and moving to
Manchester where I can be closer to the Indian people of
New Hampshire, but it's just not very feasible right now.

LH:     Well, I'd like to be more in touch with the plight that the
Indian people are going through right now.

LF:     Given your choice, which area would be more beneficial
to you, the Abenaki group in Manchester or the Indians
of Arizona and New Mexico?

LH:     Well, it would probably be more beneficial for me right
now to be in New Mexico, because I would have blood
ties there, and I could go through a lot of the rituals that a
man who would have grown up in his own tribe would go
through, none   of which I've had, except for the
introduction of the Creator.

LF:     It seems to me that your short stay in New Mexico was
important to you and that you probably did not realize its
significance until you got to Florida.

LH:     A lot of people in Florida thought I was Mexican.

LF:     So that just contributed to your identity crisis problem.

LH:     Uh huh.

LH:     One thing I'd like to pressure the Alaskan government for
is my land. I had land in Alaska.  I'm not sure how much
land, but it's valued at around two thousand dollars
because...  and I was never given the choice as to
whether I wanted that land or not.  It was just sold from
underneath me.

LF:     Did they send you the money?

LH:     My mother put that in a CD for me a long time ago.

LF:     Your mother, meaning your adopted mother?

LH:     Yeah.  And it kind of bothers me that I didn't have a

|       |                                                                                 |
|-------|---------------------------------------------------------------------------------|
|       | choice whether I wanted that land or not.                                       |
| LF:   | And if you had a choice, would you consider going to Alaska?                     |
| LH:   | Definitely.                                                                      |
| LF:   | You would go back to Alaska.                                                     |
| LH:   | Yes.                                                                             |
| LF:   | Do you still think that a trip to Alaska is in the future?                       |
| LH:   | Without a doubt. A lot of people tell me that it would be very therapeutic, a trip to Alaska, it would be like going home. But I've looked into some of the prices that it's going to cost and we're looking at well over a thousand dollars just to get there, and then we'd have to probably rent a car, and I'd need to bring somebody from here, so as not to insult any of the natives, because they have their own system and I could be seen as an outsider until they came to understand who I was. |
| LF:   | What makes you think that that's how it would work?                             |
| LH:   | Because I've not been among them since I was two months old. I mean, obviously I didn't have a choice in the matter. |
| LF:   | Right.                                                                           |
| LH:   | But that doesn't change the facts. My godmother has told me that I would need somebody with me. |
| LF:   | Okay, who's your godmother?                                                      |
| LH:   | That'd be Sharon Hunt.                                                           |
| LF:   | Has Sharon Hunt been to Alaska?                                                  |
| LH:   | No. but she has a friend who she said would go with me. I was planning on making the trip this summer, but right now money is the biggest problem. |
| LF:   | Now, you're not sure that Sharon Hunt is Indian or not, right? |
| LH:   | No. I don't. I don't believe she is. She may be.                                |
| LF:   | But she runs the Abenaki Indian Center in Manchester.                            |
| LH:   | Yeah.                                                                            |
| LF:   | Another approach would be to go there and introduce yourself. Once there, open your arms, admit that you do not know your cultural ways but that you want to learn. State that you are a son of your tribe, present your tribal number and your papers. They will see that you have a heritage, a lineage and then just take it from there. You |

       may not need someone who is of questionable heritage
       to introduce to your own people.

LH:   Uh huh.

LH:   Well, I still plan to be a practicing psychologist... to work
       with my people.

LF:   Well good luck to you.

LH:   It was good talking to you, Larry.

  Although articulate, Little Hawk seems to jump from one grand plan to the next. His godmother, the Director of the Abenaki Indian Center, claims to be Ojibway. There is a marked difference between the members of the Abenaki Indian Center and the Indians of the southwest -- most of whom are at least half-blooded. Obviously, this socio-cultural confusion does little to help Little Hawk deal with his cultural identity. Despite his special education background, he took some community college courses with mixed results. He did poorly in math and English in the state-run community college system but was able to produce an improved grade point when he transferred to a private, two-year, business college. His highest grade out of four courses, over two semesters, was an A-. It was in Introduction to Psychology. I realize my mentoring efforts may perhaps have an influence in this proposed career goal, yet, it is unlikely that he will ever be able to complete the rigors associated with an approved doctoral program.

  And, while his life seems to be stable at this time, this is not to say that he will be able to cope with future crises. Substance abuse may still become a problem in his life. It seems that Little Hawk has finally found love, if only for the present. As with any FAS client with serious associated features, the prognosis for Little Hawk is guarded at best. Continued bouts of mental illness and even substance abuse are likely factors in his life.

  The remainder of the book looks at unique clinical situations relevant to American Indians. Chapter Two addresses the delicate issue of Indian child abuse and the application of bibliotherapy. Chapter Three provides insights into the Cherokee cultural model while Chapter Four focuses on the traditional healing of the Sioux. The Navajo are covered in Chapter Five while Chapter Six looks at the role of the curandismo among the mestizo. Taken as a whole, the book provides a number of clinical stratagies relevant to a variety of

American Indian cultural situations.  We hope that it serves as a foundation for additional works in this much needed area.

Laurence French

# Chapter 2

---

# When the Snake Bites: Bibliotherapy for Traumatized Indian Children and Youth.

**Laurence French**
**T. J. Betenbough**
**Nancy Picthall-French**

## Introduction

Clinical interventions for American Indian children and youth is critical given that suicide within this population is far greater than it is for their non-Indian counterparts within American society. Another reason for effective and timely treatment is to reduce the incidence of *psychological marginality* which contribute considerably to alcohol-related cycles-of-abuse among American Indians. The Robert Wood Johnson foundation, in their pamphlet, *Healthy Nations: Reducing Substance Abuse among Native Americans* noted the extent of these problems among American Indians. In the report, it is stated that the age-adjusted, race and gender controlled death rates for Native Americans in the 33 reservation states exceeded rates for the total U.S. population in many categories including suicide. The authors note that substance abuse is a common factor in many of these mental and physical health categories (Fleming, 1992:4). The protection of Indian children and youth is of paramount concern among Native American groups. Within the Harmony Ethos children are considered to be the single most valued resource within the tribe. When a child or youth is violated this is tantamount to a wrong directed to the entire tribe.

Given that the most severe recent case of Indian child abuse involves the Hopi Pueblo Tribe, the snake, the primary vehicle of spiritual communication among this group, is used to illustrate the bad omen associated with mass child abuse. When the tribe is plagued by bad omens this is when the sacred snake bites leaving a legacy of long-termed trauma and healing for not only those children and youth afflicted but for the entire tribe. The Hopi Snake Dance is a nine-day ceremony where the first four days are spent collecting snakes from the four directions. Next, there are four days of secret rites held in the kivas. On the ninth day, the snake dancers emerge from the kivas and dance in the village square with live snakes, both poisonous and non-poisonous, held in their mouths and draped around their necks. The snakes are then released to take a request for rain to the gods. This ritual is as old as Hopi oral history itself. It symbolizes not only the strength of the Hopi's belief in their gods but also in the gods' message to them. If the snake bites, then the implication is that the gods are displeased with the Hopi. The Hopi's neighbor, the Navajo, also view snakes as a powerful symbol in their aboriginal lore. They are taught to leave snakes alone since snakes are considered to be messengers from the gods much like coyotes and owls. The message conveyed by the gods through these animals can be good or bad. This section looks at healing the traumas of child abuse and neglect among American Indians. An innovative approach, that of bibliotherapy, is explored in detail.

## Indian Child Abuse and Neglect

Clinicians need to have an understanding of the evolution of federal Indian child welfare protection laws in order to be effective counselors. In 1978, the 95th Congress passed Public Law 95-608. This was known as the "Indian Child Welfare Act of 1978." In 1989, a "Special Committee on Investigations" of the 101st Congress provided a report *A New Federalism for American Indians.* This report outlined the nature and extent of child abuse within Indian Country. Many believe that this report directly influenced the new federal requirements for better regulation of Indian child protection as well as the prevention of child abuse on Indian reservations, standards established in 1990 (P.L. 95-608, 1978; S. Prt. 101-60, 1989).

Indian child abuse was hinted at in *The Indian Child Welfare Act of 1978:*

Within these systems, two levels of abuse can and do occur. In the initial determination of parental neglect the conceptual basis for removing a child from the custody of his/her parents is widely discretionary and the evaluation process involves the imposition of cultural and familial values which are often opposed to values held by the Indian family. Second, assuming that there is a real need to remove the child from its natural parents, children are all too frequently placed in non-Indian homes, thereby depriving the child of his or htribal and cultural heritage. Non-Indian institutions apparently have a very difficult time finding Indian  foster homes and adoptive parents. In recent years, some states are making concentrated efforts to improve; however, many of the home approval criteria are rigid and inappropriate for the economy and lifestyle of many Indian families. Because of this, many fine potential Indian adoptive and foster care families are rejected or, fearing rejection, do not apply. This process can eliminate blood relatives from keeping these children as is the traditional custom.

Unless a tribe is actively involved with child welfare issues through its court system and its social service agencies, it has almost no way of knowing what is occurring with respect to its minor tribal members. Even where a tribe is actively involved with these issues, there are substantial difficulties, particularly when events occur outside of its territorial jurisdiction. There is no existing requirement that public or private social service agencies, whether they are close by or in distant cities, have to notify a tribe when they take action with respect to any tribal member. Even when a tribe seeks to aggressively assert its interests in child custody proceedings in non-Indian forums, it cannot do so as a matter of right (PL 95-608).

The fact that Indian children and youth were systematically abused by non-Indians -- notably those employed by the federal government -- first became evident in **The Executive Summary: A New Federalism for American Indians:**

The Committee found that the BIA also permitted a pattern of child abuse by its teachers to fester throughout BIA schools nationwide. For almost 15 years, while child abuse reporting standards were being adopted by all 50 states, the Bureau failed to issue any reporting guidelines for its own teachers. Incredibly, the BIA did not require even a minimal background check into potential school employees. As a result, the BIA employed teachers who actually admitted past child molestation, including at least one Arizona teacher who explicitly listed a prior criminal offense for child abuse on his employment form.

At a Cherokee Reservation elementary school in North Carolina, the BIA employed Paul Price, another confessed child molester -- even after his previous principal, who had fired him for molesting seventh grade boys, warned BIA officials that Price was an admitted pedophile. Shocked to learn several years later from teachers at the Cherokee school that Price continued to teach despite the warning, Price's former principal told several Cherokee teachers of Price's pedophilia and notified the highest BIA official at Cherokee. Instead of dismissing Price or conducting an inquiry, BIA administrators lectured an assembly of Cherokee teachers on the unforeseen consequences of slander.

The Committee found that during his 14 years at Cherokee, Price molested at least 25 students while the BIA continued to ignore repeated allegations-- including an eyewitness account by a teacher's aide. Even after Price was finally caught and the negligence of BIA supervisors came to light, not a single official was ever disciplined for tolerating the abuse of countless students for 14 years. Indeed, the negligent Cherokee principal who received the eyewitness report was actually promoted to the BIA Central Office in Washington --the same office which, despite the Price case, failed for years to institute background checks for potential teachers or reporting requirements for instances of suspected abuse. Another BIA Cherokee school official was promoted to the Hopi Reservation in Arizona without any inquiry into his handling of the Rice fiasco.

Meanwhile at Hopi, a distraught mother reported to the local BIA principal a possible instance of child sexual abuse by the remedial reading teacher, John Boone. Even though five years earlier the principal had received police reports of alleged child sexual abuse by Boone, the principal failed to investigate the mother's report or contact law enforcement authorities. He simply notified his superior, who also took no action. A year later, the same mother eventually reported the teacher to the FBI, which found that he had abused 142 Hopi children, most during the years of BIA's neglect. Again, no discipline or censure of school officials followed: the BIA simply provided the abused children with one counselor who compounded their distress by intimately interviewing them for a book he wished to write on the case.

Sadly, these wrongs were not isolated incidents. While in the past year the Bureau has finally promulgated some internal child abuse reporting guidelines, it has taken the Special Committee's public hearings for the BIA to fully acknowledged its failure. (S. Prt. 101-60, 1989: 9,10).

Boone was sentenced to life imprisonment for his crimes against these Hopi youth. Ironically, he is serving his sentence in North Carolina, the state where the other white pedophile mentioned in this federal report, Paul Price, committed his crimes. Apparently Price resides near the Eastern Band of Cherokee Indian Reservation despite a restraining order not to associate with Cherokee children and youth. Nonetheless, these legal actions merely serve to take a particular pedophile out of circulation. They do little to salve the injury either to the individual victims or to the collective tribal psyche. In Arizona, Indian/white (anglo) relations have worsened, so much so that many Hopi object to hiring any more Anglo instructors in their schools. The clinical problems associated with this violation includes individual cases of post-traumatic disorders, depression and subsequent drinking as a form of self-medication. Any combination of these clinical features serve to undermine the children's cultural persona leading to alienation and marginality. A real fear is that untreated youth will grow up not only abusing substances but also having the potential to abuse others in much the same fashion they were abused (French, 1994).

In 1990, *The Indian Child Abuse Prevention and Treatment Act* was passed. It was a reaction by the Congress to the Price and Boone cases:

> The Selection Committee on Indian Affairs and the Special Committee on Investigations have held numerous hearings which focused on the growing problems of child abuse and neglect in Indian country. In November of 1988, the Select Committee on Indian Affairs held a field hearing in Flagstaff, AZ which focused on the problems of sexual molestation of Indian children on the Navajo and Hopi reservations by Bureau of Indian Affairs employees and teachers. In February of 1989, the Special Committee on Investigations further alerted the Congress to the tragic problems of child sexual abuse in Indian country. The hearings of the Special Committee on Investigations focused primarily on three reservations, Navajo, Hopi, and Cherokee, which have suffered cases of child sexual abuse where large numbers of children were abused over a period of years.
>
> ...Section 4 of the bill establishes mandatory reporting procedures for certain professionals working in Indian country by amending Title 18 of the United States Code and providing criminal penalties for failure to report cases of child abuse or neglect. The Committee is very concerned that the reluctance of professionals working in Indian country to report instances of child sexual abuse must be corrected. The Committee has heard much testimony from tribal witnesses regarding their frustrations with the lack of timely prosecution of cases of child sexual abuse in Indian country. In many cases, Indian tribes have been unable to proceed with prosecutions in tribal court in cases of child sexual abuse where the United States Attorneys have declined prosecutions, or because of breakdowns in communications with the United States Attorneys. The Committee feels that the penalties prescribed by this section must be enforced by United States Attorneys in United States District Courts....
>
> Section 4(a)(1) sets out the reporting procedures for cases of child abuse and neglect in Indian country. This section would amend Title 18 of the United States Code to include a section 1169, which would establish mandatory reporting requirements. Under subsection (a) of 1169, if a person who is a physician,

teacher, administrative officer of any public or private school, social worker, psychiatrist, child counselor, mental health professional, law enforcement officer, or other identified person, knows or has a reasonable suspicion that a child was abused or neglected in Indian country and fails to immediately report such abuse or neglect to a local child protective services agency or local law enforcement agency, that person shall be subject to a fine of up to $5,000 or imprisonment of not more than six months or both.

Subsection (b) of 1169 provides that any person who supervises or has authority over a person described in subsection (a) and inhibits    or prevents that person from reporting a case of abuse or neglect shall be subject to a fine of up to $5,000 or imprisonment of not more that six months or both.

Subsection (d)(1) of 1169 provides that the physician-patient, psychotherapist-patient, or other health care provider-patient privileges and the husband-wife privilege shall not apply with respect to the reporting requirements of this Act and shall not constitute a defense to an action under subsection (a) or (b).

Subsection (d)(2) of 1169 provides that any person making a report of child abuse or neglect based upon their reasonable belief and    which is made in good faith shall be immune from civil and criminal liability for making that report.

Subsection 4(b)(1) provides that any local law enforcement agency shall immediately notify the local child protective services agency and shall submit copies of the written reports required under subsection (c) to said agency. Section 4(b)(2) provides that any local child protective services agency shall immediately notify the local law enforcement agency and shall submit copies of the written reports required under subsection (c) to said agency. This section also provides that where the Federal Bureau of Investigation has jurisdiction, the Bureau shall receive immediate notice of the child abuse.

Subsection (c)(1) provides that within 36 hours after receiving a report of child abuse or neglect the agency that initially received the report shall prepare an initial written report. Subsection (c)(1) further provides a description of the information that shall be included in the initial report.

Subsection (c)(2) requires any law enforcement agency or child protective agency that receives a report of child abuse or child sexual abuse as defined in the Act shall initiate an investigation of the allegations of abuse within 36 hours after receiving such report.

Subsection (c)(3) states that upon the completion of an
investigation of any report of alleged abuse or neglect the local
law enforcement agency and the local child protective services
agency shall prepare a              final written report.

Subsection (c)(4) provides that the initial written report
prepared pursuant to subparagraph (1) shall be transmitted by
that agency to the central registry on child abuse and neglect
in Indian country located within the Department of Interior
within 36 hours after the report is completed.

...Section 8 provides that the Secretary of the Interior and the
Secretary of Health and Human Services shall conduct an
investigation of the character of each individual who is
employed in or is being considered for a position that involves
regular contact with, or control over, Indian children. It further
provides that the       Secretary of Interior and the Secretary
of Health and Human Services shall prescribe by regulations
minimum standards of character for any individual who is
employed in a position that      involves regular contact with,
or control over, Indian children.

...Section 10 provides that the Secretary of Health and Human
Services through the Indian Health Service shall establish the
Indian Child Abuse Prevention and Treatment Grant Program
which shall provide grants to any Indian tribe or inter-tribal
consortium for the establishment on Indian reservations of
treatment programs for Indians who have been victims of child
sexual abuse. The maximum amount of any grant awarded
under this section shall be $500,000....(PL 101-630, 1990: 6-
9).

The Qualla Cherokee (Cherokee, North Carolina), in light of
the Price incident, felt it necessary to pass their own child sexual
abuse law, one that includes tribal members who sexually abuse
children. Tribal resolution No. 59, passed December 5, 1991,
gives the tribal council the authority to banish tribal members from
the reservation (Qualla Boundary), who are convicted of a sexual
offense against a minor on the reservation. Additional action
would be to remove the offender from the tribal rolls:

The stiff measure came after a number of 'closed' executive
sessions in which the problems of child sexual abuse were
discussed. In many cases the council found that cases

weren't getting the attention they needed from federal court officials to get these cases of alleged child abuse into the federal courts. ...Faced with that problem, the Council decided to take its own stiff measures in these cases and hoped the stiff penalty would show court officials the tribe takes the problem of child abuse as serious. The heavy law should make the authorities aware that the tribe is doing something about the problem. The new law could be used in cases where the criminal is a repeat offender or in cases it deems important enough in the first time cases. "The problem with this is the children don't deserve this type or treatment and in cases where the offender has been abused himself as a child, it gi"es them no right to abuse another child,' one member of council pointed out (Welch, 1991:4).

On the Navajo reservation the Winona Kee case illustrates the continuing problem with Indian child abuse. In January, l992, a 14-month-old Indian girl froze to death outside her home on the Navajo Reservation in China Springs, New Mexico. Apparently, Winona Kee's mother left the children alone with drunken relatives and did not return until the next day. The father stated that he had been separated from his wife since January 17, l992. (He walked out, therefore he claimed that he was not responsible for his children's welfare.) Winona's five-year-old brother tried to carry her to their grandmother's home, however she proved to be too heavy and he left her and went on alone. He failed to tell his grandmother about his sister. The baby, Winona tried to crawl back to the house, but she didn't make it. She was found in the morning by her grandmother 45 feet from her house frozen to the ground covered with mud and bare footed.

The maximum sentence for this neglect is a six-month jail term. based upon the l968 Indian Civil Rights Act. In l988, the U. S. Congress increased that to one year and a $5,000 fine (up from $500). It is not clear why the Navajo Nation has yet to adopt the stronger penalty. One reason may be the limited availability of correctional treatment facilities on the reservation. Some feel that the federal government has to increase, and not decrease, the authority of tribal courts -- the most viable vehicle for handling Indian-specific cases (French, 1994).

This problem extends off the reservation as well. Benny Diaz, a former Gallup elementary school custodian, was charged in December, l991 with 11 counts of sexual contact with girls aged 8 and 10 at the Indian Hills Elementary School.  And while over 70 percent of the off-reservation student population in the Gallup public schools is Navajo, the case is to be heard before a state trial court.  Clearly, much more needs to be done to break this cycle of Indian child abuse and its link with substance abuse among marginal American Indians (French, 1994).  In the past, these abuses were often concealed from the public by both the federal government (Bureau of Indian Affairs, Indian Health Services, Federal Bureau of Investigation, federal magistrates and district courts) and tribal officials.  These new reporting laws bring the same level of clinical/legal responsibility required of states into Indian Country.  Now that these issues of child abuse are in the open, it is felt that the snake has bitten those groups afflicted by these problems.  Phrased within the American Indian cultural context: The Great Spirit has indicated his displeasure with the abuses of his children.

## Bibliotherapy: A Cultural-Specific Treatment Modality

The most significant aspect of counseling American Indian children and youth is reinforcement of the positive elements of their cultural heritage -- that is, their *cultural persona.*  The most critical therapy issue for any Indian child or youth is the positive reinforcement of their *Indianism.*  Once this mind set has been established then other skill acquisitions can be addressed.  This secondary process is often called the acquisition of *survival skills,* the learning of activities of daily living which allow the American Indian to *walk in two worlds* -- their Indian culture as well as the larger dominant U. S. society (French, 1987; 1994).

The Bureau of Indian Affairs published a *Child Protection Reference Book* in September, 1990.  The following advice to counselors was provided in the section, "Are there special problems/resources when sexual abuse occurs in Native American communities?

One primary difference is that, in an Indian community, almost everyone knows everyone and most people are related in one way or   another.  On the negative side, this can foster denial and result in protection of the offender.  On the other hand, there are few secrets in an Indian community, a fact which can help identify acts of sexual   abuse.  In addition, the closeness of the community can provide important support to the victim and can provide a vigilance which prohibits repetition of the abuse.

A special problem which many Native Americans face is the problem of getting appropriate legal and social services to any specific child sexual abuse case.  This situation is caused by two primary factors.

First, because of past experiences in which they have been treated less than justly, many Indian people distrust the very legal, law enforcement and social authorities which are best equipped to help.  Secondly, because of complicated questions of legal jurisdiction, it is often not clear what governmental entity actually has responsibility for cases which occur on a reservation. Difficulty in obtaining proper services and prosecution result. In an attempt to solve these problems, some tribes have undertaken efforts to develop inter-governmental agreements with surrounding jurisdictions and agencies.  These agreements help to establish cooperative relations and outline responsibilities and procedures for handling Indian child sexual abuse cases.

There are also special resources within Indian communities. For example, a tribal elder who is committed to the need for developing a sexual abuse prevention and treatment program can be tremendously effective in developing community support. A traditional talking circle, in which tribal members meet to share their thoughts on a particular subject in an atmosphere of trust and acceptance, can serve as a means through which a community can identify its standards concerning the protection of children.  A closed talking circle, in which participants agree to keep the ideas expressed confidential, can provide a safe environment in which sexual abuse victims can find support.  Or, when a legal sanction against an offender is unavailable, the tribal council may perhaps choose to use its traditional right to discharge the offender from the community (See the example given above regarding the Eastern Band of Cherokee Indians.) (Adear, 1992:5-6).

Bibliotherapy specifically addresses the primary treatment

issue, that of providing a positive culturally-specific Indian persona, doing so via a powerful teaching resource -- that of storytelling. Cultural norms, during aboriginal times, were disseminated by the tribal elders (*grandparents*) through storytelling. This oral tradition began during early childhood and continued throughout the life-span. Those who had the most varied experiences in life became the teachers. The most honored teachers were the elders, the grandparents. This aboriginal honor has survived to the present among the more traditional tribes such as the Navajo and Pueblo Indians of the southwest.

Bibliotherapy takes storytelling a step further by using the written word as the medium for promoting a positive cultural identity and tribal-specific integration. It can even be used in the initial assessment of problem areas in the child or youth's life. I described this process in my article, "Adapting Projective Tests for Minority Children." Here, elements of the Draw-A-Person (D-A-P) and Thematic Apperception Tests (TAT) (Bellack & Bellack, 1989; Harris, 1963; Murray, 1971) are utilized in such a fashion so as to minimize otherwise potential ethnocentric interpretations of these instruments: "The animals may insult or mislead Indian children whose culture places considerable significance on animal clans and fetishes. (French, 1993: 17)" In this assessment procedure I use the D-A-P so that the Indian children or youth can draw a picture of themself. This provides a clinical baseline from which to interpret the next stage which is to Draw-Your-Family (D-A-F). The D-A-F then becomes the TAT projection *plate*. The TAT interview is then used modified so that the child understands what is asked: Tell me a story about this family? What is happening in the story? Who is the hero? What are the people thinking, feeling? What is the outcome of the story? I feel that this format not only gives us the children's or youth's perception of the situation, it provides a basis for clinical and legal interventions with a minimum of additional trauma. This provides a clearer picture of which stories to use within the treatment/therapy stage.

Bibliotherapy has a long history, one that extends back to the ancient Greeks and Romans. In the United States in the nineteenth century, Benjamin Rush and John Minson Galt, recommended bibliotherapy for the sick and mentally ill.

Coleman (1988) noted that bibliotherapy has been known as bibliocounseling, bibliopsychology, biblioeducation, biblioguidance, library therapeutics, biblioprophylaxis, tutorial group therapy, and literotherapy. These orientations fall into two categories: clinical bibliotherapy and educational bibliotherapy. The former is used mostly with individuals with emotional or behavioral problems while the latter is used with developmental problems or minor adjustment problems. We can see how both aspects of bibliotherapy apply to minority children, notably American Indians. The collective use of bibliotherapy allows the counselor to progress from the cognitive (awareness of problem), affective (emotional insight), and life-planning (strategies) stages of therapy.

When used with American Indian children and youth we need to employ a two-step process. Step one involves a content analysis of the stories. This includes a bio-pyramid, story pyramid and plot chart. The second step involves processing the tribal message promoted by the stories. Here, the talking circle is used. Once this psycho-cultural foundation is established, progress can be made toward establishing and reinforcing survival skills -- those activities of daily living which best prepare the Indian children or youth for two-world integration. Using the abused Hopi children situation, we can see how it is important to first reinforce their cultural self-concept and esteem (Indian persona/Indianism). Identification with story characters and situations similar to theirs allows these children to heal. Story analysis provides the benefits of the cognitive element of group processes while the talking circle allows for the transition to the critical affective stage where insight and cathartic healing occurs. Once these two stages of group processing has occurred, then specific strategies can be mapped out individually for each child. This is the function of the survival school component of the therapy process.

A major resource for the counselor is our bibliography for bibliotherapy according to treatment issue. The following categories are addressed by our bibliography.

Abuse and Neglect
Addictions
Adoptions
Alienation

Assertiveness
Attention-Deficit Disorder
Career Awareness
Children's Stories/Poems
Communication
Conflict with Adults
Diferently - Abled
Family Illness
Family Problems
Fears
Friendships
Gifted
Growing Up
Honesty
Illness
Learning Differences/Mental Illness
Loss
Motivation
Moving
Multicultural Awareness
Peer Pressure
Responsibility
School Problems
School Success
Self-Esteem
Sexuality
Sibling Relationships
Social Behavior
Stepfamilies/single parent families
Stress Management
Teens Growing Up
Teen's Problems
War/Survival
Weight Problems/Body Image

The **Bibliography for Bibliotherapy** is provided at the end of this chapter.

The story analysis component, that which draws out the cognitive recognition of the child or youth's problem, is comprised of the following steps: Bio-Pyramid, Story Pyramid, and Plot Chart. Once the reader has bonded with the book character then the reader can utilize the Bio-Pyramid format to help with character descriptions. More importantly, the evaluator will be able to identify the reader's self-descriptive terms by those character descriptions. This would in turn aid the evaluator to assess how the reader perceives self. If the reader has projected all negative descriptors for the character, then the reader may perceive self as being negative.

The Story Pyramid helps readers to not only identify the main character but also to help identify events in the story. By using descriptive words the reader projects information from his/her experiential background to the story. He/she uses his/her prior knowledge of events and characters to aid with the descriptions of the events and the characters in the story. Again, this transference from experiential background information to present-time stories can assist the evaluator with the affective intents of the reader. This begins the transition from the cognitive to affective therapeutic stages.

A Plot Chart provides readers with a story frame. Some readers have a difficult time telling or writing about a story. The Plot Chart assists the reader in the organization of the information. By having a framework for the retelling, students will be able to retrieve the story information. Plot Charts are simple devices to help readers with story grammar yet they provide a structure that is needed by many readers.

All three of the tools provided above necessitates assistance to those readers who may need help with expressive aspects of their lives. Many children and youth need to talk about family and home problems but have difficulty telling someone outside their circle. The projective tools allow those children and youth to articulate these events and characters without actually confronting the problems, and possibly reinforcing the negative elements we are attempting to overcome through therapy and counseling. Lastly, readers use vocabulary and descriptive terms that are similar to their own cultural identities.

The *Talking Circle* component, that which addresses the affective elements of the child, is comprised of a circle of children and at least one American Indian adult. It is imperative that non-Indian therapists and counselors have an adult tribal member conducting the circle. When used in this fashion, the Talking Circle becomes a *healing circle.*

The Talking Circle is a special group procedure that American Indians have used since aboriginal times. The circle represents the holistic nature of the Harmony Ethos: the interrelatedness of all living things, Mother Earth and Father Sky. The Talking Circle has variations such as the *Dance Circle*. Pow-wow dancing and the Navajo Song and Dance are examples of Dance Circles. Sioux Pow-wow *Circle Dances* can be either mixed gender or gender-specific. The gender-specific Circle Dance for Sioux women is the *Shawl Dance*. Plains Indian men have their gender-specific Circle Dance, that of the *Gord Dance* for Warriors. The *Song Circle* is comprised of *singers* sitting around a drum and singing traditional songs. Running in the four directions is known as a *Running Circle*. Talking Circles take place in sacred places (ceremonial grounds) or in blessed settings. An honored person usually conducts the Talking Circle (French, 1994).

The Talking Circle begins with a prayer to the Great Spirit from the Indian group leader. This is followed with a blessing from the Indian elder. The blessing usually involves the use of a *feather fan* made of the wing or tail feathers of the eagle, hawk, raven, turkey or snow goose. With children and youth, sweet grass, cedar, or sage provides the medium for the blessing. Tobacco is restricted to adult Talking Circles and ceremonies so as not to inadvertently promote the inappropriate use of this agent. Today, a charcoal is lit within a sea shell. The Indian adult conducting the Talking Circle walks to each child or youth and, using sweet grass, cedar or sage, fans the smoke first up and then down the youth. The Indian leader then proceeds from the child's right and blesses both shoulders, the heart and the head. The circle now is a *Sacred Circle*. The adult Indian leader now explains the significance of the circle in general, and the Talking Circle in particular. If the circle is comprised of children and youth from the same tribal groups, the tribal-specific use of the circle is disclosed. If it is a mixed group with children and youth from different tribes, a Pan-Indian approach needs to be used. The PanIndian approach is based on the Siouxan traditions. A feather or talking stick is passed around and the holder is allowed to speak without interruption. Another adaptation of the Talking Circle is for the children to sit around a powwow drum with the drum stick (talking stick) resting on top. When a child or youth desires to speak within this forum, he/she the picks up the drum stick, strikes the drum, and then speaks uninterrupted. At the conclusion of the session, the children are allowed to move around the circle and position themselves next to the person they feel closest. Now, everyone joins hands, completing the healing session. The talking circle may sound like a simplistic process, but it is quite powerful. Conduct as many of these sessions that are dictated by the bibliotherapy curriculum.

With the Hopi children, some of the stories need to be linked to their aboriginal mythology and socialization (enculturation). The Hopi have a long tradition in the three mesas area of Arizona. Oraibi is still the main village of the twelve Hopi villages or pueblos. It is considered to be the oldest continuously inhabited place in the United States. The Hopi origin myth begins with their ancestors, two female dieties (*Hurung Whuti*), who lived in an underworld sea. Eventually the two Hurung Whuti created dry land in the underworld by parting the waters. At this time, they also created life from clay. During this period another power emerged, that of Spider Woman -- the diety of the earth. She also created her own humans, scattering them across the underworld, providing each group with its own language. Thus, according to the Hopi creation myth, the Hurung Whuti created the Hopi's ancestors while Spider Woman created all other humans. Harmony was disrupted when many of Spider Woman's people began to quarrel first among themselves and then with the Hopi's ancestors. With this came dissension, corruption and brutality. This disruption in the harmony caused the rains to stop and the crops to fail. The Hopi were forced to leave the once peaceful underworld and enter the upperworld through a special opening (Sipapu). Only the good Pueblo Indians were allowed in the upperworld and each of these groups was accompanied by a female elder of great wisdom (*Sowuhti*). The arid upperworld, the current mesas where the Hopi reside, forced the Hopi to adapt to these harsh conditions. Aboriginal socialization involved an unusually early and harsh rite of passage from childhood to adult responsibilities. At about age six, boys and girls were compelled to forgo play and engage in rigorous training designed to teach them self-discipline, cooperation, and adult skills and responsibilities. Then, between ages six and ten, both boys and girls were initiated into the Kachina cult. These initiations involved ceremonial whippings clearly marking the child's ascension to adulthood.   The rationale for these rites was that if all Hopi behave properly, then the gods *(Kachinas)* will send life-giving rain and other blessings to the people (French, 1994).

The Hopi today still adhere to many tenets of their aboriginal past.   Clearly, we can see from their creation myth, that is still taught to traditional Hopi, how these abused children's guilt is exacerbated by their cultural roots.   Stories need to be both culturally-relevant and individually tailored to the particular Indian child or youth.   What follows is an American Indian bibliotherapy resource list.

# American Indian Bibliotherapy Bibliography

**Preschool-Primary (prekindergarten - grade 3)**
-Aliki (1976).  *Corn is Maize: The Gift of the Indians*, Crowell.
- Alvarez, Juan S.  (1993).  *Chocolate, Chipmunks, and Canoes: An American Indian Words Coloring Book*, Red Crane Books,
-Andrews, Jan (1985).   *Very Last First Time*, Illustrated by Ian Wallace, Atheneum.
-Baker, Betty (1981).  *Rat Is Dead and Ant is Sad*, Illustrated by Mamoru Funai, Harper & Row.
-Belknap, Barbara (1992).   *An Anasazi Welcome*, Red Crane Books.
-Bulla, Clyde Robert and Syson, Michael (1978).   *Conquista!*, Illustrated by Ronald Himler, Crowell.
-Carlstrom, Nancy White (1992).  *Northern Lullaby*, Illustrated by Leo and Diane Dillon, Trumpet Club.
-Celsi, Teresa (1989). *Squanto and the First Thanksgiving*, Illustrated by Pam Ford Johnson, Raintree Publishers.
-Connell, Kate (1993).  *These Lands are Ours:Tecumseh's Fight for the Old Northwest,* Illustrated by Jan Naimo Jones, Steck-Vaughn Co.
-Dalgliesh, Alice (1954).  *The Courage of Sarah Noble*, Illustrated by Leonard Weisgard, Macmillan Publishing Co.
-Fradin, Dennis B. (1988).  *The Shoshoni*, Childrens Press.
-(1988).   *The Pawnee*, Childrens Press.
-(1988).   *The Cheyenne*, Childrens Press.

-Gleiter, Jan and Thompson, Kathleen (1985). *Pocahontas,* Illustrated by Deborah L. Chabrian, Raintree Children's Books.
- Grossman, Virginia and Long, Sylvia (1991). *Ten Little Rabbits,* Sundance Publishers and Distributors.
-Hoobler, Dorothy, Hoobler, Thomas and Cary-Greenberg Assoc. (1992). *The Trail on Which They Wept: The Story of a Cherokee Girl,* Illustrated by S. S. Burrus, Silver Burdett Press.
-Hyde, Hazel (1990). *Maria Making Pottery,* The Sunstone Press.
-Jassem, Kate (1979). *Sacajawea, Wilderness Guide,* Illustrated by Jan Palmer, Troll Associates.
-Jeffrey, David (1992). *Geronimo,* Illustrated by Tom Redman, Raintree Publishers.
-Jumper, Moses and Sonder, Ben (1993). *Osceola Patriot and Warrior,* Illustrated by Patrick Soper, Steck-Vaughn Co.
-Keehn, Sally M. (1991). *I Am Regina,* Dell Publishing.
-Kvasnicka, Robert M. (1990). *Hole-In-The-Day,* Illustrated by Rick Whipple, Raintree Publishers.
-Lepthien, Emilie U. (1989). *The Mandans,* Children's Press.
-(1987). *The Choctaw,* Children's Press.
-(1985). *The Cherokee,* Children's Press.
-(1985). *The Seminole,* Children's Press.
-Lopez, Alonzo (1972). *Celebration,* Sundance Publishers and Distributers.
-Lowe, Felix, C. (1990). *John Ross,* Illustrated by Patrick Soper, Raintree Publishers.
-Mana, Tawa and Youyouseyah (1989). *When Hopi Children Were Bad: A Monster Story,* Illustrated by Ross Coates, Sierra Oaks Publishing Co.
-Martin, Bill, and Archambault, John (1987). *Knots on a Counting Rope,* Holt, Rinehart & Winston.
-Matiella, Ana Consuelo (1990). *The Multicultural Caterpillar: Children's Activities in Cultural Awareness,* Illustrated by Nina Paley, Network Publications.
-Mayo, Gretchen Will (1994). *Here Comes Tricky Rabbit!,* Walker and Co.
-(1994). *Big Trouble for Tricky Rabbit!,* Walker and Co.
-McDermott, Gerald, Retold by (1993). *Raven: A Trickster Tale from the Pacific Northwest,* Scholastic Inc.
-McGraw, Eliose Jarvis (1992). *Moccasin Trail,* Scholastic Inc.

-McKissack, Patricia (1985). *Aztec Indians,* Children's Press.
-(1984). *The Apache,* Children's Press.
-Medearis, Angela Shelf (1991). *Dancing with the Indians,* Illustrated by Samuel Byrd, Scholastic Inc.
-Miles, Miska (1971). *Annie and the Old One,* Illustrated by Peter Parnall, Little, Brown.
-Morrow, Mary Frances (1990). *Sarah Winnemucca,* Illustrated by Ken Bronikowski, Raintree Publishers.
-O'Dell, Scott and Hall, Elizabeth (1992). *Thunder Rolling in the Mountains,* Dell Publishing.
-Oskiski, Alice (1988). *The Nez Perce,* Children's Press.
_(1987). *The Chippewa,* Children's Press.
_(1987). *The Navajo,* Children's Press.
_(1984). *The Sioux,* Children's Press.
-Paulsen, Gary (1994). *The Legend of Red Horse Cavern,* Bantam Doubleday Dell Publishing Group, Inc.
-Peters, Russell M. (1992). *Clambake: A Wampanoag Tradition,* Photographs by John Madama, Lerner Publications Co.
-Powers, Tom (1987). *Osceola: Seminole War Leader,* Illustrated by James Balkovek, Quercus Corp.
-Rand, Jacki Thomson (1993). *Wilma Mankiller,* Illustrated by Wayne Anthony Still, Raintree Publishers.
-Regguinti, Gordon (1992). *The Sacred Harvest: Ojibway Wild Rice Gathering,* Photographs by Dale Kakkak, Lerner Publications Co.
-Robbins, Ruth (1980). *How the First Rainbow Was Made,* Parnassus.
-Scott, Ann Herbert (1993). *On Mother's Lap,* Illustrated by Glo Coalson, Scholastic Inc.
-Sharpe, Susan (1991). *Spirit Quest,* Scholastic Inc.
-Smith, A. G. (1994). *Plains Indians: Punch-Out Panorama,* Dover Publications, Inc.
-Smith, A. G. and Hazen, Josie (1992). *Easy-to-Make Pueblo Village,* Dover Publications, Inc.
-Stein, R. Conrad (1989). *The Trail of Tears,* Children's Press.
_(1983). *The Story of The Little Bighorn,* Childrens Press.
-Steptoe, John, Retold by (1993). *The Story of Jumping Mouse,* Scholastic Inc.
-Stone, Deborah (1989). *Tecumseh,* Illustrated by James Balkovek, Quercus Corp.

-Swentzell, Rina (1992). *Children of Clay: A Family of Pueblo Potters,* Photographs by Bill Steen, Lerner Publications Co., NF.
-Tierney, Tom (1992). *Little Indian Girl Paper Doll,* Dover Publications, Inc.
-Tomchek, Ann Heinrichs (1987). *The Hopi,* Children's Press.
-Viola, Herman J. (1990). *Sitting Bull,* Illustrated by Charles Shaw, Raintree Publishers.
-Wittstock, Laura Waterman (1993). *Ininatig's Gift of Sugar: Traditional Native Sugar Making,* Photographs by Dale Kakkak, Lerner Publications Co.

**Intermediate (grades 4-6)**
-Anderson, Bernice G. (1979). *Trickster Tales from Prairie Lodgefires,* Illustrated by Frank Gee, Abingdon.
-Batherman, Muriel (1981). *Before Columbus,* Houghton Mifflin.
-Bird, E. J. (1993). *The Rainmakers,* Carolrhoda Books, Inc.
-Beaulieu, David and Hamley, Jeffrey (1993). *Native Americans: The Struggle for the Plains,* Glove Book Co.
-Borland, Hal (1985). *When The Legends Die,* Bantam Books.
-Cleaver, Elizabeth (1985). *The Enchanted Caribou,* Atheneum.
-Coatsworth, Emerson and Coatsworth, David, Eds. (1980). *The Adventures of Nanbush: Ojibway Indian Stories,* Illustrated by Francis Kagige, Atheneum.
-Curtis, Edward S. (1978). *The Girl Who Married a Ghost and Other Tales from the North American Indian,* Edited by John Bierhorst, Four Winds.
-Dorame, Anthony (1993). *Peril at Thunder Ridge,* Red Crane Books.
-Dressman, John (1984). *On the Cliffs of Acoma,* Spanish Translation by Pedro Ribera-Ortega, Illustrations by Glen Strock, Sunstone Press.
-Dubois, Muriel L. (1994). *Abenaki Captive,* Carolrhoda Books, Inc.
-Dudley, Joseph Iron Eyes (1992). *Choteau Creek: A Sioux Reminiscence,* University of Nebraska Press.
-Freedman, Russell (1988). *Buffalo Hunt,* Holiday House.
_(1987). *Indian Chiefs,* Holiday House.
-George, Jean Craighead, (1987). *Water Sky,* Harper & Row.
-(1983). *The Talking Earth,* Harper & Row.
-(1972). *Julie of the Wolves,* The Trumpet Club.

-Goble, Paul (1989). *Beyond the Ridge,* Bradbury.
-(1989). *Iktomi and the Berries,* Watts.
-(1988). *Iktomi and the Boulder: A Plains Indian Story,* Orchard.
-(1987). *Buffalo Woman,* Bradbury.
-(1987). *Death of the Iron Horse,* Bradbury.
-(1980). *The Gift of the Sacred Dog,* Bradbury.
-(1978). *The Girl Who Loved Wild Horses,* Bradbury.
-Harris, Christie (1982). *The Trouble with Adventurers,* Illustrated by  Douglas Tait, Atheneum.
_(1976). *Mouse Woman and the Vanished Princesses,* Illustrated by  Douglas Tait, Atheneum.
-Haseley, Dennis (1983). *The Scared One,* Illustrated by Deborah Howland, Warne.
-Haviland, Virginia (1979). *North American Legends,* Illustrated by Ann Stugnell, Philomel.
-Highwater, Jamake (1986). *I Wear the Morning Star,* Harper & Row.
_(1985). *The Ceremony of Innocence,* Harper & Row.
_(1977). *Anpao: An American Indian Odyssey,* Illustrated by Fritz Scholder, Lippincott.
-Hirschfelder, Arlene (1986). *Happily May I Walk: American Indians and Alaska Natives Today,* Scribner's Sons.
-Hobbs, Will (1989). *Bearstone,* Atheneum.
-Holling, Holling Clancy (1989). *Paddle-to-the-Sea,* The Trumpet Club.
-Hoven, Leigh (1990). *Native Americans: A Thematic Unit,* Illustrated by Blanqui Apodaca and Paula Spence, Teacher Created Materials, Inc.
-Hoyt-Goldsmith, Diane (1991). *Pueblo Storyteller,* Photographs by Lawrence Migdale, Scholastic Inc.
-Hudson, Jan (1990). *Dawn Rider,* Scholastic Inc.
_(1984). *Sweetgrass,* Tree Frog.
-Luenn, Nancy (1990). *Nessa's Fish,* Atheneum.
-Marrin, Albert (1984). *War Clouds in the West: Indians & Cavalrymen, 1860-1890,* Atheneum.
-Matthews, Kay (1992). *An Anasazi Welcome,* Illustrated by Barbara Belknap, Red Crane Books.
-Mayo, Gretchen Will (1993). *Meet Tricky Coyote!,* Walker and Co.
_(1993). *That Tricky Coyote!,* Walker and Co.

-Momaday, Natachee Scott (1975). *Owl in the Cedar Tree,* Illustrated by Don Perceval, University of Nebraska Press.
-Morrison, Dorothy Nafus (1980). *Chief Sarah: Sarah Winnemucca's Fight for Indian Rights,* Atheneum.
-Mowat, Farley (1984). *Lost in the Barrens,* Illustrated by Charles Geer, McClelland & Stewart.
-O'Dell, Scott (1988). *Black Star, Bright Dawn,* Houghton Mifflin
_(1970). *Sing Down the Moon,* Houghton Mifflin.
Otis, Alicia (1987). *Spiderwoman's Dream,* The Sunstone Press.
-Paulsen, Gary (1988). *Dogsong,* Bradbury Press.
_(1986). *Sentries,* Bradbury Press.
-Powell, Mary, Ed. (1992). *Wolf Tales,* Ancient City Press.
-Prusski, Jeffrey (1988). *Bring Back the Deer,* Illustrated by Neil Waldman, Harcourt Brace Jovanovich.
-Reed, Evelyn Dahl (1988). *Coyote Tales from the Indian Pueblos,* Illustrations by Glen Strock, The Sunstone Press.
-Richter, Conrad (1990). *The Light in the Forest,* Bantam.
-Robinson, Gail (1982). *Raven the Trickster: Legends of the North American Indians,* Illustrated by Joanna Troughton, Atheneum.
-Rockwood, Joyce (1978). *Groundhog's Horse,* Illustrated by Victor Kalin, Rinehart & Winston.
-Seeley, Virginia, Ed. (1994). *Native American Biographies,* Globe Fearon, NF.
_(1993). *Plains Native American Literature,* Globe Fearon.
-Sneve, Virginia Driving Hawk (1993). *The Chichi Hoohoo Bogeyman,* Illustrations by Nadema Agard, University of Nebraska Press.
_(1993). *When Thunders Spoke,* Illustrated by Oren Lyons, University of Nebraska Press.
_(1989). *Dancing Teepees: Poems of American Indian Youth,* Illustrated by Stephen Gammell, Holiday House.
_(1972). *Jimmy Yellow Hawk,* Illustrated by Oren Lyons, Holiday House.
_(1972). *High Elk's Treasure,* Illustrated by Oren Lyons, Holiday House.
-Speare, Elizabeth George (1983). *The Sign of the Beaver,* Houghton Mifflin.
-Sutter, Joanne (1992). *World Myths and Legends: Native Americans,* Fearon/Janus.

-Vallo, Lawrence Jonathan (1987). *Tales of a Pueblo Boy,* The Sunstone Press.
-VanEtten, Teresa, Retold by, (1985). *Ways of Indian Magic,* The Sunstone Press.
_(1987). *Ways of Indian Wisdom,* The Sunstone Press.

## Junior High/Senior High (grades 7-12)
-Aaseng, Nathan (1992). *Navajo Code Talkers,* Walker and Co.
-Blake, Michael (1991). *Dances with Wolves,* Newmarket Press.
-Broker, Ignatia (1983). *Night Flying Woman: An Ojibway Narrative,* Minnesota Historical Press.
-Boissiere, Robert (1985). *The Hopi Way: An Odyssey,* The Sunstone Press.
_(1983). *Po Pai Mo: The Search for White Buffalo Woman,* The Sunstone Press.
-Costner, Kevin, Blake, Michael and Wilson, Jim (1990). *Dances with Wolves: The Illustrated Story of the Epic Film,* Newmarket Press.
-Edelman, Sandra A. (1986). *Summer People Winter People,* The Sunstone  Press.
-Folsom, Franklin (1989). *Red Power on the Rio Grande: The Native American Revolution of 1680,* Council for Indian Education.
-Freedman, Russell (1994). *An Indian Winter,* Illustrations by Karl Bodmer, Scholastic Inc.
_(1992). *Buffalo Hunt,* Scholastic Inc.
-Fritz, Jean (1983). *The Double Life of Pocahontas,* Illustrated by Ed Young, Putnam.
-Garmhausen, Winona (1988). *History of Indian Arts Education in San Fe,* The Sunstone Press.
-Highwater, Jamake (1981). *Moonsong Lullaby,* Photographs by Marcia Keegan, Lee & Shepard.
-Hillderman, Tony (1973). *Dance Hall of the Dead,* Avon.
-Hirschfelder, Arlene and Singer, Beverly R. (1993). *Rising Voices: Writings of Young Native Americans,* Ivy Books.
-Hodge, Gene Meany, Collected by (1993). *Kachina Tales From the Indian Pueblos,* The Sunstone Press.
-Hudson, Jan (1991). *Sweetgrass,* Scholastic Inc.

-Monroe, Jean Guard and Williamson, Ray A. (1987). *They Dance in the Sky: Native American Star Myths,* Illustrated by Edgar Stewart, Houghton Mifflin.

-Morris, Richard B. (1985). *The Indian Wars,* Illustrated by Leonard Everett Fisher, Lerner Publications Co.

-Morrison, Dorothy Nafus (1980). *Chief Sarah: Sarah Winnemucca's Fight for Indian Rights,* Atheneum.

-Otis, Alicia (1990). *The First Koshare,* The Sunstone Press.

-Parsons, Elsie Clews, Ed. (1992). *North American Indian Life: Customs and Traditions of 23 Tribes,* Dover Publications, Inc.

-Paulsen, Gary (1991). *The Night the White Deer Died,* Dell.

-Poatgieter, Alice Hermina (1981). *Indian Legacy: Native American Influences on World Life and Culture,* Messner.

-Rausch, David A. and Schlepp, Blair (1994). *Native American Voices,* Baker Books.

-Spinden, Herbert Joseph, Collected and Translated by (1993). *Songs of the Tewa,* The Sunstone Press.

Underhill, Ruth (1991). *Life in the Pueblos,* Ancient City Press.

-Whitaker, Muriel, Ed. (1980). *Stories from the Canadian North,* Illustrated by Vlasta van Kampen, Hurtig.

## All Ages

Appleton, Le Roy H. (1971). *American Indian Design and Decoration,* Dover Publications, Inc.

-Ashabranner, Brent (1984). *To Live in Two Worlds: American Indian Youth Today,* Photographs by Paul Conklin, Dodd, Mead.

_(1982). *Morning Star, Black Sun: The Northern Cheyenne Indians and America's Energy Crisis,* Photographs by Paul Conklin, Dodd, Mead.

-Baker, Olaf (1981). *Where the Buffaloes Begin,* Illustrated by Stephen Gammell, Warne.

-Baylor, Byrd (1982). *Moonsong,* Illustrated by Ronald Himler, Scribner's Sons.

_(1981). *A God on Every Mountain Top: Stories of Southwest Indian Mountains,* Illustrated by Carol Brown, Scribner's Sons.

_(1978). *The Other Way to Listen,* Illustrated by Peter Parnall, Scribner's Sons.

_(1976). *Hawk, I'm Your Brother,* Illustrated by Peter Parnall, Scribner's Sons.

_(1975). *The Desert Is Theirs,* Illustrated by Peter Parnall, Scribner's Sons.

_(1972). *When Clay Sings,* Illustrated by Tom Bahti, Scribner's Sons.

-Beyer, Don E. (1991). *The Totem Pole Indians of the Northwest,* Franklin Watts.

-Bierhorst, John, Ed. (1983). *The Sacred Path: Spell, Prayers, and Power Songs of the American Indians,* Morrow.

_(1982). *The Whistling Skeleton: American Indian Tales of the Supernatural,* Illustrated by Robert Andrew Parker, Four Winds.

_(1979). *A Cry from the Earth: Music of the North American Indians,* Four Winds.

_(1970). *The Ring in the Prairie, A Shawnee Legend,* Illustrated by Leo and Diane Dillon, Dial.

-Clark, Ann Nolan (1992). *There Still Are Buffalo,* Illustrated by Stephen Tongier, Ancient City Press.

-Culin, Stewart (1975). *Games of the North American Indians,* Dover Publications, Inc.

-Cushing, Frank Hamilton (1901, 1986). *Zuni Folk Tales,* University of Arizona Press.

-de Paola, Tomie (1983). *The Legend of the Bluebonnet,* Putnam.

-Esbensen, Barbara Juster, Ed. (1988). *The Star Maiden,* Illustrated by Helen K. Davie, Little Brown.

-Green, John (1993). *Indian Designs,* Dover Publications, Inc.

-Hamilton, Virginia (1988). *In the Beginning: Creation Stories From Around the World,* Illustrated by Barry Moser, Harcourt Brace Jovanovich.

-Hayes, Joe ( Retold by) (1983). *Coyote,* Illustrated by Lucy Jelinek, Mariposa Publishing.

-Highwater, Jamake (1981). *Moonsong Lullaby,* Lothrop, Lee & Shepard.

-Hodge, Gene Meany (1988). *Four Winds: Poems from Indian Rituals,* The Sunstone Press.

-Kennedy, Paul E. (1993). *Fun with Southwest Indian Stencils,* Dover Publications, Inc.

-Krenz, Nancy and Byrnes, Patricia (1979). *Southwestern Arts and Crafts Projects,* The Sunstone Press.

-Liptak, Karen (1992). *North American Indian Ceremonies,* Franklin Watts.

_(1992). *North American Indian Tribal Chiefs,* Franklin Watts.
_(1992). *North American Indian Sign Language,* Franklin Watts.
-Metayer, Maurice, Ed. (1972). *Tales from the Igloo,* Illustrated by Agnes Nanogak, Hurtig.
-Newman, Shirlee P. (1993). *The Inuits,* Franklin Watts.
-Parker, Arthur C. (1954). *The Indian How Book,* Dover Publications, Inc.
-Sneve, Virginia Driving Hawk, Selected by (1989). *Dancing Teepees: Poems of American Indian Youth,* Illustrated by Stephen Gammell, Holiday House.
-Spencer, Paula Underwood (1983). *Who Speaks for Wolf,* Illustrated by Frank Howell, Tribe of Two Press.
-Steptoe, John (1984). *The Story of Jumping Mouse,* Lothrop, Lee & Shepard.
-Toye, William (1977). *The Loon's Necklace,* Illustrated by Elizabeth Cleaver, Oxford.
-Wallace, James (1981). *Kwakiutl Legends,* Recorded by Pamela Whitaker, Hancock House.
-White Deer of Autumn (1983). *Ceremony - In the Circle of Life,* Illustrated by Daniel San Souci, Raintree.
-Wolfson, Evelyn (1988). *From Abenaki to Zuni: A Dictionary of Native American Tribes,* Illustrated by William Sauts Bock, Walker and Co.
-Yoder, Walter D. (1993). *The Big New Mexico Activity Book,* The Sunstone Press.
_(1994). *The American Pueblo Indian Activity Book,* The Sunstone Press.

## Bibliography for Bibliotherapy:

### Abuse and Neglect

-Booher, Dianna (1991). *Rape: What Would You Do If...?,* Messner.
-Chetin, Helen (1977). *Frances Ann Speaks Out: My Father Raped Me,* New Seed Press.
-Howard, Ellen (1986). *Gillyflower,* Atheneum.
Hyde, Margaret (1986). *Cry Softly!: The Story of Child Abuse,* Westminster.
-Irwin, Hadley (1985). *Abby, My Love,* Macmillan.

-Len, Dan and Howard, Marie (1990). *Sexual Assault: How to Defend Yourself,* Frederick Fell.
-Levy, Barry (1993). *In Love and in Danger: A Teen's Guide to Breaking Free of Abusive Relationships,* Seal Press.
Martin, Katherine (1989). *Night Riding,* Knopf.

## Addictions

-Anonymous (1976). *Go Ask Alice,* Avon.
-Bonham, Frank (1972). *Cool Cat,* Dell.
-Childress, Alice (1974). *A Hero Ain't Nothin' but a Sandwich,* Avon.
-Cohen, Susan and Cohen, Daniel (1988). *What You Can Believe About Drugs: An Honest and Unhysterical Guide for Teens,* Evans.
-Cormier, Robert (1991). *We All Fall Down,* Delacorte.
-Due, Linnea A. (1980). *High and Outside,* Harper and Row.
-Ehrlich, Amy (1991). *The Dark Card,* Viking.
-Greene, S, (1980). *The Boy Who Drank Too Much,* Dell.
-Hall, Lindsay and Cohn, Leigh (1988). *Dear Kids of Alcoholics,* Gurze Books.
-Hinton, S. E. (1980). *That Was Then, This Is Now,* Dell.
-Holland, Isabelle (1979). *Heads You Win, Tails I Lose,* Dell.
-Irwin, Hadley (1990). *Can't Hear You Listening,* McElderrry Books.
-Leite, Evelyn and Espeland, Pamela (1987). *Different Like Me: A Book for Teens Who Worry About Their Parents' Use of Alcohol,* Johnson Institute.
-Levy, M. (1988). *Touching,* Fawcett.
-Major, Kevin (1981). *Hold Fast,* Dell.
-Miklowitz, Gloria D. (1989). *Anything to Win,* Delacorte.
-Orgel, Doris (1989). *Crack in the Heart,* Juniper.
-Ryan, Elizabeth (1989). *Straight Talk About Drugs and Alcohol,* Dell.
-Scoppettone, Sandra (1977). *The Late Great Me,* Bantam.
-Strasser, Todd (1981). *The Angel Dust Blues,* Dell.
-Talbert, Marc (1985). *Dead Birds Singing,* Little, Brown.
-Thompson, Thomas (1981). *Richie,* Dell.
-Trivers, J. and Davis, A. (1977). *I Can Stop Anytime I Want,* Dell.
-Wagner, R. (1975). *Sarah T. - Portrait of a Teenage Alcoholic,* Ballentine.

-Wojciechowska, M. (1971). *Tuned Out,* Bantam.

## Adoption
-DuPrau, Jeanne (1990). *Adoption: The Facts, Feelings and Issues of a Double Heritage,* Messner.
-Gravelle, Karen and Fischer, Susan (1993). *Where are My Birth Parents?: A Guide for Teenage Adoptions,* Walker.
-Okimoto, Jean Davies (1990). *Molly By Any Other Name,* Scholastic Inc.
-Rosenberg, Maxine (1989). *Growing up Adopted,* Bradbury Press.

## Alienation
-Cormier, Robert (1986). *The Chocolate War,* Dell.
-Hall, Lynn (1972). *Sticks and Stones,* Dell
-Miklowitz, Gloria D. (1988). *Good-Bye Tomorrow,* Dell.
-Sebestyen, Ouida (1983). *Words by Heart,* Bantam.

## Assertiveness
-Knudson, R. R. (1972). *Zanballer,* Dell.
-Marek, Margot (1988). *Matt's Crusade,* Knopf.
-Pfeffer, Susan Beth (1982). *A Matter of Principle,* Dell.
-Rostkowski, Margaret I. (1986). *After the Dancing Days,* Harper Trophy.

## Attention-Deficit Disorder
-Gordon, Michael (1993). *I Would If I Could: A Teenager's Guide to ADHD/Hyperactvity,* GSI Publications.

## Career Awareness
-Bernstein, Daryl (1992). *Better Than a Lemonade Stand: Small Business Ideas for Kids,* Beyond Words.
-Farr, J. Michael and Christophersen, Susan (1991). *Career Preparation: Getting the Most From Training & Education,* JIST Works.
_(1991). *Your Career: Thinking About Jobs and Careers,* JIST Works.
-Henderson, Kathy (1990). *What Would We Do Without You?: A Guide to Volunteer Activities for Kids,* Betterway.

-Johnson, Neil (1989). *All in a Day's Work: Twelve Americans Talk About Their Jobs,* Joy Street Books.
-Riehm, Sarah (1990). *The Teenage Entrepreneur's Guide: 50 Money-Making Business Ideas,* Surrey Books.

### Children's Stories/Poems
-Bourgeois, Paulette (1986). *Franklin in the Dark,* Scholastic Inc.
-Bunting, Eve (1989). *The Wednesday Surprise,* Clarion Books.
-Carlson, Nancy (1990). *Arnie and the New Kid,* Viking Penguin.
-dePaola, Tomie (1981). *Now One Foot, Now the Other,* G. P. Putnam's Sons.
_(1979). *Oliver Button is a Sissy,* Harcourt Brace Jovanovich, Inc.
-Frasier, Debra (1991). *On The Day You Were Born,* Harcourt Brace.
-Jukes, Mavis (1989). *Blackberries in the Dark,* Houghton Mifflin Company.
-Quackenbush, Robert (1982). *First Grade Jitters,* J. B. Lippincott Junior Books.
-Silverstein, Shel (1976). *The Missing Piece,* HarperCollins.
_(1964). *The Giving Tree,* HarperCollins.
-Varley, Susan (1984). *Badger's Parting Gifts,* William Morrow & Company, Inc.
-Wachter, Oralee (1983). *No More Secrets for Me,* Little, Brown and Company.
-Warburg, Sandol Stoddard (1969). *Growing Time,* Houghton Mifflin Company.
-Zolotow, Charlotte (1969). *The Hating Book,* Harper & Row Junior Books.

### Communication
-Gilbert, Sara (1991). *You Can Speak Up In Class,* Beech Tree Books.
-Stern, Zoe and Stern, Ellen (1993). *Questions Kids Wish They Could Ask Their Parents,* Celestial Arts.

### Conflicts with Adults
-Arrick, F. (1986). *Nice Girl From Good Home,* Dell.
-Bennett, J. (1986). *To Be a Killer,* Scholastic Inc.

-Hayes E, K. and Lazzarino, A. (1978). *Broken Promises*, Fawcett.
-Heyman, A. (1983). *Final Grades*, Dodd, Mead.
-Hughey, R. (1984). *The Question Box*, Delacorte.
-Kerr, M. E. (1978). *Gentlehands*, Harper and Row.
-Lowry, Lois (1990). *Find a Stranger, Say Goodbye*, Dell.
-Mazer, Norma Fox (1981). *Taking Terri Mueller*, Avon.
-Paterson, Katherine (1979). *The Great Gilly Hopkins*, Avon.
-Shreve, S. (1981). *The Masquerade*, Dell.
-Shusterman, N. (1991). *What Daddy Did*, Little, Brown.
-Slepian, J. (1987). *Something Beyond Paradise*, Philomel.
-Sweeney, J. (1984). *Center Line*, Delacorte.
-Wolitzer, H. (1980). *Toby Lived Here*, Bantam.
-Wolverton, L. (1987). *Running Before the Wind*, Houghton Mifflin.

**Differently-Abled**
-Albert, L. (1976). *But I'm Ready to Go*, Dell.
-Blume, Judy (1973). *Deenie*, Bradbury.
-Brancato, Robin (1977). *Winning*, Knopf.
-Bridges, Sue Ellen (1989). *Notes for Another Life*, Bantam.
_(1979). *All Together Now*, Knopf.
-Brown, H. (1976). *Yesterday's Child*, New American Library.
-Brown, Irene (1992). *Before the Lark*, Blue Heron.
-Cassedy, Sylvia (1987). *M. E. and Morton*, Crowell.
-Covington, Dennis (1991). *Lizard*, Delacorte.
-Crutcher, Chris (1987). *The Crazy Horse Electric Game*, Greenwillow.
-Feuer, Elizabeth (1992). *Paper Doll*, Farrar, Straus & Giroux.
-Gerson, C. (1978). *Passing Through*, Dell.
-Greenberg, Joanne (1988). *Of Such Small Differences*, Holt.
_(1972). *In This Sign*, Avon.
-Guccione, Leslie D. (1989), *Tell Me How the Wind Sounds*, Scholastic Inc.
-Guest, J. (1980). *Ordinary People*, Ballentine.
-Haar, J. (1977). *The World of Ben Lighthart*, Delacorte.
-Hall, Lynn (1990). *Halsey's Pride*, Scribner's.
_(1985). *Just One Friend*, Scribner's.
-Hamilton, Virginia (1982). *Sweet Whispers, Brother Rush*, Philomel.

-Helfman, Elizabeth (1992). *On Being Sarah,* Whitman.
-Holland, I. (1989). *The Unfrightened Dark,* Little, Brown.
-Kent, Deborah (1989). *One Step at a Time,* Scholastic Inc.
-Kerr, M. E. (1981). *Little, Little,* HarperCollins.
-Keyes, Daniel (1966). *Flowers for Algernon,* Bantam Book.
-Kingman, L. (1981). *Head Over Wheels,* Dell.
-Krementz, Jill (1992). *How It Feels To Live With a Physical Disability,* Simon & Schuster.
-Krentel, M. (1972). *Melissa Comes Home,* Popular Library.
-Kriegsman, Kay, et. al. (1992) *Taking Charge: Teenagers Talk About Life and Physical Disabilities,* Woodbine House.
-Levenkrom, S. (1989). *The Best Little Girl in the World,* Warner.
-Little, Jean (1972). *From Anna,* Bantam Doubleday Dell Publishing Group, Inc.
_(1962). *Mine for Keeps,* Little Brown and Company.
-Mandel, S. (1981). *Change of Heart,* Dell.
-Martin, Ann M. (1984). *Inside Out,* Holiday House.
-Mazer, Harry (1979). *The War on VIlla Street,* Dell.
-McNair, Joseph (1989). *Commander Coatrack Returns,* Houghton Mifflin.
-Melton, D. (1977). *A Boy Caled Hopeless,* Scholastic Inc.
-Meyer, Donald, et. al. (1985). *Living with a Brother or Sister with Special Needs: A Book for Sibs,* Univeristy of Washington.
-Mohr, Nicholasa (1979). *In Neuva York,* Dell.
-Naylor, Phyllis Reynolds (1987). *The Keeper,* Bantam.
-Paulsen, Gary (1983). *Dancing Carl,* Scholastic, Inc.
-Platt, Kin (1971). *Hey, Dummy,* Dell Publishing Company.
-Roberts, Willo Davis (1980). *The Girl with the Silver Eyes,* Scholastic, Inc.
-Sallis, S. (1980). *Only Love,* Harper & Row.
-Savitz, Harriet May (1979). *Run, Don't Walk,* The New American Library, Inc.
_(1979). *On the Move,* The New American Library, Inc.
_(1975). *The Lionhearted,* The New American Library, Inc.
-Silsbee, P. (1987). *The Big Way Out,* Dell.
-Slepian, Jan (1990). *Risk n' Roses,* Philomel.
_(1980). *The Alfred Summer,* Macmillan.
-Terris, S. (1987). *Nell's Quilt,* Farrar, Straus & Giroux.
-Voigt, Cynthia (1986). *Izzy, Willy-Nilly,* Ballentine.
-Willey, M. (1983). *The Bigger Book of Lydia,* Harper & Row.

-Wojciechowska, M. (1971). *A Single Light,* Bantam.
-Wolf, Virginia Euwer (1988). *Probably Nick Swanson,* Macmillan.

### Divorce/Separation
-Angell, Judie (1981). *What's Best for You,* Bradbury.
-Arnold, William V. (1980). *When Your Parents Divorce,* Westminster.
-Blume, Judy (1972). *It's Not the End of the World,* Bantam.
-Byars, Betsy (1982). *The Animal, the Vegetable, and John D. Jones,* Delacorte.
-Cameron, Eleanor (1975). *To the Green Mountains,* Dutton.
-Holland, Isabelle (1973). *Heads You Win, Tails I Lose,* Lippincott.
_(1972). *The Man Without a Face,* Lippincott.
-Irwin, Hadley (1980). *Bring to a Boil and Separate,* Atheneum.
-Johnson, Annabel and Johnson, Edgar (1964). *The Grizzly,* Harper.
-Kerr, M. E. (1975). *Is That You, Miss Blue,* Harper.
-Klein, Norma (1982). *It's Not What You Expect,* Avon.
_(1980). *Breaking Up,* Pantheon.
_(1974). *Taking Sides,* Avon.
_ (1972). *Mom, the Wolf Man and Me,* Avon.
-Konigsburg, E. L. (1982). *Journey to an 800 Number,* Atheneum.
-Krementz, Jill (1984). *How It Feels When Parents Divorce,* Knopf.
-Rofes, Eric (editor) (1981). *The Kids' Book of Divorce: By, For and About Kids,* Random House.
-Smith, Doris Buchanan (1974). *Kick a Stone Home,* Crowell.
-Stolz, Mary (1972). *Leap Before You Look,* Dell.

### Families
-Bawden, Nina (1989). *The Outside Child,* Lothrop, Lee and Shepartd.
-Brooks, Bruce (1986). *Midnight Hour Encores,* HarperCollins.
-Byars, Betsy (1982). *The Two-Thousand Pound Goldfish,* HarperCollins.
-(1980). *The Night Swimmers,* Delacorte.
-(1977). *The Pinballs,* Scholastic, Inc.
-(1963). *The House of Wings,* Viking Penguin, Inc.
-Childress, Alice (1981). *Rainbow Jordan,* Putnam.

-Cleaver, Vera and Bill (1977). *Trial Valley,* Lippincott.
_(1969). *Where the Lilies Bloom,* Harper Collins.
-Davis, Jenny (1987). *Good-bye and Keep Cold,* Orchard.
-Deaver, Julie Reece (1988). *First Wedding, Once Removed,* HarperCollins.
-Ferris, Jean (1993). *Relative Strangers,* Farrar, Straus & Giroux.
-(1990). *Across the Grain,* Farrar, Straus & Giroux.
-Fleischman, Paul (1986). *Rear-View Mirror,* HarperCollins.
-Fox, Paula (1986). *The Moonlight Man,* Bradbury.
-Grant, Cynthia (1991). *Keep Laughing,* Atheneum.
-Hall, Barbara (1990). *Dixie Storms,* Harcourt Brace Jovanovich.
-Hinton, S. E. (1979). *Tex,* Delacorte.
-Kerr, M. E. (1972). *Dinky Hocker Shoots Smack,* HarperCollins.
-Kincaid, Jamaica (1985). *Annie John,* Farrar, Straus & Giroux.
-Konigsburg, E. L. (1982). *Journey to an 800 Number,* Atheneum.
-Levitin, Sonia (1986). *A Season For Unicorns,* Atheneum.
-Mazer, Harry (1985). *When the Phone Rang,* Scholastic Inc.
-Mazer, Norma Fox (1984). *Downtown,* Morrow.
-(1980). *Mrs. Fish, Ape, and Me, The Dump Queen,* Avon Books.
-Myers, Walter Dean (1992). *Somewhere in the Darkness,* Scholastic Inc.
-Naylor, Phyllis (1990). *Send No Blessings,* Macmillan.
-Paterson, Katherine (1979). *The Great Gilly Hopkins,* Crowell.
-Peck, Richard (1978). *Father Figure,* Viking.
-Peck, Robert Newton (1973). *A Day No Pigs Would Die,* Knopf.
-Robinson, Nancy K. (1981). *Mom, You're Fired!,* Scholastic Inc.
-Rodowsky, Colby (1989). *Sydney, Herself,* Farrar, Straus & Giroux.
-Rylant, Cynthia (1988). *A Kindness,* Orchard.
-Smith, Doris Buchanan (1986). *Return to Bitter Creek,* Viking.
-Talbert, Marc (1991). *Pillow of Clouds,* Dial.
-Tolan, Stephanie (1988). *A Good Courage,* Morrow.
-Voigt, Cynthia (1983). *A Solitary Blue,* Atheneum
-(1982). *Dicey's Song,* Atheneum
-Wyss, Thelma Hatch (1988). *Here at the Scenic-Vu Motel,* HarperCollins.

## Family Illness
-Cannon, A. E. (1991). *Amazing Gracie,* Delacorte.
-Dinner, Sherry (1989). *Nothing to be Ashamed of: Growing Up with Mental Illness in Your Family,* Lothrop.
-Fine, Judylaine (1986). *Afraid to Ask: A Book for Families to Share About Cancer,* Morrow.
-Green, Hannah (1964). *I Never Promised You a Rose Garden,* Holt.
-Hermes, Patricia (1982). *You Shouldn't Have to Say Good-bye,* Scholastic Inc.
-Johnson, Julie (1989). *Understanding Mental Illness: For Teens Who Care About Someone with Mental Illness,* Lerner.
-McDaniel, Lurlene (1992). *When Happily Ever After Ends,* Bantam Book.
-Naylor, Phyllis Reynolds (1986). *The Keeper,* Atheneum.
-Oneal, Zibby (1980). *The Language of Goldfish,* Penguin Books.
-Riley, Jocelyn (1983). *Crazy Quilt,* Morrow.
-Stowe, Rebecca (1992). *Not the End of the World,* Pantheon.
-Voigt, Cynthia (1988). *Tree By Leaf,* Random House Inc.

## Family Problems
-Hinton, S. E. (1979). *Tex,* Dell Publishing.
-Hunter, Bernice Thurman (1981). *That Scatterbrain Booky,* Scholastic Inc.
-Myers, Walter Dean (1992). *Somewhere in the Darkness,* Scholastic Inc.
-O'Dell, Scott (1978). *Kathleen, Please Come Home,* Dell Publishing Inc.
-Roberts, Willo Davis (1991). *Scared Stiff,* Macmillan Publishing Co.
-Voigt, Cynthia (1982). *Dicey's Song,* Fawcett.
-(1981). *Homecoming,* Ballantine Books.

## Fears
-Hyde, Margaret (1987). *Horror, Fright & Panic: Emotions That Affect Our Lives,* Walker.
-Stolz, Mary (1963). *The Bully of Barkham Street,* Harper and Row.

-(1960). *A Dog on Barkham Street,* Harper & Row Junior Books.

## Friendships
-Clements, Bruce (1993). *Coming About,* Aerial.
-Cole, Brock (1991). *Celine,* Sunburst.
-Derby, Pat (1989). *Visiting Miss Pierce,* Sunburst.
-Ferris, Jean (1986). *The Stainless Steel Rule,* Farrar, Straus & Giroux.
-Feuer, Elizabeth (1987). *One Friend to Another,* Farrar, Straus & Giroux.
-French, Michael (1987). *Us Against Them,* Bantam Books.
-Garden, Nancy (1986). *Peace O River,* Farrar, Straus & Giroux.
-Greenberg. Jan (1985). *Bye, Bye, Miss American Pie,* Farrar, Straus & Giroux.
-Hermes, Patricia (1984). *Friends are Like That,* Scholastic Inc.
-Herzig, Alison Cragin (1985). *Shadows on the Pond,* Little, Brown and Company.
-LeShan, Eda (1990). *When Kids Drive Kids Crazy: How to Get Along With Your Friends and Enemies,* Dial.
-Mazer, Norma Fox (1987). *B, My Name is Bunny,* Scholastic Inc.
-Mazzio, Joann (1992). *The One Who Came Back,* Houghton Mifflin.
-McDonnell, Christine (1991). *Lucky Charms and Birthday Wishes,* Houghton Mifflin.
-Pfeffer, Susan Beth (1982). *Starting with Melodie,* Scholastic Inc.
-Powell, Randy (1992). *Is Kissing a Girl Who Smokes Like Licking an Ashtray?,* Farrar, Straus and Giroux.
-Rochman, Hazel, editor (1993). *Who Do You Think You Are?: Stories of Friends and Enemies,* Joy Street Books.
-Sachs, Marilyn, (1965). *Laura's Luck,* Doubleday & Co., Inc.
-Varenhorst, Barbara (1983). *Real Friends: Becoming the Friend You'd Like to Have,* HarperCollins.
-Youngs, Bettie (1990). *Friendship is Forever, Isn't It?,* Learning Tools.

## Gifted
-Cooney, Carolyn (1987). *Among Friends,* Bantam.
-Delisle, James and Galbraith, Judy (1987). *The Gifted Kids Survival Guide II,* Free Spirit.

-Galbraith, Judy (1983). *The Gifted Kids Survival Guide: For Ages 11 - 18,* Free Spirit.
-Oneal, Zilpha (1986). *In Summer Light,* Bantam.
-Paterson, Katherine (1985). *Come Sing, Jimmy Jo,* Avon.
-Stone,B. (1988). *Been Clever Forever,* Harper & Row.
-Voigt, Cynthia (1987). *Sons from Afar,* Atheneum.

## Growing Up

-Blume, Judy (1977). *Starring Sally J. Freedman as Herself,* Dell Yearling.
-(1974). *Are You There God? It's Me, Margaret,* Dell.
-Derby, Pat (1989). *Goodby Emily, Hello,* Farrar, Straus & Giroux.
-Seuss, Dr. (1990). *Oh, The Places You'll Go,* Random House.
-Ullman, James Ramsey, (1954). *Banner in the Sky,* Scholastic.
-Waber, Bernard (1971). *Nobody is Perfick,* Houghton Mifflin.

## Honesty

-Clements, Bruce (1984). *I Tell a Lie Every So Often,* Sunburst.
-Kincher, Jonni (1992). *The First Honest Book About Lies,* Free Spirit.
-Weiss, Ann (1988). *Lies, Deception and Truth,* Houghton Mifflin.

## Illness

-Abt, Samuel (1990). *LeMond: The Incredible Comeback of an American Hero,* Random House.
-Blinn, William (1972). *Brian's Song,* Bantam.
-Bombeck, Erma (1989). *I Want to Grow Hair, I Want to Grow Up, I Want to Go to Boise,* HarperCollins.
-Brancato, Robin (1977). *Winning,* Knopf.
Center for Attitudinal Healing (1978). *There is a Rainbow Behind Every Dark Cloud,* Celestial Arts.
-Cohen, Barbara (1974). *Thank You, Jackie Robinson,* Scholastic Inc.
-Cormier, Robert (1974). *The Bumblebee Flies Anyway,* Pantheon.
-Ferris, Jean (1987). *Invincible Summer,* Farrar, Straus & Giroux.
-Gaes, Jason (1987). *My Book for Kids with Cancer,* Melius and Peterson.
-Gunther, John (1949). *Death Be Not Proud,* HarperCollins.

-Hunter, Bernice Thurman (1984).  *A Place for Margaret,* Scholastic-TAB Publications, Ltd.
-Jewell, Geri with Stewart Winer (1984). *Geri,* Morrow.
-Kellogg, Marjorie (1993).  *Tell Me That You Love Me, Junie Moon,* Aerial.
-Klein, Norma (1974). *Sunshine,* Avon Flare.
-Kremitz, Jill (1989).  *How It Feels to Fight For Your Life,* Little, Brown
-Lancaster, Matthew (1985). *Hang Tough,* Paulist.
-Landau, Elaine (1990). *We Have AIDS,* Franklin Watts.
-LeVert, Suzanne (1993).  *Teens Face to Face with Chronic Illness,* Messner.
-Lund, Doris (1974). *Eric,* Lippincott.
-McDaniel, Lurlene (1993). *Baby Alicia is Dying,* Bantam Books.
-(1992). *Mother, Help Me Live,* Bantam Books.
-(1992). *Sixteen and Dying,* Bantam Books.
-(1990). *Time to Let Go,* Bantam Books.
-(1985). *Six Months to Live,* Willowisp Press Inc.
-(1983). *If I Should Die Before I Wake,* Willowisp Press Inc.
-Osius, Alison (1991). *Second Ascent: The Story of Hugh Herr,* Stackpole.
-Peck, Richard (1978). *Something for Joey,* Bantam.
-Stolp, Hans (1992). *The Golden Bird,* Bantam Doubleday Dell Publishing Group, Inc.
-White, Ryan and Cunningham, Ann Marie (1991). *Ryan White: My Own Story,* Dial.
-Young, Alida E. (1993). *Losing David,* The Trumpet Club.

**Learning  Differences/Mental  Illness**
-Brown, Roy (1978). *The Swing of the Gate,* Clarion.
-Bulla, Clyde Robert (1979).  *Daniel's Duck,* Harper and Row, Publishers.
-Byars, Betsy (1970). *The Summer of the Swans,* Scholastic Inc.
-Donovan, John (1973). *Remove Protective Coating a Little at a Time,* Harper.
-Garden, Nancy (1972). *The Loners,* Viking.
-Grace. Fran (1981). *Branigan's Dog,* Bradbury.
-Nelson, Carol (1980). *Dear Angie, Your Family's Getting a Divorce,* David C. Cook.
-Neufield, John (1969). *Lisa Bright and Dark,* Phillips.

-Oneal, Zibby (1980). *The Language of Goldfish,* Viking.
-Platt, Kin (1971). *The Boy Who Could Make Himself Disappear,* Dell.
-Potter, Marian (1979). *The Shared Room,* Morrow.
-Riley, Jocelyn (1982). *Only My Mouth Is Smiling,* Morrow.
-Shreve, Susan (1980). *The Masquerade,* Knopf.
-Shyer, Marlene (1978). *Welcome Home, Jellybean,* Scholastic Inc.
-Wells, Rosemary (1972). *The Fog Comes on Little Pig Feet,* Dial.
-Winthrop, Elizabeth (1978). *Knock, Knock, Who's There?,* Dell.

**Loss**
-Arrick, Fran (1980). *Tunnel Vision,* Bradbury.
-Blume, Judy (1981). *Tiger Eyes,* Dell Publishing Co., Inc.
-Bode, Janet (1993). *Death is Hard to Live With: Teenagers and How They Cope with Loss,* Delacorte.
-Buscaglia, Leo (1982). *The Fall of Freddie the Leaf,* Charles Slack.
-Carter, Alden R. (1987). *Sheila's Dying,* Putnam.
-Clements, Bruce (1992). *Tom Loves Anna Loves Tom,* Aerial.
-Davis, Jenny (1988). *Sex Education,* Orchard.
-Deaver, Julie Reece (1988). *Say Goodnight, Gracie,* HarperCollins.
-Donovan, John (1971). *Wild in the World,* HarperCollins.
-Ferris, Jean (1993). *Across the Grain,* Aerial.
-(1987). *Invincible Summer,* Farrar, Straus & Giroux.
-Gravelle, Karen and Haskins, Charles (1989). *Teenagers Face to Face with Bereavement,* Messner.
-Greenberg, Jan (1979). *A Season In-Between,* Farrar, Straus & Giroux.
-Grollman, Earl (1993). *Straight Talk About Death for Teenagers: How to Cope with Losing Someone You Love,* Beacon Press.
-Guest, Judith (1976). *Ordinary People,* Viking.
-Hyde, Margaret and Lawrence (1989). *Meeting Death,* Walker.
-Johnson, A. E. (1969). *A Blues I Can Whistle,* Four Winds.
-Jonsson, Reidar (1993). *My Life as a Dog,* Noonday.
-Jukes, Mavis (1985). *Blackberries in the Dark,* Dell Publishing Co., Inc.
-Klein, Norma (1975). *The Sunshine Years,* Dell Publishing Co., Inc.

-LeShan, Eda (1988). *Learning to Say Good-By: When a Child's Parent Dies,* Avon.
-McDaniel, Lurlene (1989). *Goodbye Doesn't Mean Forever,* Bantam Books.
-Naughton, Jim (1989). *My Brother Stealing Second,* HarperCollins.
-Paterson, Katherine (1977). *Bridge to Terabithia,* HarperCollins.
-Paulsen, Gary (1984). *Tracker,* Scholastic Inc.
-Peabody, Barbara (1986). *The Screaming Room,* Avon Books.
-Peabody, Kathleen and Mooney, M. (1993). *Swinging in the Wind: Kids-Survivors of a Crisis,* Sharp Publishing.
-Peck, Richard (1981). *Close Enough to Touch,* Delacorte.
-Peck, Robert Newton (1972). *A Day No Pigs Would Die,* Knopf.
-Pershall, Mary K. (1990). *You Take the High Road,* Dial.
-Richter, Elizabeth (1986). *Losing Someone You Love: When a Brother or Sister Dies,* Putnam.
-Schotter, Roni (1979). *A Matter of Time,* Philomel Books.
-Smith, Doris Buchanan (1973). *A Taste of Blackberries,* Scholastic Inc.
-Tyler, Anne (1991). *Saint Maybe,* Knopf.
-Zindel, Paul (1989). *A Begonia for Miss Applebaum,* HarperCollins.

## Motivation
-DeVenzio, Dick (1989). *Smart Moves: How to Succeed in School, Sports, Career, and Life,* Prometheus Books.
-Shusterman, Neal (1991). *Kid Heroes: True Stories of Rescuers, Survivors, and Achievers,* Tor Books.
-Zerafa, Judy (1982). *Go For It!,* Workman.

## Moving
-Grove, Vicki (1988). *Goody-bye My Wishing Star,* Scholastic Inc.
-Nida, Patricia and Heller, Wendy (1985). *The Teenager's Survival Guide to Moving,* Collier Books.
-Wilson, Budge (1986). *A House Far From Home,* Scholastic-TAB Publications Ltd.

## Multicultural Awareness
-Arrick, Fran (1981). *Chernowitz!,* Bradbury.

-Bawden, Nina (1969). *The Runaway Summer,* Puffin Books.
-Brooks, Bruce (1986). *The Moves Make the Man,* HarperCollins.
-Buss, Fran Leeper and Cubias, Daisy (1991). *Journey of the Sparrows,* Dutton/Lodestar.
-Crew, Linda (1989). *Children of the River,* Dell Publishing.
-Crutcher, Chris (1987). *The Crazy Horse Electric Game,* Greenwillow.
-Guy, Rosa (1992). *The Music of Summer,* Delacorte.
-Hamilton, Virginia (1987). *A White Romance,* Putnam.
-Houston, Jeanne Wakatsuki and Houston, James D. (1973). *Farewell to Manzanar,* Bantam Books.
-Kerr, M. E. (1973). *If I Love You, Am I Trapped Forever?,* HarperCollins.
-Major, Kevin (1981). *Far from Shore,* Delacorte.
-Myers, Walter Dean (1988). *Fallen Angels,* Scholastic Inc.
-(1987). *Crystal,* Viking.
-(1984). *Motown and Didi: A Love Story,* Viking.
- (1979). *The Young Landlords,* Viking.
-(1978). *It Ain't All for Nothin',* Viking.
-Thomas, Joyce, editor (1990). *A Gathering of Flowers: Stories About Being Young in America,* HarperTrophy.
-*Yolen, Jane (1991). The Devil's Arithmetic,* Penguin Books.

**Peer Pressure**
-Alcock, Vivien (1990). *The Trial of Anna,* Cotman.
-Cormier, Robert (1985). *Beyond the Chocolate Wars,* Knopf.
-(1974). *The Chocolate Wars,* Pantheon.
-Knowles, John (1959). *A Separate Peace,* Dell.
-Peck, Richard (1987). *Princess Ashley,* Delacorte.
-Rogers, Thomas (1980). *At the Shores,* Simon & Schuster.
-Stevens, Janice (1982). *Take Back the Moment,* New American Library.

**Responsibility**
-Collier, James Lincoln (1986). *When the Stars Begin to Fall,* Delacorte.
-Cooney, Caroline B. (1992). *Flight #116 Is Down,* Scholastic Inc.
-Duncan, Lois (1978). *Killing Mr. Griffin,* Dell Publishing.
-Hughes, Dean (1989). *Family Picture,* Atheneum.
-Phipson, Joan (1985). *Hit and Run,* Macmillan.

## School Problems
-Haas, Jessie (1992). *Skipping School,* Greenwillow Books.
-Snyder, Zilpha Keatley (1990). *Libby on Wednesday,* Dell Publishing.
-Vedral, Joyce (1991). *My Teacher is Driving Me Crazy,* Ballantine.

## School Success
-Bautista, Veltisezar (1990). *Improve Your Grades: A Practical Guide to Academic Excellence,* Bookhaus.
-Geoffrion, Sondra (1993). *Get Smart Fast: A Handbook for Academic Success,* R & E Publishers.
-Jensen, Eric (1989). *Student Success Secrets,* Barron's.
-McCutcheon, Randall (1985). *Get Off My Brain: A Survival Guide for Lazy Students,* Free Spirit.
-Schneider, Zola and Kalb, Phyllis (1989). *Countdown to College: Every Student's Guide to Getting the Most Out of High School,* The College Board.

## Self-Esteem
-Greene, Betty (1974). *Summer of My German Soldier,* Bantam.
-Johnson, Julie (1991). *Celebrate You: Building Your Self-Esteem,* Lerner.
-Kerr, M. E. (1978). *Dinky Hocker Shoots Smack!,* Dell.
-Malecka, Janina (1992). *Valuing Yourself: 22 Ways to Develop Self-Esteem,* J. Weston Walch.
-McKillip, Patricia (1980). *The Night Gift,* Atheneum.
-Palmer, Pat and Froehner, Melissa (1989). *Teen Esteem: A Self-Direction Manual for Young Adults,* Impact Publishers.
-Paterson, Katherine (1981). *Jacob Have I Loved,* Avon.
-Sheperd, Scott (1990). *What do You Think of You?: And Other Thoughts on Self-Esteem,* CompCare.
-Zindel, Paul (1977). *Pardon Me, You're Steppin gon My Eyeball,* Bantam.

## Sexuality
-Arrick, Fran (1978). *Steffie Can't Come Out to Play,* Bradbury.
-Arthur, Shirley (1991). *Surviving Teen Pregnancy: Your Choices, Dreams, and Decisions,* Morning Glory Press.

-Bell, Ruth, et. al. (1987). *Changing Bodies, Changing Lives: A Book for Teens on Sex and Relationships,* Vintage.

-Blume, Judy (1975). *Forever,* Bradbury.

-Borich, Michael (1985). *A Different Kind of Love,* Holt.

-Cohen, Susan and Cohen, Daniel (1989). *When Someone You Know is Gay,* Dell.

-Colman, Hila (1984). *Happily Ever After,* Scholastic.

-Crutcher, Chris (1989). *Chinese Handcuffs,* Greenwillow.

-Dizenso, Patricia (1976). *Why Me? The Story of Jenny,* Avon.

-Donovan, John (1969). *I'll Get There. It Better Be Worth the Trip,* HarperCollins.

-Duberman, Martin (1994). *Lives of Notable Gay Men and Lesbians,* Chelsea House.

-Ferris, Jean (1988). *Looking for Home,* Farrar, Straus & Giroux.

-Foreman, Matt (1994). *Homophobia,* Chelsea House.

-Garden, Nancy (1991). *Lark in the Morning,* Farrar, Straus & Giroux.

-(1984). *Annie on My Mind,* Sunburst.

-Gardner-Loulan, JoAnn, et. al. (1991). *Period: Revised and Updated with a Parents' Guide,* Volcano Press.

-Gravelle, Karen and Peterson, Leslie (1992). *Teenage Fathers,* Messner.

-Hacker, Sylvia (1993). *What Every Teenager Really Wants to Know About Sex: With the Startling New Information Every Parent Should Read,* Carroll & Graf.

-Guy, Rosa (1976). *Ruby,* Viking.

-(1973). *The Friends,* Holt.

-Hall, Lynn (1972). *Sticks and Stones,* Follett.

-Hautzig, Deborah (1978). *Hey, Dollface,* Alfred A. Knopf.

-Hill, Marjorie (1994). *Growing Up Gay or Lesbian,* Chelsea House.

-Holland, Isabelle (1972). *The Man without a Face,* Lippincott.

-Homes, A. M. (1989). *Jack,* Macmillan.

-Irwin, Hadley(1985). *Abby, My Love,* Atheneum.

-Jakobson, Cathryn (1993). *Think About Teenage Pregnancy,* Walker.

-Kelly, Gary (1993). *Sex & Sense: A Contemporary Guide for Teenagers, Revised Edition,* Barron's.

-Kerr, M. E. (1986). *Night Kites,* HarperCollins.

-Klein, Norma (1979). *Love is One of the Choices,* Dial.

-Koertge, Ron (1988). *Where the Kissing Never Stops,* Dell.
-Kuklin, Susan (1991). *What Do I Do Now?: Talking About Teenage Pregnancy,* Putnam.
-Levoy, Myron (1981). *Three Friends,* HarperCollins.
-Lowry, Lois (1988). *Rabble Starkey,* Dell.
-Luger, Harriet (1981). *Lauren,* Dell.
-Mazer, Norma Fox (1989). *Silver,* Avon.
-(1979). *Up in Seth's Room,* Delacorte.
Minkowitz, Donna, editor (1994). *AIDS and Other Health Issues,* Chelsea House.
-(1993). *Issues in Gay and Lesbian Life,* Chelsea House.
-Paton, Alan (1953). *Too Late the Phalarope,* Scribner's.
-Peck, Richard (1976). *Are You in the House Alone?,* Dell Publishing.
-Rench, Janice (1990). *Understanding Sexual Identity: A Book for Gay and Lesbian Teens and Their Friends,* Lerner.
-Rylant, Cynthia (1990). *A Kindness,* Dell.
-Scoppettone, Sandra (1974). *Trying Hard to Hear You,* HarperCollins.
-Silverstein, Herma (1989). *Teenage and Pregnant: What You Can Do,* Messner.
-Strasser, Todd (1985). *A Very Touchy Subject,* Delacorte.
-Voigt, Cynthia (1983). *A Solitary Blue,* Atheneum.

**Sibling Relationships**
-Blume, Judy (1976). *Tales of a Fourth Grade Nothing,* Dell.
-Bradbury, B. (1963). *The Loner,* McKay.
-Hinton, S. E. (1980). *The Outsiders,* Dell.
-Johnson, A. (1968). *Count Me Gone,* Simon & Schuster.
-Konigsburg, E. L. (1977). *From the Mixed Up Files of Mrs. Basil E. Frankweiler,* Dell.
-Mathis, Sharon (1987). *Teacup Full of Roses,* Puffin.
-Myers, Walter Dean (1988). *Scorpions,* HarperCollins.
-Pevsner, S. (1981). *And You Give Me a Pain, Elaine,* Pocket Books.
-Spinelli, Jerry (1984). *Who Put That Hair in My Toothbrush?,*Little, Brown.
-Voigt, Cynthia (1982). *Homecoming,* Fawcett Junior.
-(1982). *Dicey's Song,* Atheneum.

## Social Behavior
-Re, Judith and Schneider, Meg (1991). *Social Savvy: A Teenager's Guide to Feeling Confident in Any Social Situation,* Summit Books.

## Stepfamilies/Single Parent Families
-Gardner, Richard (1982). *The Boys and Girls Book About Stepfamilies,* Creative Therapeutics.
-Martin, Ann M. (1983). *Bummer Summer,* Scholastic Inc.
-Rosenberg, Maxine B. (1990). *Talking About Stepfamilies,* Bradbury.

## Stress Management
-Cohen, Daniel and Cohen, Susan (1984). *Teenage Stress,* Laurel-Leaf
-Fleming, Alice (1992). *What, Me Worry?: How to Hang in When Your Problems Stress You Out,* Scribner.
-Hipp, Earl (1991). *Feed Your Head: Some Excellent Stuff on Being Yourself,* Hazeldon.
-(1985). *Fighting Invisible Tigers: A Stress Management Guide for Teens,* Free Spirit.
-Maloney, Michael and Kranz, Rachel (1991). *Straight Talk About Anxiety and Depression: High School Help Line,* Dell.
-Newman, Susan (1991). *Don't be S.A.D.: A Teenage Guide to Handling Stress, Anxiety, & Depression,* Messner.
-VanWie, Eileen (1987). *Teenage Stress: How to Cope in a Complex World,* Messner.

## Teens Growing Up
-Bell, Alison and Rooney, Lisa (1993), *My Body, Myself: A Girl's Guide,* Lowell House.
-Byars, Betsy (1981). *The Cybil War,* Scholastic Inc.
-Cahill, Susan, editor (1993). *Growing Up Female,* Mentor.
-Childre, Doc Lew (1992). *The How-To Book of Teen Self-Discovery: Helping Teens Find Balance, Security, & Esteem,* Planetary Publications.
-Douthit, Gretchen (1991). *Inside Out: My Book About Who I Am and How I Feel,* Hazelden.
-Eichoness, Monte (1989). *Why Can't Anyone Hear Me?: A Guide for Surviving Adolescence,* Monroe Press.

-Espeland, Pamela and Espeland, Rosemary (1991). *Making the Most of Today: Daily Readings for Young People on Self-Awareness, Creativity and Self-Esteem*, Free Spirit.

-Gordon, Sol (1990). *Why Love is Not Enough: Second Edition*, Bob Adams.

-Harmon, Ed and Jamin, Marge (1988). *Taking Charge of My Life: Choices, Changes and Me*, Barksdale Foundation.

-Johnson, Julie (1992). *Making Friends, Finding Love: A Book About Teen Relationships*, Lerner.

-LeMieux, A. C. (1993). *The TV Guidance Counselor*, Morrow.

-Levinson, Nancy and Rocklin, Joanne (1992). *Feeling Great: Reaching Out to Live, Reaching in to Yourself -- Without Drugs*, Hunter House.

-Lewis, Barbara (1992). *Kids with Courage: True Stories About Young People Making a Difference*, Free Spirit.

-Lipsyte, Robert (1967). *The Contender*, HarperCollins Publishers..

-Madaras, Lynda (1993). *My Feelings, My Self*, Newmarket Press.

-Mayer, Barbara (1986). *The High School Survival Guide: An Insider's Guide to Success*, VGM Career Horizons.

-McCoy, Kathy (1992). *The New Teenage Body Book*, Perigee.

-Newton, Suzanne (1991). *Where Are You When I Need You?*, Puffin Books.

-Packer, Alex (1992). *Bringing Up Parents: The Teenager's Handbook*, Free Spirit.

-Parsley, Bonnie (1992). *The Choice is Yours: A Teenager's Guide to Self-Discovery, Relationships, Values, and Spiritual Growth*, Fireside.

-Spethman, Martin (1992). *How to Get Into and Graduate from College in 4 Years with...: Good Grades, A Useful Major, A Lot of Knowledge, A Little Debt, Great Friends, Happy Parents, Maximum Part Attendance, Minimal Weight Gain, Decent Habits, Fewer Hassles, A Career Goal, and a Super Attitude, All while Remaining Extremely Cool!*, Westgate Publishing.

-Wilson, Budge (1990). *The Leaving and Other Stories*, Scholastic Inc.

## Teen's Problems

-Adderholdt-Elliot, Miriam (1987). *Perfectionism: What's Bad About Being Too Good,* Free Spirit.

-Avi (1991). *Nothing But the Truth,* Avon Books.

-Bridgers, Sue Ellen (1987). *Permanent Connections,* Harper Keypoint.

-Colman, Warren (1990). *Understanding and Preventing Teen Suicide,* Children's Press.

-Gardner, Sandra (1990). *Teenage Suicide,* Messner.

-Glick, Stephen (1990). *Little by Little, The Pieces Add Up: Daily Readings for Teens,* Deaconess Press.

-Gordon, Sol (1985). *When Living Hurts,* Laurel-Leaf.

-(1981). *The Teenage Survival Book,* Times Books.

Greenberg, Harvey (1989). *Emotional Illness in Your Family: Helping Your Relative, Helping Yourself,* Macmillan.

-Johnson, Kendall (1992). *Turning Yourself Around: Self-Help Strategies for Troubled Teens,* Hunter House

-Kuklin, Susan (1993). *Speaking Out: Teenagers Take on Race, Sex, and Identity,* Putnam.

-Lang, Denise (1990). *But Everyone Else Looks So Sure of Themselves: A Guide to Surviving the Teen Years,* Shoe Tree Press.

-Nixon, Joan Lowrey (1985). *The Stalker,* Dell Publishing Co., Inc.

-Owen, Lonny (1991). *What's Wrong With Me?: Breaking the Chain of AdolescentCodependency,* Deaconess Press.

-Ryan, Elizabeth (1989). *Straight Talk About Parents,* Dell.

-Salzman, Marian, editor (1991). *Greetings From High School,* Peterson's.

-Stone, J. David and Keefauver, Larry (1990). *Friend to Friend: Helping Your Friends Through Problems,* Educational Media.

-Switzer, Ellen (1992). *Anyplace But Here: Young, Alone and Homeless - What to Do,* Atheneum Books.

-Toma, David and Biffle, Christopher (1992). *Turning Your Life Around: David Toma's Guide for Teenagers,* HarperPerennial.

-Van Raven, Pieter (1989). *The Great Man's Secret,* Puffin Books.

-Vedral, Joyce (1987). *I Can't Take It Any More: How to Get Up when You're Really Low,* Ballantine.

-(1986). *My Parents are Driving Me Crazy,* Ballantine.
-Wesson, Carolyn (1988). *Teen Troubles: How to Keep Them from Becoming Tragedies,* Walker.
-Wirths, Claudine (1987). *I Hate School: How to Hang in & When to Drop Out,* HarperTrophy.

## War/Survival
-Blackwood, Gary L. (1987). *Wild Timothy,* Macmillan Inc.
-Bosse, Malcolm (1993). *Deep Dream of the Rain Forest,* Farrar, Straus and Giroux.
-Cridle, Joan and Mann, Teeda Butt (1987). *To Destroy You Is No Loss,* Atlantic Monthly Press.
-Dawidowicz, Lucy S. (1989). *From That Place and Time: A Memoir, 1938-1947,* Norton.
-Frank, Anne (1952). *The Diary of a Young Girl,* Doubleday.
-Jens, Inge, editor (1987). *At the Heart of the White Rose: Letters and Diaries of Hans and Sophie Scholl,* HarperCollins.
-Jury, Mark (1986). *The Vietnam Photo Book,* Vintage.
-Kehret, Peg (1989). *Nightmare Mountain,* Simon and Schuster Inc.
-Kheridan, David (1979). *The Road from Home,* Greenwillow.
-Lasker, Lawrence and Parkes, Walter F. (1983). *WarGames,* Dell Publishing Co., Inc.
-Mathabane, Mark (1990). *Kaffir Boy,* New American Library.
-Miklowitz, Gloria D. (1985). *After the Bomb,* Scholastic Inc.
-O'Brien, Tim (1990). *The Things They Carried,* Houghton Mifflin.
-Roth-Hano, Renee (1988). *Touch Wood: A Girlhood in Occupied France,* Four Winds.
-Safer, Morley (1990). *Flashbacks: On Returning to Vietnam,* Random House.
-Sender, Ruth Minsky (1986). *The Cage,* Macmillan.
-Wallace, Terry (1984). *Bloods: An Oral History of the Vietnam War by Black Veterans,* Random House.

## Weight Problems/Body Image
-Blume, Judy (1986). *Then Again, Maybe I Won't,* Dell Publishing Co., Inc.
-(1982). *Deenie,* Bradbury.

-(1974). *Blubber,* Dell Publishing Co., Inc.

-Cormier, Robert (1979). *After the First Death,* Pantheon.

-Danziger, Paula (1974). *The Cat Ate My Gymsuit,* Dell Publishing Co., Inc.

-Erlanger, Ellen (1988). *Eating Disorders: A Question and Answer Books About Anorexia Nervosa and Bulimia,* Lerner.

-Kerr, M. E. (1972). *Dinky Hocker Shoots Smack,* Harper and Row.

-Kolodny, Nancy (1992). *When Food's a Foe: How to Confront and Conquer Eating Disorders,* Little, Brown.

-Lee, Mildred (1969). *The Skating Rink,* Seabury.

Lipsyte, Robert (1977). *One Fat Summer,* Harper and Row.

-Lukes, Bonnie (1986). *How to be a Reasonably Thin Teenage Girl: Without Starving, Losing Your Friends, or Running Away from Home,* Athenneum Books.

-Maloney, Michael and Kranz, Rachel (1991). *Straight Talk About Eating Disorders: High School Help Line,* Dell.

-Meyer, Carolyn (1978). *C. C. Poindexter,* Atheneum.

-Miles, Betty (1979). *The Trouble with Thirteen,* Knopf.

-Ojeda, Linda (1993). *Safe Dieting for Teens: Design Your Own Diet, Lose Weight Effectively,and Feel Good About Yourself,* Hunter House.

-Peck, Richard (1972). *Don't Look and It Won't Hurt,* Holt, Rinehart and Winston.

-Phifer, Kate (1987). *Tall & Small: A Book About Height,* Walker.

-Powers, John R. (1975). *Do Black Patent Leather Shoes Really Reflect Upwards?,* Regnery.

-Sachs, Marilyn (1984). *The Fat Girl,* Dutton.

-Silverstein, Alvin & Virginia (1991). *So You Think You're Fat?,* HarperCollins.

-Stren, Patti (1985). *I Was a Fifteen Year Old Blimp,* Harper & Row, (F).

# Chapter 3

---

# The Cherokee Cultural Therapy Model

**Laurence French**
**Jim Hornbuckle**

## Introduction

The Cherokee are a unique American Indian group because of their culture and history. Their aboriginal heritage represents an intact traditional culture which had been in existence for over a thousand years (their ancestors have been traced back to at least 15,000 years in the southeast). Moreover, the aboriginal Cherokee culture was widely and richly documented providing an untarnished view into the workings of the *Harmony Ethos* (sometimes referred to as the Harmony Ethic). Also, a brief history of the Cherokee provides the counselor with a flavor of the long tradition of deceit the U.S. has perpetuated upon American Indians. It is imperative that we understand this history so that we can better empathize with the Indian client's general distrust of dominant societal laws, rules, regulations, policies and promises. In turn, we need to be certain that we can provide the services that we promise to American Indian clients. Trust is the most significant factor in a viable client/therapist relationship when working with American Indians.

The Cherokee were the largest of the seven *Civilized Tribes,* yet were subjected to extreme psychological and physical suffering at the hands of whites. Their removal in 1838 is still know as *the Trail of Tears.* Today they are the second largest Indian tribe with most of the population affiliated with the Western Tribe. The Eastern Band of Cherokee Indians represents the remnants of the 1,000 or so mountain Cherokees allowed to remain behind in 1838. And, while the aboriginal and traditional roots of both groups of Cherokee remain the same, our focus is on the Eastern Band of Cherokee. Unlike their Oklahoma counterparts, the Eastern Cherokee did not have an opportunity to assimilate with other Indian tribes when Oklahoma was *Indian Territory.* The Eastern Cherokee remained isolated until the Great Depression when plans were made for opening up a large eastern National Park -- the Great Smoky Mountains National Park. The dilemma facing the contemporary Eastern Cherokees is twofold. On the one hand, they have preserved their traditional language and customs more so than their western counterparts. On the other hand, they have been co-opted, by both the federal and local governments, into playing a stereotypical *movie Indian* role for the purpose of attracting tourists to this otherwise economically deprived region. This process has led to a bi-polar social environment whereby the Qualla Boundary, the main tourist section of the 56,000 acre reservation, is assaulted with millions of tourists from April to Labor Day. For the rest of the year, the reservation reverts back to a rural, mountain environment with chronic unemployment and a host of social and health problems, including mental health problems. It is as if the Qualla Boundary suffers from a manic-depressive disorder with the manic stage occurring during the tourist season quickly followed by the depressive stage during the off-season. Interestingly, the off-season coincides with the already dreary winter season. Thus, both psycho-cultural and environmental factors serve to fuel the high need to self-medicate among the Eastern Cherokees. During the tourist, manic season, traditional Cherokee customs, language, and cultural images are challenged with the false role they are compelled to portray. During the depressive, off-season, the collective, weakened cultural self-image attempts to recharge. Many cannot muster sufficient psyche energy to do so. These are the marginal Cherokees who turn to alcohol as a means of self-medication and escapism. This is the challenge that we faced over twenty-years ago when Jim Hornbuckle, a former Cherokee Police Officer who just recently earned his BS in Psychology, took over as Director of the Cherokee Alcohol and Mental Health Program. I became a clinical consultant to this program. Jim, and his wife Suzanne, also were the Cottage Parents of the tribal-run Girls' Cottage. This was part of the Cherokee Children's Home, facilities (three homes) on the reservation which provide cultural-specific care for neglected and/or abused enrolled children. I also served as a clinical consultant to the Hornbuckles in their role as Cottage Parents. It was within these environments that our Cherokee Cultural Therapy Model emerged.

## Cherokee Culture and Traditions

Linguistically, the Cherokees are related to numerous other tribes, including both the Iroquois and Tuscarora Indians. The Iroquois were and still are the largest northeastern confederacy of tribes, while the Tuscarora (part of the Iroquois Confederacy) were related to the Cherokees. The Cherokees were the largest southeastern tribe at the time of white contact with a population estimated of over 20,000. Today the Tuscarora, along with the remnants of numerous other smaller tribes and escaped black slaves, comprise the 40,000 strong, non-tribal Lumbee Indian confederation located in North Carolina. It is speculated that thousands of years ago the ancestors of both the Iroquois and Cherokees were comprised of the same parent tribe which ranged from the Saint Lawrence River to the Florida Everglades.

The aboriginal Cherokee were recorded as being of middle stature with light brown or olive complexions. Lieutenant Henry Timberlake considered them to be both handsome and proud. He went on to say they had erect posture and were well built with small hands and feet. Females dressed in mid-length buckskin skirts, waistcoats, leggings and moccasins. The women wore their hair long, braided or coiled on top of their heads. Men wore buckskin loin cloths, shirts and moccasins during warm weather, adding leggings during the winter. The men shaved their head and face except for a patch on the back of their head. Here they wore one feather which indicated their clan affiliation. Children went unclad, weather permitting, until puberty, at which time they followed the prescribed dress pattern for their sex group. The aboriginal Cherokees called themselves, *Ani-Yun-Wiya,* or the "real or principal people." Other tribes referred to them as *the Tsalagi,* meaning Cave People. The English translation of Tsalagi became *Cherokee.*

The aboriginal world-view and creation myth of the Cherokee was one where they believed that the earth was a great island floating in a sea of water. Above the earth island was the "sky vault" made of solid rock. The earth island, according to this belief, was secured to the sky vault by four cords, each attached to one of the four corners of the earth island. The Cherokee considered themselves to be the principal people on the earth island. The Cherokee, like other American Indian groups, respected the natural phenomena that played such an important role in their survival. Nature, and not humans, was the predominant force within this aboriginal belief system.

The Cherokees, at the time of white contact, claimed some 40,000 square miles of territory encompassing areas in eight states-- Georgia, Alabama, South Carolina, North Carolina, Tennessee, Kentucky, Virginia and West Virginia. The Cherokee had some 60 permanent villages within this vast territory. For the most part, the Cherokees exercised local autonomy within their villages. The larger link between the villages was the clan structure, comprised of seven matrilineal clans. Cherokees identified themselves according to their clan affiliation. The seven clans are the *Wolf Clan*, the *Deer Clan*, the *Bird Clan*, the *Red Paint Clan*, the *Blue Paint Clan*, the *Wild Potato Clan* and the *Long Hair* or *Twister Clan*.

The clan structure held the Cherokees together as a people. It provided their identity and regulated marriages and mobility as well. The Cherokees had a matrilineal/matrilocal system. Within this structure the female played a dominant role within both the family and village structure. Equally significant, Cherokees traced their lineage through the female's mother's clan. When a Cherokee couple married, they moved to the home of the bride.

An unmarried male would refer to his mother, in particular, and her clan, in general, for his family identification. Once married, he would then also refer to his mother-in-law and her clan for his identity. Females merely associated with their own clan and with the clan of their immediate female superior (mother, grandmother). During aboriginal times most of the 60 villages had all seven clans represented. Those few that did not have all seven clans represented became known as *neutral villages* for those fugitives whose clan was not represented. The 60 villages were organized into four districts. Each district, in turn, had at least one strong village which acted more or less as its district capital. Similarly, each clan had a *mother village* where the ultimate matriarch resided. Clans, regardless of district affiliation, consulted with their respective mother village concerning family norms, regulations and sanctions.

Each village had a *Town House* which was used for public meetings. The importance of this structure was stressed by both its size and design. It was the largest village structure and was often elevated on a mound so as to emphasize its significance. It consisted of seven sides, one for each of the Cherokee clans. The Town House represented the heart of the village, and to signify this a symbolic flame was kept burning in the Town House throughout the year. The Town House also served as the village religious center and the most important social institution within the aboriginal Cherokee society. It provided the binding force necessary for this otherwise highly decentralized people to stay together as a tribe. All important matters were discussed publicly within the Town House. No one was omitted, and all adults, both males and females, could participate. Each adult, regardless of gender, had a vote in village/clan/tribal matters. Decisions were based upon consensus, and once agreement was reached, all concurred, even the dissenters. Within these meetings the Cherokee grouped themselves according to clan affiliation and not by sex, age or viewpoint. They sat in their respective clan sections with the arbiters seated in the center, close to the flame of vitality.

Each village had two chiefs who represented white and red factions typical of southeastern Indians, and the nature of the discussion determined which chief presided over the town meeting. The "white chief" regulated domestic affairs, which were especially important from spring planting until the fall harvest. The *red chief*, or warrior chief, was more important during the winter season, which was the time for war. Females played an important role in both domestic and war councils, with evidence indicating that on occasion they even served as *white chiefs*. The fact that most village chiefs were males does not, however, imply that the females played subordinate roles to men. Females seem to have had an equal voice in all village councils, in addition to playing a very crucial role in the social regulation and enculturation of the traditional ways. The males played the dominant role in external affairs such as wars, hunting and intervillage competition while the females regulated intravillage domestic affairs as well as intervillage clan matters. The females may have even had the upper hand since males had little say regarding clan regulations and sanctions while females played an important role even on the war council where an assemblage of *war women*, or *pretty women*, offered counsel concerning strategy, time of attack, fate of captives and other important matters.

The major external check on taboos, custom violations and the administering of sanctions was the intratribal clan structure. The Cherokee ethos or value system helped to sustain their harmonious domestic lifestyle. This society had no policemen, courts, social workers, or written laws. It was regulated by custom, dictated and enforced through consensus and not through formal law. Gearing (1962) summarized the Cherokee ethos as "Old equals good equals honor." This represented a complicated psychology and social process which served to perpetuate both harmony and the status quo. Deference, ritual purification and avoidance were the three most crucial values associated with the Cherokee ethos, which stressed cooperation rather than competition. Thomas (1958) labeled the Cherokee ethos *The Harmony Ethic*, thereby setting it apart from the western-oriented, *Protestant Ethic*. The Cherokees' early belief system must indeed have been a strong and powerful one since attributes of it have survived up until the present.

Deference, then as today, was expressed in terms of respect, especially when complying with a friend or relative's wishes and not in terms of formal obligation such as exists in the larger dominant U.S. society (civil, criminal and/or juvenile adjudication).

The contemporary Cherokees, like all federally-recognized tribal entities, are now compelled to use social and legal agencies in resolving certain matters determined by tribal and/or federal codes.

Within the traditional Cherokee culture, avoidance represented the actual implementation of the deference value. Here, elaborate networks of avoidance provided the needed regulatory sanctions, thereby minimizing the need for and use of formal controls such as police power, courts and corporal punishment. Ostracism was the most common control mechanism while death was reserved only for the most serious transgressions. Ostracism as a control sanction also included disapproval and ridicule while death fell into the realm of vengeance. Both types of control were administered by the clan. Serious transgressions included murder, violation of mourning taboos and the abusing of women and children. In these instances, vengeance became a clan responsibility. The clans involved (both victim's and offender's) acted as "corporate individuals" in resolving these matters. Often they sought a reasonable compromise regarding the obligatory avenging of the transgression. Clan obligations and not emotions prevailed within the aboriginal Harmony Ethos, creating an environment of rational justice. If the two clans could not reach a satisfactory compromise, then the issue was brought before the village council for advice, again leaving the ultimate solution to the respective clans involved.

During aboriginal times, summer stick ball competition and winter war parties provided temporary escape from the dictates of the Harmony Ethos, allowing both males and females an outlet for pent-up frustrations. The new year purification ritual (consumption of the *black drink* which induced vomiting, hence internal cleansing) and its week-long celebration culminated in a total emotional purge of any tensions acquired during the year. This system seemed to work well for the early Cherokees. White insistence on eliminating these ritualistic tension outlets, while not replacing them with any viable alternative, has greatly increased the frustration level of many contemporary Cherokees, making them susceptible to excessive stress and its corresponding personal and social problems.

Among the aboriginal Cherokees, personal freedom was best expressed in terms of the family process. Young Cherokee children were socialized to play the appropriate sex role via modeling and instructions from the *grandparents*. Once children reached puberty and acquired the necessary skills for their gender and age cohort, they were eligible for marriage. Contrary to the popular Indian stereotype, Cherokee brides were not bought, given away or bargained for. Dowries were unknown among the Cherokees. They practiced free mate selection centuries before it became a popular European and American practice. The decision was ultimately left up to the prospective bride. Her hand was asked for, and only she could consent. Once married, males had to move into the home and village of the bride's mother. The only constraints on the free choice in selecting mates were the rules of exogamy which prohibited a Cherokee from marrying within one's own or one's father's clan. Corresponding rules of endogamy encouraged Cherokees to marry into either of one's grandfather's clans.

Marriages were regulated by the women in the village. The female members of the clan adhered sanctions to both male and female marital offenders when they violated sacred clan taboos. The most serious transgressions were those involving neglect of wife and children and the violation of widow's and widower's mourning customs. When a husband neglected his wife or children other males were not involved in the dispute unless authorized by their clan matriarchs. Records indicate that violators of family taboos, including men, were often publicly beaten by female members of the abused person's clan.

Moreover, the wife had considerable license regarding family size. Not having today's knowledge of birth control or abortion, a mother was allowed to perform infanticide if she wanted to rid herself of an unwanted child. A male's doing the same thing constituted murder and likely the death sentence. Divorce was a rather simple process. The female merely placed her husband's belongings outside the dwelling if she chose to divorce him while the husband simply moved out if he chose to initiate divorce. Since brothers-in-laws and other male relatives did not get involved in these matters, the male peer group was seldom disrupted by a marital breakup. Children were cared for by the wife's clan and seldom posed a problem. If a mother wanted to relieve herself of older dependent children, she merely gave them to someone within her clan who would provide for them.

This system allowed maximum personal license among adults with minimum trauma for the children. After the death of a spouse during aboriginal times, widows were expected to marry their deceased husband's brother, the *levirate* while widowers were expected to marry their deceased wife's sister, the *sororate.* It is not known how rigidly this custom was enforced given the ease with which Cherokees could divorce their spouse. The fact of the matter is that the aboriginal Cherokee females operated from a position of social and personal strength, a phenomenon which has survived to the present.

## Cherokee History of Accommodation

Contact with the European culture had many shortcomings including the unexpected such as disease. In 1738, a smallpox epidemic decimated the Cherokee making them more susceptible to attacks from other tribes and Indian slave dealers, a new activity encouraged by the British. Nonetheless, by the early 1700s, the Cherokees had the guns, goods, and illnesses of the white man. White/Indian contact also forced the Cherokee to become more tolerant of other groups especially since eastern Indian groups were being pushed into their territory. It was during this time that whites, notably of Scottish, Irish, and English descent, moved among the Cherokee contributing to the emergence of *mixed bloods,* a group that played an important role in future developments of the Cherokee Nations.

It was during this time of early contact that the Cherokee were forced to reassess their international policies which eventually led to the creation of the new Cherokee Nation, patterned after that of the American republic. Prior to the unification of the Cherokee villages, Kituwah and Chota come the closest to representing any Cherokee capital. The former was the largest and oldest *Mother Town* while the latter was the most significant village in the Overhill section. During times of tribal crises spokespersons from one or both of these villages mediated until the situation abated.

In the late 1700s, increased white contact instituted a situation of perpetual crises. There was now a demand for permanent leadership. Little Turkey, of the Ustanali village, emerged as the tribe's *beloved man,* or tribal Red Chief. Subsequently, a Grand Cherokee National Council was developed in 1792 in order to deal specifically with the issues of national leadership, centralized government, and a new political philosophy sufficient to prepare the Cherokee for continuous Indian/white relationships. Little Turkey was selected as the first *Principal Chief,* a title still in use among both the Eastern and Western Cherokees (Malone, 1956; Reid, 1970; 1976).

In 1817, a national bicameral legislature consisting of an upper house (*Standing Committee*) and a lower house (*National Council,* later renamed the *National Committee*) replaced the old National Council which was comprised of area and village chiefs. The Standing Committee was much like the U.S. Senate while the National Council reflected our U.S. Congress. By 1822, the mold for the Cherokee Nation was set. Path Killer was Principal Chief while Charles Hicks was Vice Chief, John Ross was President of the National Committee and The Ridge was Speaker of the Council. Hicks, Ross, and The Ridge later played crucial roles within the Nation. A year later the Cherokee Nation developed a Supreme Court. Finally, in 1827, a National Constitution was adopted and ratified and a new national capital, New Echota, was selected (Rights, 1974; Sheehan, 1974).

This movement toward a European-styled "civilization" was designed with self-preservation in mind. The cost of this western-type democracy was at the expense of certain aboriginal freedoms. Females who were once the political peers of male Cherokees were now disenfranchised like their white counterparts. Now only male descendants of Cherokee females, with the exception of black mixed-bloods, were eligible candidates for the General Council, or for any elected or appointed office, providing they were at least twenty-five years of age. All males, except those of black mixed-blood, eighteen years of age or older could vote. Accordingly, the Principal and Vice Chiefs, the Treasurer, the three Supreme Court Justices, and the National Marshalls were elected by the General Council to serve for four-year terms. The General Council could also override the Chiefs' veto by a two-third margin or more. Due process, a Bill of Rights, trial by jury, and religious freedom were also incorporated into the New Cherokee constitution. Clearly, this was an exact copy of the U.S. federal government ideals at that time. The major difference was that the chief executive position was that of *Chief* instead of *President*. (It was not until the 1990s that a major recognized tribe, the Navajo or *Dine'*, changed from Chief to President.)

The success of the Cherokee Nation was remarkable by any standard. By 1825, the Cherokee were successful farmers, herdsmen and merchants. There were large herds of cattle, horses, hogs, and sheep with crops of cotton, tobacco, wheat and corn. Indeed, Cherokee merchants had a favorable trade balance with international exports extending as far west as New Orleans. Financially the Cherokee Nation operated in the black. They also owned well over a thousand African slaves. Eastern liberals were proud of the Cherokees' separate, yet equal, civilization that parallelled that of the larger U.S. society.

Despite these changes and adaptations, southern whites wanted all American Indians removed from the southeast. Moreover, these same whites coveted the farms, villages, and plantations that the Cherokee Nation created. The Cherokee removal had its start with the1802 Georgia Compact and the 1803 Louisiana Purchase. Georgia soon tired of waiting for the Cherokee to be removed and embarked on a campaign designed to drive them out. White vigilantes, known as *pony clubs,* raided Cherokees with the consent of the state government. Cherokees, on the other hand, had no legal recourse to combat this harassment.

In 1830, the Indian Removal Bill was passed by Congress compelling all southeastern Indians to move to Indian Territory (Oklahoma) west of the Mississippi River. The U.S. Supreme Court ruled in favor of the Cherokee but they were forcefully removed in 1838. On May 23, 1838 the U.S. Army began the roundup of Cherokees placing them in stockades while white settlers first looted and then claimed their abandoned homes, farms, plantations, and villages.

The cost of removal was expensive in terms of human lives and suffering, over four thousand, one-fifth of the Cherokee Nation, died as a direct result of removal. Some died in the stockades where little attention was given to their welfare while thousands more died en route along the *Trail of Tears*. Hundreds more died immediately upon arrival in Oklahoma (Indian Territory) due to illness associated with removal. About a thousand Cherokees who fled into the Appalachian mountains were allowed to stay behind after their leaders were executed by the U.S. Army. Those who were removed comprise the Western Cherokees while those who stayed behind constitute the ancestors of the contemporary 8,000 Eastern Cherokees (Bedford, 1972; Fleischmann, 1971; Forrest, 1956; French, 1981; 1987; 1994; Mooney, 1972; Woodward, 1963).

As a brief post-script, the Western Cherokees rebuilt their Nation only to have it destroyed again during the War Between the States (Civil War). Reconstruction and then the onslaught of white settlers soon served to destroy the Western Cherokee Nation. The destructive blow crushing the Western Cherokee Nation came with the Dawes Act (1887) which, among other things, abolished common ownership of Indian land virtually destroying Indian tribes as autonomous entities. Land was now allotted to white settlers (Boomers) and, in 1890, the Territory of Oklahoma emerged and became a state in 1907. The Eastern Cherokees remained culturally dormant until the Great Depression when the federal government now had better use of them and their land -- the creation of the Great Smoky National Park (Collier, 1973, French & Hornbuckle, 1981; French, 1987; 1994).

## Cherokee Cultural Therapy Model

Increased white contact among the Eastern (Qualla) Cherokees, although delayed nearly a century, quickly challenged their traditional heritage which, unlike their Western cousins, survived forced removal, the Civil War, Reconstruction, and the destruction of Indian Territory. Within a decade of their completion, the Great Smoky National Park and the Blue Ridge Parkway brought thousands of tourists as well as shops, motels and restaurants to the Qualla Boundary. The Cherokee's role in this master plan was to nurture the popular media Indian stereotype as an attraction for the tourist industry. The overall effort was successful in that this plan opened up a once barren and isolated area, bringing prosperity to many of its inhabitants as well as making the area's beauty accessible to millions of tourists (Bauer, 1970; French & Hornbuckle, 1981; French, 1987;

1994).

This tourist role and the bi-polar circumstances of their lives has seen a marked increase in marginal Cherokees. Since the 1950s, several generations of Cherokees have been enculturated within this tourist milieu. The end result has been the creation of a self-fulfilling prophecy whereby they come to believe the tourist Cherokee image as being their true heritage. Lost, for many, is the native language, customs, rituals, and crafts. This was the situation when we first began the Cherokee Cultural Therapy Model in the early 1970s.

The Cherokee Alcohol and Mental Health Program until this time was run by a succession of recovering Indian Alcoholics. These individuals were usually lay Christian preachers who lacked any formal training or education in the fields of substance abuse or mental illness. Clearly this was a token program designed to meet minimal federal, state and local concerns so that additional monies could be brought into the tribal coffers. At the same time, every effort was made not to draw public attention to the true nature of the problem. The general feeling was that addressing the real issues of substance abuse and mental illness would hurt the tourist industry and the lucrative profits being made by the white-dominated Cherokee Historical Association consortium.

Jim Hornbuckle became the Director of the Cherokee Alcohol and Mental Health Program shortly after completing his BS in Psychology at Western Carolina University (WCU) in 1973. I was the faculty advisor for the Native American Student Organization at WCU at this time and also became the clinical advisor for the Cherokee Alcohol and Mental Health Program. Under Jim Hornbuckle's direction, the Cherokee Alcohol and Mental Health Program adopted a new approach to these problems among the Eastern Cherokees. First, a prevention outreach component was added. In the past, the Program only dealt with "walk ins." It was more a club for drinking buddies which often included the Program Director. Now, two full-blooded Cherokee leaders, one a female clan leader and herbalist and the other a former Tribal Chairman and Medicineman, were added to the staff. Both were fluent in Cherokee and knew the traditional ways. They operated the outreach component of the Program traveling to remote Cherokee villages such as Big Cove and Snow Bird. Meanwhile, the base program, housed on the Qualla Boundary, began to target potential clients who, in the past, avoided treatment. We even proposed a tribal community facility where Cherokees could go to avoid the temptations of alcohol, drugs, and violence. This was known as Cherokee House. The proposal was never endorsed by the tribe, again due to the feared stigma this would bring them but was picked up by the surrounding white community and renamed Hawthone House.

The next stage in the Cherokee Cultural Therapy Model was a plan to involve those traditional women who still knew the aboriginal arts and crafts. This reflected the traditional method of the clan elders teaching the younger generation the cultural ways. The therapeutic rationale for this element of the Program was twofold. One, it would reinforce the significance of the traditional female role within contemporary Cherokee society. Secondly, this interaction would provide the non-traditional generations of Cherokee females with critical aspects of their heritage. Both groups would then be better armed to avoid the pitfalls of marginality, notably that affiliated with the cycle-of-abuse such as fetal alcoholism.

A significant element of this project was the assistance we received from Jeannette Henry-Costo and Rupert Costo, Directors of the American Indian Historical Society and publishers of *Wassaja, The Wee Wish Tree*, and the *Indian Historian* as well as books by American Indians about Indian history and culture (The Indian Historian Press). Given the Cherokees matrilineal tradition, this became an excellent medium for teaching and preserving lost aspects of the traditional culture to the marginal females who know little about these skills. With the informal apprenticeships came valuable interactions and the dissemination of the traditional ways. Included in these sessions were the skills of pottery, sash weaving, basketry, bead work and quill work in addition to the preparation of traditional foods. The Cherokees are famous for their unique pottery and basketry. At this time, only a few women knew how to use the old coil method where designs were made with a stamping paddle and the pottery fired over an open fire producing a beautiful black finish. Cherokee baskets, those made of rivercane, white oak splints, sugar maple splints and hickory bark adorned with natural dyes are beautiful. Of these the Cherokee double-weave baskets are highly valued. Again, this was a dying tradition in the early 1970s. The traditional foods were one of the most popular elements of this program. This element allowed the younger non-traditional Cherokee females to participate in aboriginal rites and customs where traditional meals played such an important role. The traditional Cherokee elders taught their younger non-traditional counterparts how to gather and prepare the indigenous wild spring plants such as poke, sochan, dandelions, sweet grass, artichokes, ramps and sweet potatoes. In the fall, nature provides buckberries, huckleberries, raspberries, blackberries, strawberries, gooseberries and elderberries as well as persimmons and wild grapes. Wild nuts include hazelnuts, chestnuts, butternuts, Chinquapins, black walnuts and hickory nuts. Cress is also found during the winter. PreColumbian horticulture included crops of corn, cabbage, various beans, apples and other fruits and honey.

One of the most popular traditions taught by the elders was the preparation of traditional breads. Now that these skills are no longer in jeopardy of being lost forever, these breads are currently being prepared for numerous Cherokee rites and customs. Bean bread is made of corn flour mixed with boiled dry beans (leather breeches) which is then boiled in water. It can be eaten either cold or warm. Hot bean bread is often used as dumplings and added to stews and soups. Chestnuts, sweet potatoes and carrots can be substituted for beans creating a number of variations of bean bread. These were naturally preserved and could be taken on long trips before the advent of horses. Sweet bread was also popular. It is a bean bread flavored with honey. Fried breads are not traditional foods among any American Indian group. They are an adaptation to "reservation commodity foods" when wheat flour and cooking oils (fats) were part of the government supplies. Other traditional foods preserved by the Cherokee female elders during these cultural interactions were fish soups and fish dishes and yellow jacket soup. Yellow jacket soup requires that the bees be gathered in the winter when they are not active. The comb is then boiled to loosen the bees. The grubs, or bees, can then be boiled right in the soup broth or they can be fried and eaten as a snack. Locusts (grasshoppers) can also be either boiled into a soup or fried (browned) and eaten as a snack. Turtle soup is also popular as is squirrel gravy, a combination of parboiled squirrel meat and corn mush.  This project served to preserve these traditional meals which continue to be popular today.  Rupert and Jeannette Costo aided in the preservation of these traditions and customs provided in this project by publishing them in a special issue of *The Wee Wish Tree,* entitled "The Qualla Cherokees of North Carolina"(French & Crowe, 1976).

Another lesson gained from the American Indian Historical Society was the need for multiculural education among the Cherokee, or any American Indian group for that matter.  In my capacity as faculty advisor for American Indian students at Western Carolina University, I fought so that more Cherokees would be admitted into and encouraged to complete degrees at WCU.  This led to the establishment of a WCU site on the Qualla Boundary.  We also saw the first substantial number of Cherokee Indians complete their degrees.  Jim Hornbuckle was among this cohort.

Part of the cultural philosophy embraced by the Costos was the need for multicultural instruction.  Toward this end we developed a Cherokee Teacher Preparation and Counseling Proposal.  We argued that multicultural instruction requires that teachers be trained as counselors.  Taken a step further we felt that all teachers should be exposed to multicultural counseling especially given the heterogeneous composition of the larger dominant U.S. society.  Parochial education, regardless of the racial, ethnic, or religious groups involved, tends to enhance group-specific ethnocentrism, hence exacerbating minority/ majority strain.  Multicultural education, on the other hand, attempts to preserve unique cultural, ethnic and/or religious orientations while at the same time preparing all members of society to function within the larger majority society.  This is the basic tenet of our *survival school* concept.

What was happening among the Eastern Cherokees up until the early 1970s was a condescending approach.  We felt that majority teachers who patronize Indian students are not teaching with the multicultural perspective regardless of how helpful they may think they are.  Murray and Rosalie Wax portrayed this situation as they experienced it while working among the Sioux and Chippewa:

A major assumption of certain professional and semi-professional Helpers is that the giving of assistance is an entirely one-sided process.   It is the Helper who determines who needs help and what type of help is needed, it is they who then plot the strategy of administering help....   But it is not working today...and it never worked with traditional Indians (Wax & Wax, 1972:190).

It is clear to us that it is often counterproductive when teachers and/or counselors attempt to apply the tenets of the Protestant Ethic to Indian students and/or clients.   This ethnocentrism can result in a situation whereby teachers and/or counselors exacerbate the same problems the schools are mandated to resolve.   A basic consideration in counseling American Indians is to attempt to interpret their situation from their particular tribal orientation as well as within the larger pan-Indian orientation.

Based on this philosophy, I was instrumental in helping Western Carolina University in obtaining a million dollar federally-funded counseling and advisement center on campus.   Next came college courses offered at the Qualla Boundary some 26 miles away.   This project has survived to the present but is now threatened by the tribe due to coveted land designed for their planned expansion of the gambling program.  If this occurs then it will be yet another example of the tourist image winning out over the cultural-specific needs of the Cherokees themselves.   The gains of a few will again prevail over preserving tribal traditions.

The influence of the Cherokee female elders program quickly expanded to the tribal schools.   In the day care program, Cherokee children were introduced to traditional dances and songs.   This effort continues in kindergarten with the addition of Cherokee crafts, language and folklore.   Not only are these programs taught by local traditionalists, continued community input is maintained through parent advisory groups.   Cultural programs continue throughout grades 4 to 12 along with traditional western-oriented courses.   Moreover, Indian input continued throughout these years as well as in the neighboring elementary and secondary schools off the reservation.   This input in off-reservation schools is a condition of Johnson-O'Malley and Title IV government subsidies to public schools which have significant Indian student populations.   The tribe also has a Cherokee Advisory School Board which is comprised of elected members.

We also applied the Cherokee Therapy Model to the Girls' Cottage of the Cherokee Children's Home. As stated earlier, our cultural therapy program incorporated the craft skills of traditional females who otherwise came from alcohol-prone families. Here their cultural status was greatly enhanced by virtue of their new role as "teachers" of the traditional past. They, in turn, were encouraged to interact with the targeted group of Cherokee children with the goal of providing positive cultural role models for these girls. The targeted girls themselves stayed on the reservation and attended the reservation schools (they lived in the Girls' Cottage with Jim and Suzanne Hornbuckle from infancy until adulthood). All completed high school (Cherokee High School) while five attended college (one obtained a BA degree while two others completed the AA degree). Eight of these Cherokee females bore children (three have a single child; four have two children; and one has three children), seven during wedlock. One resident of the Girls' Cottage was crowned "Miss Cherokee" and "Miss Fall Festival" (the highest traditional status for a Cherokee teenage female). All continue to live on the reservation (Qualla Boundary) and only one has manifested any signs of alcohol-related problems (the "girls" now range in age from 25 to 33). One of the former residents of the Cherokee Children's Home is now an Associate Judge of the Cherokee Tribal Court. Most significantly, all of these Cherokee females continue to maintain a positive relationship with their Cherokee foster parnts (Jim and Suzanne Hornbuckle) while many have also reestablished positive adult-to-adult relationships with their biological parents (French, 1990).

The Native American Student Organization at Western Carolina University provided the incentive for tribal discussions of higher education, an area long represented at WCU by indifference and a high Cherokee drop-out rate. Our Cherokee adult education model and the cultural-specific objectives were published in 1977 in the *Indian Historian.*

1. To promote a sense of unity among Cherokee students attending college.

2. To encourage other Cherokee, both adults and high school students, to go to college.

3. To establish a tutorial and counseling program designed to help the Cherokee student adapt to this new cultural and academic setting.

4. To establish a Cherokee studies minor or concentration for Cherokee students.

5. To actively promote the Cherokee culture.

6. To gain recognition for the Cherokee's academic accomplishments and to use the Native American Student Organization as a vehicle for obtaining grants, scholarships...as well as exploring potential job prospects and graduate studies.

Cherokee input included suggestions for the following programs:

1. The Development of a summer preparatory program for Cherokee high school students and adults anticipating furthering their education.

2. Academic year tutorial programs for enrolled students.

3. Development of a special adult extension program on the reservation.

4. On-going Native American cultural workshops.

5. Establishment of a student companionship program.

6. Utilization of a Cherokee advisory group at the college and university level.

7. Creation of Cherokee and/or Native American curriculum at neighboring colleges and universities (French & Hornbuckle, 1977:39).

The Cherokee student cohort at Western Carolina University during the early 1970s soon became teachers, social workers and counselors among their own people. A scholarship was named for Richard (Yogi) Crowe, president of the Native American Student Organization when I served as faculty advisor during this critical era twenty years ago. Yogi attended Western Carolina University from 1973 until 1976 and went on to earn his B.S. Ed in 1979 and a M.P.H. in 1982, both at the University of Tennessee at Knoxville. A year later, in 1983, he was killed in an automobile accident at age 36. Yogi Crowe was the Director of the American Indian Recruiting Program for the School of Public Health at the University of North Carolina at Chapel Hill at the time of his death. To be eligible for the Richard (Yogi) Crowe Memorial Scholarship, a student must:

> 1. Be an enrolled member of the Eastern Band of Cherokee Indians;
>
> 2. Have been accepted into graduate school with preference going to those needy individuals in the areas of law, medicine, health, business and education, and
>
> 3. Be willing to return to Cherokee and contribute toward the betterment of the tribe for a minimum of two (2) years if employment is available.

Twenty years of these efforts have resulted in the reintroduction of the traditional Cherokee culture so that today Cherokees can discern between their original heritage and the tourist Indian image introduced over fifty years ago. Equally significant was the tribe's formal recognition of the destructive role of alcohol and substance abuse among the Eastern Cherokee. Credit for this is due more to federal influences than our efforts. Nonetheless, on July 16, 1987 Tribal Resolution No. 680 was passed.

> Whereas: Alcoholism and substance abuse is the most severe health and social problem facing Indian people today, and nothing is more costly to Indian people than the consequences of alcohol and substance abuse measured in physical, mental, social and economic terms; and
>
> Whereas: The Anti-Drug Act of 1986, PL 99-570 declares four (4) of the top ten (10) causes of death among Indians are alcohol and drug related injuries (18% of all deaths) chronic liver disease and cirrhosis (5%0,suicide (3%) and homicide (3%); and
>
> Whereas: Indian tribes have the primary responsibility for protecting and insuring the well-being of their members; and
>
> Whereas: the Eastern Band of Cherokee Indians elect to join with the Federal Government to combat the damaging effects of alcoholism and substance abuse, and to recognize the intend of the Memorandum of Agreement.
>
> Whereas: The Tribal Council has authorized t h e establishment of a Tribal Coordinating Committee per Resolution No. 422 (1986) to assume the primary responsibility for the implementation of efforts to combat

the effects of alcoholism and substance abuse within the tribal community.

Whereas: The Tribal Council has charged the Tribal Coordinating Committee to provide top priority services to Indian youth consistent with the Tribal Action Plan.

Whereas: The Tribal Coordinating Committee is provided full Tribal Council support with the authority to develop and implement the attached Tribal Action Plan.

Whereas: The purpose of the Tribal Action Plan is to coordinate a comprehensive prevention and treatment program for alcoholism and substance abuse and includes not only the existing resources, but will identify the additional resources necessary to combat these problems.

Now therefore be it resolved, by the Eastern Band of Cherokee Indians in annual council assembled at which a quorum is present, that the Tribal Coordinating Committee has identified alcoholism and substance abuse prevention and treatment as a priority, has developed a comprehensive Tribal Action Plan and hereby request the attached plan be adopted as it is in compliance with Anti-Drug Abuse Act of 1986, PI 99-570.

Dualism continues among the Eastern Cherokees. For the past decade the Principal Chiefs have supported the white-run tourist industry as do many other influential Cherokees. However, in fairness to the first elected female Princial Chief of the Eastern Band of Cherokee Indians, the current Chief, a special education teacher and school administrator by training and education, is also a strong advocate for education. Marginality, substance abuse and associated mental and physical health problems continue to plague the Cherokees. However, we would like to think that our efforts and the evolving Cherokee Cultural Therapy Model did much to reduce the negative effects of cultural marginality. Today, the federal government, through the Indian Health Services (IHS), had selected the Qualla Boundary for its Indian youth substance abuse program. Jim Hornbuckle is the Treatment Services Supervisor for the UNITY Regional Youth Treatment Center. He was also recently appointed by the Governor of North Carolina to serve as Chairman of North Carolina Commission on Substance Treatment and Prevention. Jim will serve in this capacity until April 30, 1998.

# The UNITY Regional Youth Treatment Center at Cherokee.

Interestingly, this program is similar to the Cherokee House Program we proposed to the tribe twenty years ago. The major difference is that this is a federally-funded, IHS program which serves the entire southeast and beyond. IHS has twelve area offices. There are ten Indian Health Service Youth Regional Treatment Centers. One program is *UNITY* located in Cherokee, North Carolina. The others are:

> *Raven's Way*
> 222 Tongas Drive
> Sitka, Alaska 99835
> *Nanitch Sahallie Program*
> 5119 River Road, NE
> Keizer, Oregon 97303
> *Jack Brown Treatment Center*
> Cherokee Nation of Oklahoma
> P.O. Box 948
> Tahlequah, Oklahoma 74465
> *Phoenix/Tucson Regional Treatment Center*
> 198 South Skill Center Road
> Sacaton, Arizona 85247
> *FNN/TCC Adolescent Treatment Program*
> P. O. Box 80450
> Fairbanks, Alaska 99708
> *New Sunrise Regional Treatment Center*
> P. O. Box 219
> San Fidel, New Mexico 87049
> *Four Corners Adolescent Treatment Center*
> P. O. Box 567
> Shiprock, New Mexico 87420
> *Inland Tribal Consortium Treatment Center*
> North 1617 Calispel
> Spokane, Washington 99205
> *California Youth Treatment Center*
> 1825 Bell Street, Suite 200
> Sacramento, California 95825

The Nashville Area provides services for all the recognized

eastern tribes. There are two Indian hospitals within the Nashville Area, one at Cherokee and the other in Philadelphia, Mississippi (Choctaw). There are also 13 health centers within this area ranging from Maine and New York in the northeast to Alabama, Louisiana, Texas and Florida in the south. UNITY RYTC (Regional Youth Treatment Center) is an adolescent residential treatment program for chemically dependent Native American youth within the Nashville Area.

UNITY opened its doors to the Nashville Area in October, 1989. The UNITY RYTC is a 20-bed co-ed facility with a capacity to serve 10 males and 10 females. The goal of UNITY RYTC is to provide a home-like environment, a place of healing where the physical, mental, emotional and spiritual receive equal attention. UNITY RYTC is a long-term, intensive residential treatment program which utilized the 12 Step program of recoverers along with a focus on the cultural uniqueness of Indian youth. A third component is Adventure Based Counseling. Chemical dependent education and individual and group counseling are the therapy techniques used in this program. The cultural component involves a cultural/spiritual assessment, Native American arts and crafts, legend telling, traditional dancing and participation in Sweat Lodge purifications. Clients must be referred through a Tribal Alcohol and Drug Program within the Nashville Area and be eligible to receive services from Indian Health Service. Clients can also be referred from outside of the Nashville Area if they are Indian Health Service eligible. Clients referred must be between the ages of 12 and 24. UNITY RYTC is located in the old Cherokee hospital. It is located on a hill overlooking the tribal council house, war memorial, elementary school and Oconoluftee River. Both the Sweat Lodge and Ceremony Wheel are located east of the hospital building facing the war memorial and parallel to the river.

The Sweat Lodge was developed by Lloyd Carl Owle, another of the Cherokees involved in our efforts twenty years ago. The entrance of the Sweat Lodge faces East looking down directly on the Cherokee War Memorial, a symbol of strength for the participants. Purifications rituals are held every Wednesday, at 6:00 for male clients and staff and at 7:00 for female clients and staff. Lloyd Carl Owle conducts all purifications in the Sweat Lodge. The fire, which is located directly in front of the entrance, is lit three hours in advance so as to provide sufficient coals to heat the stones for both sweat sessions. Once inside, the Fire Tender brings four stones into the Sweat Lodge. Prayers, meditation and stories about Indian culture and customs follow. Later, a fifth stone is brought in, this one representing Mother Earth. A sixth stone, representing the "people" who inherit Mother Earth, is brought into the Sweat Lodge. Lastly, the seventh stone, that representing Father Sky or the Great Spirit, is placed in the Sweat Lodge. The initial four stones and subsequent seven stones are symbolic representations of Mother Earth and Father Sky and the Sacred Circle of the Harmony Ethos. Purification is now in progress. Lloyd Carl Owle often recites one of his poems in the purification process.

### Indian Shoes
These shoes are old and worn
These shoes are old and torn,
These shoes have seen many miles
While tears haunted Indian styles.
These shoes have seen the years
These shoes know the Trail of Tears,
As many wore away
These shoes realized the need to stay.
These shoes are old and pitiful
Their roads were cruel and scornful
These shoes have walked in pain
They endured life with nothing to gain.
These shoes are Indian shoes
And as the end of life nears
These shoes will fade away
They walked the Trail of Tears one day.
Lloyd Carl Owle (French & Hornbuckle, 1981:145).

The Ceremony/Medicine Wheel is a spiritual circle with the four directions indicated by four animals and color rocks; the Deer (South/black), Wolf (West/yellow), Bear (North/green) and Eagle (East/purple). The red, Coyote, rock is kept outside the Ceremonial Wheel indicating that Coyotes are marginal Indians who have not yet been integrated into the Circle of Harmony. The East represents the most sacred of the four directions among American Indians.

The *twelve steps* to recovery for American Indians use the *Great Spirit* in place of the Judaic/Christian reference to *God*.

1. We admitted we were powerless over alcohol; that we had lost control of our lives.

2. We came to believe that a power greater than ourselves could help us regain control.

3. We made a decision to ask for help from a higher power and others who understand.

4. We stopped and thought about our strengths and our weaknesses and thought about ourselves.

5. We admitted to the Great Spirit, to ourselves and to another person the things we thought were wrong about ourselves.

6. We are ready, with the help of the Great Spirit, to change.

7. We humbly ask a higher power and our friends to help us change.

8. We made a list of people who were hurt by our drinking and want to make up for these hurts.

9. We ar making up to those people whenever we can, except when to do so would hurt them more.

10. We continue to think about our strengths and weaknesses and when we are wrong we say so.

11. We pray and think about ourselves, praying only for strength to do what is right.

12. We try to help other alcoholics and to practice these principles in everything we do.

American Indian youth enrolled in the UNITY RYTC progress through five levels each with its own treatment objectives and corresponding client privileges. These five stages in the treatment progression include the Coyote, Deer, Wolf, Bear, and Eagle. Note that all but the Coyote are represented within the Ceremony Wheel.

## Coyote

All youth enter the program at the Coyote level. At this stage of the treatment, the Indian youth is allowed one supervised (five minutes) phone call home to let his/her family know that the

Coyote is O.K. The treatment requirement associated with this
stage includes the following expectations.

    1. Client reads characteristics of the Coyote (marginal,
    ambiguous and isolated from his/her cultural heritage)
    and then writes what he/she thinks is expected of
    him/her as a Coyote.

    2. "Welcome to Our World" group within 2 hours
    of admission. Introductions of each patient in their
    respective groups. A generalized, enthusiastic
    welcome of each new patient to Unity.

    3. Evening "Celebration" Ceremony at the Medicine
    Wheel. The new Coyote will be welcomed onto the
    wheel. Following this activity the community will
    participate in a "Celebration Feast" (snacks and a
    welcome cake in honor of the new member).

    4. Client reads "Bill's Story" in the Big Book
    and/or watches "The Story of Bill W." video (depending
    upon the patient's ability to read and comprehend).
    He/she then answers five questions regarding the story.

    5. The client describes, in his/her own words, the
    philosophy of the 12 Steps.

    6. The client reads Chapter 5 of the Big Book, "The
    Promises."

    7. The client makes the initial Solace Walk with a staff
    member. This is intended to orient the new Coyote to
    the earth/creation environment and the way that UNITY
    incorporates ecology into the program.

    8. During "Coyote Time" (free time), the new Coyote will
    meet with the Coyote group and staff to talk about
    expectations of the group, expectations at UNITY,
    laundry schedules, clean-up schedules, room
    responsibilities, etc.

    9. The case manager meets with the Coyote for
    assessments, orientation to Patient Rights and
    Responsibilities, Group Norms, etc.. The client reads,
    sign, and receives a copy of this process.

    10. Other Coyotes are accountable for all new members
    at all times.

    11. New Coyotes are introduced to the Cultural/Spiritual
    Specialists and are given a tour of the purification lodge

(Sweat Lodge), and are oriented to the Medicine Wheel
as well as other outdoor areas that are used frequently.
12. The new Coyote is oriented to the Master
Treatment Plan. It is necessary to sign the treatment
plan and meet with three additional staff members, other
than the Case Manager. During these meetings the
client needs to convey his/her understanding of the
treatment plan.
13. The new Coyote is instructed to begin and maintain
a daily journal. The journal entries need to describe what
it feels like to be at UNITY. The Coyote is also expected
to log his/her willingness to commit to the treatment
progression.

### Deer

As a Deer, the client is allowed one 15-minute supervised phone
call to the tribal case worker from his/her reservation. They are
also allowed a five-minute unsupervised phone call to a family
member. Deers are also allowed to read a newspaper in the
morning between chores and 9:00 A.M. Deers may also request
to have house plants in their room.

The theme for the Deer stage is self-esteem and hope and
involves the following steps.

1. The client now describes how it tells to be a Deer and
what he/she thinks is expected of a Deer.
2. The Deer is required to describe, in writing, why
his/her life is out of control.
3. The Deer is expected to complete a collage based
on the promises of the Big Book, depicting what his/her
life can become from these promises. Each will share
the collage with the Deer group.
4. Deer participate in daily solace activity with staff
members. Solace therapy involves meditation and
connection with Mother Earth.
5. During Deer time the group works on specific activities
that teach them how to take care of basic needs and
practical living skills (survival skills).
6. Deer participate in *Stump Therapy* for one hour per
week. Here the Deer is taken to his/her stump for stump
therapy. A tree stump is selected and turned so that

it fits flat on the ground with the roots facing up. The idea is to identify inner and outer conflicts among the roots. Over time one is to eliminate these conflicts and therefore free the roots so they will be pure enough to hold the sacred drum which represents the *circle of harmony* within our life and our *Indianism.* The treatment goal is to provide insight to the client the aspects (roots) of the personality that have been masked by chemicals. This is a highly individualized process.

7. Didactic session on addiction as a disease is introduced at this stage using a multitude of approaches and techniques (lectures, role-playing films, group discussions).

8. As a group, Deer present brief weekly skits on the aspects of addiction as a disease thereby demonstrating their understanding of this clinical concept.

9. As a Deer, focus is placed on the affective component of treatment. There are specific Deer "Feelings" Groups where the clients act out, sculpt and use other creative techniques to experience their feeling and to process the significance of their affective understanding.

10. As a Deer, the client is required to write his/her understanding of the 12 Steps.

11. Deers must also write how they can apply the 12 Steps to both their lives and their cultural universe.

12. Each Deer develops a shield that depicts what he/she is currently "shielding" (anger, fear, hopelessness etc.).

13. As a Deer, the client experiences a preliminary *vision quest*, which involves an overnight expedition to get in touch with the basics of life. The client needs to fast for a minimum of 12 hours and prepare for the quest with a minimum of gear. The Deer will experience hunger, thirst and other depravations. Upon the return, the Deer is requested to identify in either words (written) or actions (demonstrating) the understanding of the experience. This activity will be noted in the personal

journal.
14. Academic studies begins at this level.
15. Self-hygiene skills are introduced at this level.
16. Issues discussed during Deer Groups include
sexual abuse, sexual identity, family violence and
how these situations occur and can best bedealt with
emotionally. Individual disclosures and situations
are avoided at this stage.
17. Discussions begin concerning one's *Indianism* and
how one feels about it. Marginality is not only
challenged, but replaced with a positive cultural-specific
self-image.
18. Deer are required to make at least three entries
daily concerning positive aspects of self, someone else,
or the surroundings.
19. Deer Group therapy identifies specific group goals.
20. Individual therapy addresses issues emerging from
group therapy goals as well as from the restructuring of
one's positive self-image, their Indianism.

### Wolf
At the Wolf stage, the client is allowed two five-minute
unsupervised phone calls and one 15-minute call to the tribe or
family per week. Clients may request musical instruments. They
are allowed to request a half-hour of private time per week. They
can request the use of an iron.
     The theme for the Wolf is trust and care. The program for this
stage includes the following twenty-three components.
     1. As a Wolf, the client is required to write how it  feels to
     have become a Wolf and what he/she thinks the
     expectations are of a Wolf.
     2. They are now requested to write how it feels to be
     "back in control" of their thoughts, feelings, and actions.
     These elements cover the cognitive, affective, and
     planning (strategies) components of the treatment plan.
     3. Wolves begin trust activities with experiential
     activities. These occur within the group context with day
     outings.
     4. Clients participate in Wolf "feeling" Groups.
     5. Clients participate in Wolf "Issues" Groups.

6.  A Wolf is required to make a two-sided shield where one side reflects what the Wolf is using to protect him/herself (defense mechanisms) and identify what that side of the shield is keeping in and why it is shuting out these issues to significant others. The other side reflects what things that the shield is keeping out from the Wolf (love, care etc.).

7.  The Wolf writes about an experience that felt like love and how he/she felt to love and be loved.

8.  A Wolf is required to write his/her understanding of the 12 Steps or on a particular step weekly.

9.  Daily journal entries need to reflect two themes: (1) positive entries about himself/herself, his/her surroundings or someone else, and (2) entries on things that happened today (here and now focus) where he/she shared a caring feeling.

10.  A Wolf engages in Stump Therapy for an hour and a half a week.

11.  The client engages in Trust Walks with another Wolf or with a staff for one to two hour sessions in an outdoor setting (with Mother Earth). Upon the return, the Wolf describes the experience to the Wolf Group and logs this experience in the journal.

12.  The Wolf Group presents a weekly skit that depicts some aspect of trust.

13.  Wolves go on outings to work on trust building skills.

14.  Wolves participate in creative "how I feel about myself" activities that they can demonstrate to others. The medium for this expression can be acting, singing, music, dance, etc..

15.  Academic instruction continues during this stage.

16.  Wolf "time" focuses on daily living (survival) skills.

17.  Wolves participate in communication skills classes designed to improve both verbal and non-verbal skills. Modeling and practice are used with staff and Wolves.

18.  Wolves prepare a dinner for the Deer Group as a demonstration of their care for others.

19.  Wolves participate in individual outings. Here the client is transported to an area and is left alone with no supplies (staff stay in the general vicinity in case of

emergencies). The Wolf now has the opportunity to practice his/her survival skills and to trust in his/her abilities to survive on his/her own. The Wolf then processes this experience before the Wolf Group upon his/her return using some creative means. This experience is also logged in his/her journal.

20. The client learns to express in writing about care and compassion toward himself/herself, others and Mother Earth.

21. "Earth Activities" are conducted weekly where Wolves participate in an activity that involves taking care of the earth.

22. The Wolf Group contributes to the beautification of the UNITY bank. Here, they maintain a section of the Oconoluftee River which represents the life-blood of Mother Earth on the reservation.

23. Wolves act out weekly how it feels to be an American Indian.

### Bear

At this level, the client is allowed two five-minute unsupervised phone calls and one 15-minute call to the tribe or family per week. Jewelry and make-up may be worn while a member of this group. Private time is now one and a half hours per week when requested. Bears may also stop at McDonald's Restaurant on the reservation after A.A. meetings on Tuesdays.

The theme for this level is gratitude and self-appreciation. The following seventeen components are addressed at the Bear level.

1. The client writes how it feels to be a Bear.

2. The new Bear writes his/her understanding of the 12 Steps as he/she comes into this level.

3. Bears need to address four categories in their daily journal entries: (1) positive entries, (2) trust, (3) care and compassion, and (4) gratitude and self-appreciation.

4. Clients attend Bear "feeling" Groups.

5. Bears participate in Stump Therapy two hours per week.

6. The Bear Group takes responsibility for the care of the Ropes course.

7. Bears need to develop a personal talent that they share with the group weekly.

8. Bears write on how it feels to be clean and on the road to recovery.

9. The Bear Group presents group lectures, plays and other creative activities to the Wolf and Deer Groups demonstrating their level of self- awareness, gratitude and self-appreciation.

10. Bears host a talent show where participants are staff and Bear members.

11. The Bears are responsible for displaying talent items from both the Bear and Eagle groups. They are responsible for the care and upkeep of the display.

12. Bears go on group outings that focus gratitude and self-appreciation.

13. Bears complete a collage on "what I like about me, and why I'm thankful for being me." They present their collage to the Bear Group.

14. Clients engage in daily "appreciation" activities which include walks to collect tokens of gratitude. They then describe why these items represent gratitude and appreciation.

15. Clients participate in an "Awakening Ceremony," whereby the Bear Group takes their old ways and issues and hibernate them for good (bury them, etc.). Bears then purify themselves in the Sweat Lodge. Later, the Bears feast on a dinner prepared by the Eagle Group.

16. Bears receive one hour of "pamper me" time where they engage in some wholesome, pleasurable activity.

17. Bears present brief skits that identify the attributes of each group member. This is done on a weekly basis.

## Eagle

At this level, clients are allowed music, if available and with headphones. They have cooking privileges. Eagles may go shopping for personal items once every two weeks. They may serve as staff assistants at staff request and can request four hours of private time per week.

The theme for the Eagle is self-sufficiency as an American Indian. At this level there should be an awareness of their cultural identity -- their Indiansim. There are thirteen steps which prepare the Eagle client for graduation from the UNITY program.

1. Clients write about how it feels to be an Eagle.
2. Eagles write about their understanding of the 12 Steps or one particular step.
3. Journal entries need to integrate their feelings while being a Coyote, Deer, Wolf and Bear. They also need to make entries which address how they can apply what they have learned at UNITY back home within their particular cultural environment.
4. Eagles engage in Stump Therapy for a minimum of three hours per week. They should now be able to place the sacred drum on the root base and complete their Circle of Inner Harmony -- their Indianism.
5. Clients participate in Eagle "feelings" Groups where they elaborate and demonstrate about their ability to take positive risks outside of treatment.
6. Eagles assist the other groups in working through Stump Therapy.
7. Eagle group members conduct plays and skits for the entire staff and the other groups. Here, they depict the wisdom that they have received while in treatment.
8. Clients sit on the Eagle Council where they ponder animal problems and suggest solutions designed to aid Mother Earth.
9. Eagles write their memoirs of the treatment program at UNITY expressing feelings of growth and progression.
10. Time is spent on learning independent living (survival) skills.
11. Relapse prevention is addressed during Eagle Groups.
12. Eagles demonstrate, via group interactions, the skills they have acquired while in treatment and how they can use these skills back home.
13. Eagles participate in a two-day "Spirit Wings" outing. This is designed so that the clients can process their vision quest while at UNITY and to internalize the positive aspects of the program so that they can take these thoughts, feelings and skills home with them. The last

stage of being an Eagle is to graduate from UNITY.
An individualized aftercare plan is prepared for each client prior
to discharge (graduation).  The aftercare plan is designed to
utilize services available at their home tribes.  After leaving
treatment at UNITY clients are monitored at routine intervals and
given support to encourage sobriety.  UNITY is the only
accredited Indian Health Service Regional Youth Treatment
Center.  Moreover, it has met its last two JCHO accreditations with
"commendations."  This has been due, to a great extent, to the
quality staff and especially due to the Program Director Dr. Mary
Ann Farrell and Jim Hornbuckle, its Clinical Supervisor.  Because
of its status; out of region tribes make referrals to UNITY.  This
includes Navajo, Apache, Hopi and other Pueblo Indians,
Papago and Paiute in addition to those tribes served by the
Nashville Area.  Indeed, this is an ideal model upon which to
pattern an effective Indian treatment program.

# Chapter 4

---

# Traditional Healing Among The Sioux

**Laurence French**
**Charles LaPlante**

## Introduction

The Sioux, perhaps more than any other Plains Indian group, have come to represent the *stereotypical* Indian within North American culture, even among American Indians themselves. The horse, buffalo, mobility on the plains, teepees, full-headdresses and the fierce warrior *counting coup* are all images of the *typical* Indian embodied in the American psyche. Years of federal policies outlawing traditional customs, rituals and language coupled with mass removal of Indians off their tribal lands led to the creation of a substantial population of off-reservation and urban Indians -- most who were devoid of their traditional heritage. This group of American Indians were at-risk for cultural marginality as well. In the 1960s, the Pan-Indian movement emerged with the creation of the National Indian Youth Council (NIYC). This was a reaction to the more conservative National Congress of American Indians (NCAI) which subscribed to the dictates of the federal government notably the Bureau of Indian Affairs (BIA). The NIYC served as the parent organization of the more militant American Indian Movement (AIM) -- the radical Indian counterpart to the Weathermen and Black Panthers. AIM was founded and chartered by two Chippewa Indians, George Mitchell and Dennis Banks. By the time of the 1973 Wounded Knee uprising, Russell Means, an Oglala Sioux, and Leonard Peltier, an Anishinabe/Lacota Sioux, were prominent leaders, along with Banks, of AIM. AIM, in turn, was widely accepted by American Indians, especially among marginal Indians, in that it provided a more positive alternative to the otherwise socially-impotent, *drunken Indian* image. By the same token, the dress and customs of the Plains Indians, notably the Sioux, came to represent the Pan-Indian movement. Over time the Pan-Indian movement also influenced more traditional Indians especially in the area of *traditional healing*. Today we see Sioux songs chanted in purification sweats by Navajo, Apache, Pueblo Indians and Cherokees in addition to the Sioux. Indeed, the Sioux have taken on a new role as trainers of *traditional healers* regardless of tribal affiliation. This phenomenon has had a significant impact in the area of mental health counseling. In this section, we look at the history and culture of the Sioux as well as Pan-Indian therapy models.

## The Aboriginal Roots of the Siouan Tribes

The aboriginal Sioux were a large and diverse family, second only to the Algonquians. At the time of white contact, they were both neighbors of the Cherokee and the Athapaskans. They were Knoll people (mound-builders) who resided in the Ohio Valley as woodland natives engaging in hunting and gathering with some horticultural endeavors. Archaeological evidence suggests that the early Sioux migrated slowly from the Ohio/Kentucky region into what is now the states of Alabama, North and South Carolina, Virginia, Indiana and Illinois. From this initial migration, four basic

Siouan groups emerged: the Eastern Sioux, Southern Sioux, Midwestern Sioux, and the Northern Woodlands/Great Plains Sioux. It is the Plains Sioux which history remembers. Anthropologists feel that the Great Plains Sioux were nomadic hunters hundreds of years prior to white contact and horse transportation. Once they migrated from the northern woodlands and crossed the Missouri River, the Great Plains Siouan culture changed markedly. They soon claimed a vast region of the Great Plains from the Missouri River to the Black Hills (Holder, 1970; French, 1987). Altogether, nineteen distinctive Siouan groups migrated from the northern woodlands to the Great Plains. In addition to the Winnebago, who initiated from eastern Wisconsin, there were the Hidatsa and Crow. The Mandan, Hunkpapa, Sans Arcs and Blackfeet (Sikika or Sihasapa) also shared the areas in what is now the state of North Dakota while the Assiniboins resided in that section of Canada just north of Montana and North Dakota. The Mdewkanton, Wahpeton, Wahpekute, and Sisseton, collectively known as the Santee Sioux, were all from Minnesota as were the Yankton, Yanktonai, and Hunkpatina. The Brule, Miniconjou, Oglala, and Oohenonpa, on the other hand, were from what is now the state of North Dakota and are known collectively as the Lacota Sioux.

While there was never a Sioux nation per se prior to white domination, the Teton Sioux (Seven Bands or Fires) did meet periodically to map and to reinforce their common culture. If anything, the Great Plains Siouan groups were adaptable, and it was this flexibility that accounted for their perseverance even in the face of tremendous odds. Today the Sioux tribes are located in Nebraska (Ponca, Omaha, Santee and Winnebago) in addition to those listed above residing in North and South Dakota, Wyoming and Canada.

## The Great Plains Siouan Culture

The Plains Sioux were warrior-oriented societies, and for obvious reasons, theirs was a nomadic, hunting and raiding culture with only periodic, albeit intense, tribal interaction (Teton Seven Fires). The summer pow wow welded the seven bands together in unity and it was at this time that the Sun Dance was performed.

The Sioux belief system focused about the numbers four and seven. There are the four directions: east, west, north, and south; four elements above the earth: sky, sun, moon, and stars; four parts of time: day, night, month, and year; four phases of life: infancy, childhood, maturity, and old age; four parts to plants: roots, stem, leaves, and fruit; four classes of animals: crawling, flying, two-legged, and four-legged; and four Sioux virtues: bravery, fortitude, generosity, and wisdom.

*Wakan Tanka* represents the *Great Mystery* to the Sioux and has four titles, that of Chief God, Great Spirit, Creator, and Executive. Yet, this Great Mystery, like life itself, is full of paradoxes according to Sioux beliefs. It controls both the good and evil forces within the universe. There is *Iya*, the chief of all evil, personified by the cyclone as well as *Iktomi,* the son of Rock -- a despised god, who plays the role of trickster; *Waziya,* the Old Man; *Wakonaka,* his wife -- the witch; and *Anog-Lte*, the double-faced woman, their daughter.

*Sicun*, on the other hand, represents the power of good and is associated with the four superior gods. These gods are *Inyan,* the Rock, which represents authority; *Maka,* the Earth, which is the protector; *Skan,* the Sky, which reflects force and power; and *Wi,* the Sun, which denotes bravery. Next are the four associate gods: *Hanwi,* the Moon and associate of the Sun; *Tate,* the Wind and associate of the Sky; *Whoope,* the Beautiful One and associate of the Earth; and *Wakinyan*, the Winged One and associate of the Rock.

Next in the hierarchy of universal powers come the Sioux subordinate gods and gods-like. As would be expected, there are four subordinate gods or *gods-kindred:* Buffalo, Bear, Four Winds, and Whirlwind. These are followed by the four gods-like, or *Wanalapi:* Spirit, Ghost, Spirit-like, and Potency. Overall there are sixteen Sioux gods in one, and all representing the *Great Mystery.*

In addition to the annual (Summer) Seven Council Fires pow wow, the Plains Sioux had seven sacred ceremonies: Purification, Vision Seeking, Sun Dance, Ball Throwing, Making a Buffalo Woman, Making as Brothers, and Owning a Ghost. Of these, the Sun Dance is undoubtedly the most significant. It is a warrior ceremony with four specific purposes. It is the vehicle for fulfillment of a warrior's vows, to help him and others to secure supernatural power and to seek visions. These events are paramount to the Plains Sioux since traditionalists believe that they do not directly possess power but rather they seek it from Wakan Tanka, hence, the considerable focus placed on the Sun Dance. This world-view, like all world views, draws its strength of conviction from a metaphysical source -- the Sioux creation myth In the beginning, before any other thing or time, there was *Inyan* and his spirit was *Wakan Tanka*. *Hanhepi* was there also, but only as the black darkness. It was *Inyan*, although soft and shapeless at this time, who possessed all the powers and these powers were his blood -- which was blue like water is today. Inyan eventually decided to use his powers to create another form for company since it was lonely existing alone. He created *Manka* – what is now called Earth, and he made it in his image.

But making Earth was a more demanding task than Inyan anticipated. He ruptured himself in the process and spilled his blood, his power, upon Manka where it now became water. But Inyan's powers could no longer survive out of his veins so they separated themselves from the Earth, water becoming the great spirit *Mahpiyato* -- the sky. Inyan now became hard without either his power or his blood, forming the rocks and mountains on his creation -- Manka. This is how the earth, water and sky come about according to the Sioux creation myth.

Mahpiyato was then selected to be the supreme judge of all things, and he created *Anpetu* (day) to help him differentiate between time and space. Next he added *Wi*, the Sun, to add warmth to the red light of Anpetu. He also provided Wi with a wife, *Hanwi* (moon), and ordered Anpetu to follow Hanhepi (night), hence providing the present units of time: days, months, and seasons.

The first people, according to this myth, were the *Pte*, who initially lived in the underworld. The chief of the Pte at this time was *Wazi;* and he and his wife, *Wankanda,* had a beautiful daughter, *Ite*-- the most beautiful of all women. Although merely a mortal human, Ite was sought out by the god *Tate* (Wind) who eventually married her; and this liaison produced quadruplets -- the Four Winds: North, West, East, and South. The first born, North Wind, was cruel and unruly so Tate denied him his birthright reordering his sons so that West Wind was first followed by North Wind, East Wind, and South Wind.

Wazi, having seen the success of his daughter, coveted supernatural powers like those of his in-laws for himself. To this end, he conspired with *Ikotmi,* the Trickster, to cause discord among the other gods. Ikotmi made Ite even more beautiful and seductive causing her to ignore her husband, Tate, and her children, the Four Winds. She now consorted with *Wi,* the Sun, causing considerable embarrassment to his wife, *Hanwi* (the Moon).

In judgment of these indiscretions, Wi was separated from his wife Hanwi with the former now ordered to rule only during the day thus giving Hanwi authority over the night. Ite was also punished for her vanity and maternal and connubial neglect. She was separated from her supernatural family and returned to earth, banished to live alone without friends. To insure that she would not seduce again, her beauty was destroyed by making half of her so ugly and repulsive that she became known as the *Two-Faced Woman.* Her parents suffered a similar fate, both being banished to the edge of the earth; and they were now known respectively as the *Old Man* or *Wizard (Wazi)* and *the Witch (Wakonaka). Iktomi,* the Trickster, was also banished but continued his trickery, doing so vicariously through other mediums such as birds and animals.

Tate, the Wind, was forced to raise his son (the Four Winds) alone. The sons traveled widely during this time and eventually formed the four directions. Once when the sons were away, *Woope,* a beautiful young woman, appeared at their home. She stayed performing the women's work long neglected by Tate since Ite's banishment. When the sons returned, they all fell in love with Woope, but she selected *Okaga,* the South Wind, as her partner. All the gods were invited to the wedding feast at which time they granted Woope her request for a home for her and her husband and his other three brothers. To this request, the gods created the World for them.

At this time the *Pte,* or people, lived below the earth and not on the surface. But once the world was created *Anog-Ite* and Iktomi, the Trickster, again conspired to do evil. This time they enticed *Tokahe,* of the Pte, to taste meat and know of the beauty of the world as seen from the surface of the earth (Manka). Here Iktomi used the form of the wolf to bring these offerings to Tokahe. After the wolf brought the food and clothing to the Pte,

Tokahe, and three others ventured out to the surface to see where these things came from. Once on the surface, Iktomi and Anog-Ite deceived them into thinking that living on the surface would perpetuate youth among the Pte.

But once the Pte migrated to the surface, they soon suffered from exhaustion, hunger and thirst. And it was Wazi and his wife, Wakanka, who saved them from destruction, bringing them to the planes where they taught them how to hunt and survive on Manka. Once established in the ways of the world, Woope visited the Pte, appearing in the form of the White Buffalo Maiden, telling the Pte of their powers and their relationship with the gods. These surface Pte (*Ikce*) were the ancestors of the Lacota according to the Sioux creation myth.

According to the Plains Sioux, White Buffalo Maiden (*Woope*) was also responsible for introducing the sacred pipe to the Lacota (*Ikce*). Woope gave the pipe to *Tokahe*, their first medicine man. The pipe is a symbolic representation of the universe. The bowl, made from red pipestone, represents both Manka (earth) and man's blood while the colors red (west), blue (north), green (east), and yellow (south) reflect the four directions. The shell, leather, and feather decorations represent, respectively, those things of the water, the land, and the sky. The smoke itself is the medium of spiritual communication with Wakan Tanka (the Great Mystery). The sacred pipe is the Sioux's form of Communion with their gods (Hassrick, 1967; French, 1987).

This origin myth provides the moral philosophy for the traditional Plains Sioux and it is from this that their aboriginal lifestyle was patterned. Like other native groups this belief system was an integral and inseparable part of their existence. The traditional moral code is clearly stated: "good outweighs evil." Good means intragroup harmony and cooperation where the virtues of bravery, fortitude, generosity, and wisdom lead to high status and recognition for the male while bravery, generosity, truthfulness, and childbearing are the corresponding positive female virtues.

*Bravery:* This is the most significant Siouan virtue for both males and females. It involves self-sacrifice. Counting coup, dog soldiering and the Sun Dance are prime examples of bravery among Sioux warriors. It was considered more honorable to die on the battlefield than to die of old age.  Examples of this philosophy are found in accounts of Standing Bear and Black Elk where both make mention of the warrior sentiment: it is a good thing to die in battle.  This value helps to explain the often volatile lifestyle of many contemporary Sioux "warriors."

*Fortitude:* This virtue is actually a corollary of bravery in that it specifies how one should be brave.  Again, this virtue affected both males and females in that it spells out the dictates of acceptable public behavior.  Whites have long referred to these behavioral traits as being stoical when, in fact, they reflect intense physical and psychological conditioning (socialization) and self-discipline.  Public displays of affection, even among lovers or married couples, is taboo; and a complex set of rules (customs) govern public behavior and the nature of harmonious intragroup interaction, especially during aboriginal times.

*Generosity:* The Plains Sioux had a unique system for determining generosity -- the *giveaway.*  During aboriginal times wealth was not accumulated as it is within Western societies, thus subscribing to the Protestant Ethic.  Instead, Sioux accumulated wealth so that it could be distributed within the group with high status given the benefactor.  Inheritance was virtually unheard of among these people, and any surviving personal property was often buried along with the deceased.  This practice continues today among traditional Plains Sioux.  The giveaway was an institutional form of Sioux generosity whereby the more people gave, the greater was their prestige within the group.  For this system to work reciprocity must exist between successful and indigent members of the group with the latter often being a necessity for the former to achieve prestige.  This relationship does much to reduce any sense of alienation or marginality among tribal members.  During aboriginal times its purpose was to guarantee care for the sick, crippled, and feeble--those otherwise likely to be abandoned by a mobile society.

*Wisdom:* This virtue is acquired through the life-process itself. Life experiences, augmented by spiritual insight, help cultivate this elusive virtue.  For most aboriginal groups, age was an important consideration in the acquisition of wisdom.  Age and one's life accomplishments determine the elder's status.  Among these accomplishments was sufficient participation in the major Siouan rituals and success as a warrior, for males, and childbearing, industry and fidelity for females.

Accordingly, these virtues of self-sacrifice, self-discipline and restrained personal behavior were openly displayed within prescribed public forums, ceremonies and rituals. An important function of most public ceremonies among aboriginal and contemporary traditional Sioux is lauding the bravery, fortitude, generosity and wisdom of accomplished tribal members. Besides, these events are avenues of communication between the Sioux and the supernatural powers. This interaction between man and the supernatural is important since the Sioux believe that power is obtained indirectly from the gods through Wakan Tanka's intermediaries. The original myth illustrates this relationship by portraying man as being helpless without the aid of supernatural powers. Man, by himself, is viewed as being relatively helpless. Traditional Sioux believe that they acquire strength only through cooperation with the other forces within the universe. Moreover, only the pure can acquire this necessary power, hence the significance of the purification ritual -- the sweat bath.

The sweat bath preceded any quest for power. According to the Sioux myth, the sweat lodge provides protection from the evil family: *Iya* the chief of all evil, his wife *Unk* the mother of all evil, and their son *Gnaski*. Tohaha, the Locota leader who led his people to the earth's surface is credited as being the first Sioux medicine man. He is also credited with initiating the use of steam as a purification medicine against the forces of evil, a ritual which has survived to the present not only among the Sioux and among PanIndians but has been widely adopted by most other tribes.

The purification process involves steam being generated within the *Initi* (sweat lodge) by sprinkling water over hot stones. The stones, in turn, flush the spiritual impurities from the person in the form of sweat cleaning both the body and soul. The sweat lodge is a low-profile dome-shaped construction comprised of a willow frame, usually covered with animal skins with a floor of sage and a pit for receiving the hot stones. The entrance of the sweat lodge, like that of the camp tipis, always faces east, along the *red road* or *power path*. The fire pit along the power path outside the entrance to the sweat lodge is used to heat the stones. If an altar is used, such as a buffalo skull, it is placed between the fire pit ne sweat lodge entrance. This now makes the path a sacred path which cannot be crossed. Participants in the purification sweat enter the sweat lodge clockwise with the leader entering first. The last person to enter serves as the "door tender." Outside, a "fire tender" brings the heated rocks as requested by the individual directing the purification rite. Sage, sweet grass, cedar or Indian tobacco are used to bless the fire pit, its participants and the rocks once they are placed within the sweat lodge. Four rocks at a time are usually placed into the pit. This sweat period constitutes a "door." This process is usually repeated four times with the last door concluding with the smoking of the sacred pipe or a home-rolled cigar made of Indian tobacco (tobacco, herb, grass, bark, root mixture).

One of the most significant uses of the purification sweat was for the *Vision Quest.* In its traditional application, the Vision Quest candidates would enter the lodge naked carrying only a sage branch for concealment. Once inside the lodge an attendant provides the heated stones from the fire pit. The mentor (Shaman-in-charge) then passes the candidate the sacred pipe and generates the purification steam by sprinkling water upon the stones. The pipe and steam ritual is conducted four times (doors), each time accompanied by a song (chant). Following the fourth session the candidate leaves the lodge to retire to a designated elevated place known as *Vision Hill.* This is the vantage point from which the candidates seek their visions. These visions are, in fact, guided states of disassociation, much like clinical hypnosis. Abstinence from food and water aid in this process as do cultural-parameters which influence the type of image (vision) they will experience. From the vision comes the traditional Sioux's power and adult identity.

Black Elk noted that he received his *power vision* at the age of nine. His vision provided him with a life-orientation from which to interpret later events in his life including the Ghost Dance movement and the 1890 Wounded Knee slaughter. Black Elk also gave the impression that his initial power vision was somewhat ambiguous causing him to seek additional visions whenever dramatic events threatened his identity.

Among traditional Sioux, the Sun Dance was, and remains, the single most significant ritual. Historically it occurred during the summer camp when the seven tribes of the Lacota met.

Today the Sun Dance occurs during late summer, notably August. The Sun Dance lasts twelve days with sweat baths taken each day by both the candidate and the shaman (sponsor). These purification sweats also aid the candidates in preparatory visions for the *gazing at the sun* ritual which occurs on the last day of the Sun Dance ceremony.

The aboriginal purpose of the Sun Dance was to gain widely recognized status and prestige among the larger Lacota group. Often it was used to fulfill a vow to the gods or as an attempt to seek power for another person. The Sun Dance reinforced the Sioux male's status and identity. It was a public dramatization of one's courage and self-discipline. Besides giving recognition to male candidates, the ceremony also bestowed considerable status upon those women selected to participate in the ritual. Virtuous females were selected to chop the sacred cottonwood trees used in the ceremony, as well as being selected to attend the dancers. They were also honored by the buffalo dance which was performed at this time along with war dances and the gaze at the Sun Dance. Male attendants included symbolic hunters -- who selected the sacred cottonwood tree, diggers, escorts and singers. Usually one shaman (medicine man) was in charge of the entire ritual having total authority over the proceedings.

The twelve days of the Sun Dance ceremony are divided into three, four-day intervals with the first period being one of festivity during which time the camp is established. During this time, attendants and other assistants are selected. The next period is used to instruct the candidates and medicine men as well as to select the mentor (medicine man-in-charge). The final period, known as the holy days, is when the ritual actually occurs. During the first holy day, the cottonwood tree (the symbolic enemy) is hunted by the *symbolic hunter,* marked and reported to the mentor. This is followed by the buffalo dance and a feast. The second holy day is devoted to the capture of the enemy -- the cottonwood tree. Four warriors count coup on the tree in order to neutralize its spirits (*Nagila).* The Honored Woman then fells the tree and this activity is again followed by festivities. The cottonwood tree is prepared and erected as the ritual pole on the third holy day. Painted and decorated with the enlarged symbolic genitalia of members of the evil family, *Iya* and *Gnaske,* this symbolizes a period of behavioral license whereby both males and females are allowed to discuss, joke about and initiate sexual activity which would otherwise be taboo according to traditional Sioux customs. This brief licentious period terminates later that day with the performance of the war dance. The participating warriors conclude the dance by bringing down the genitalia with their arrows, hence destroying the power of the evil family.

On the fourth, and last, holy day, the candidates are painted and otherwise prepared for the *gaze at the sun* ritual. The candidates are fastened to the cottonwood pole by leather thongs and wooden pins which are embedded in the flesh of their chests. They now dance about the pole until they tear themselves free. This requires ripping the wooden pins through the flesh. Interestingly, Standing Bear drew parallels between the Sun Dance and Christ's sacrifice upon the cross. He viewed both as constituting similar forms of torturous self-sacrifice for the purpose of religious recognition.

Essentially these religious ceremonies are all related to the power and status relationships within the Plains Sioux society. Prestige and self-sacrifice are directly related and emphasized in the seven sacred ceremonies: purification (sweats and the pipe), Vision Quest, Sun Dance, ball throwing, making a Buffalo Woman, making a brother, owning a ghost. This system is the antithesis of that prescribed by the Protestant Ethic from which most contemporary counseling techniques are based. Instead of wealth and status being directly related, these variables are inversely related within the Harmony Ethos. To the Plains Sioux, wealth is a means to an end, not an end in itself as it is in most Western societies. Wealth is a means for acquiring prestige among traditional Sioux only if it is accumulated for disposal through *giveaways*.

## Warriors and Shaman: Antecedents of Indian Violence

That which has been written on violence among American Indians often involves the Plains Indians, notably the Sioux. And this is not without justification. To the contemporary Sioux, American Indians of other tribal affiliations, and the general public, Sitting Bull, Big Foot, Crazy Horse, The Little Big Horn, Wounded Knee and the Ghost Dance all clearly illustrate the violent, last gasp effort of the Plains Indians to ward off the contamination and influence of Western ways. Indeed, these events of the latter part of the 19th century play a significant part in the revitalization of traditional, including Pan-Indian, customs, rituals and religions -- all of which must be understood by both Indian and non-Indian counselors alike when working with A merican Indian clients.

A brief history of these events (an Eriksonian psychohistorical analysis approach) helps the counselor understand not only the significance of these events as they reflect the blatant attempt at Siouan cultural genocide but also provides insights into the complexities of the warrior persona as it is exemplified by counting coup and dog soldiering (Eirkson, 1975).

Following Red Cloud's attempt at working out reasonable solutions to ending the Indian wars in the Plains, many traditional Plains Indians felt that the only honor left was to fight, to the death if needed. Chief Red Cloud, an Oglala (Lacota) Sioux, mustered an Indian force comprised of all the Lacota bands as well as the Cheyenne. His group fought a hit-and-run guerilla war forcing the U.S. government to concede to the Sioux and Cheyenne a large reservation which included much of what is now South Dakota and the northwestern portion of Nebraska. It was the Fort Laramie Treaty of 1868 which provided the Great Sioux Reservation. This 35,000 square mile plot of sacred hills and buffalo plains was home to some 20,000 Sioux. It was similar to Oklahoma Indian Territory where a sizeable tract of land was set aside solely for Indian use, where they could live in perpetuity without white settlers or military intervention (Prucha, 1990).

The treaty held until gold was discovered in the Black Hills in 1874. This, plus the belligerent actions of the U.S. Army (Lieutenant Colonel Custer and the 7th Calvary), caused a split within the Lacota ranks with Red Cloud and Spotted Tail representing the peace faction while Sitting Bull, Crazy Horse, Gall and Hump went on the warpath. White violations of the Fort Laramie Treaty culminated in the June 25, 1876 Little Big Horn battle best known as *Custer's Last Stand.* This was to be the Lacota's last great victory over the white man. It also spelled the end to the Plains lifestyle and the beginning of forced accommodation.

The United States was shocked by Custer's death and the defeat of the Seventh Calvary. The shock and fear generated by white settlers and the general public on the eve of their centennial mandated that the government pursue and punish the Sioux and their Cheyenne allies. The army pursued the militant Sioux and Cheyenne forcing Sitting Bull and Gall to hide in Canada while Crazy Horse and Hump continued to fight generals Crook and Miles, the same generals who were engaged in the Apache campaign. Things worsened for the militant Sioux in October, 1876 when the reservation faction, *Hang-Around-the-Fort Sioux,* signed away the Black Hills and all the land west of them (Yellow Stone) to the U.S.

Crazy Horse was murdered while in the stockade at Fort Robinson on May, 1877. In 1881, Crow Dog killed Spotted Tail leading to passage of the Major Crimes Act (aka FBI's Index Crimes)in 1885. From then on conditions on the new concentration-like reservations worsened. These events generated a situation of despair for the significant number of traditionalists who were either deliberately excluded from, or chose not to participate in, the new order of things. Confined on restricted land bases already subdivided into deeded lots, denied their traditional forms of subsistence as well as the source (buffalo), and forbidden their cultural spiritualism (purification sweats, Vision Quests, Sun Dances...), these despairing Sioux were susceptible for an escape to a world like that provided by the Ghost Dance.

The Ghost Dance originated among the Indians of Nevada in 1888 where Wovoka (Jack Wilson), a Paiute, had a vision that foretold that things would soon change: that the white man would vanish, the buffalo would return and all the departed Indians would again be reborn. Word of Wovaka's vision spread across the Plains and he soon became known as *Wanekia:* The Messiah--Son of the Great Spirit. The Ghost Dance consisted of wearing ribbon shirts and dresses and dancing slowly in a circle with the participants, both men and women, holding hands while facing into the circle. They sang without drums or any other instruments and often went into trances. Clearly, this process represented a religiously-engendered, shared, collective delusional state. (It would be diagnosed as Axis I: 297.3 --

Shared Psychotic Disorder according to the DSM-IV if the Ghost Dance occurred today.) The Ghost Dance movement gained momentum as the Sioux anticipated the *return of the buffalo* and their traditional ways, all of which culminated in 1891. So great was their despair and the need for a traditionally-based alternative that many Sioux became preoccupied with the Ghost Dance ritual and little else. This sent shock waves through white communities while the U.S. Army prepared to battle the Sioux once again.

All the great Sioux leaders supported the Ghost Dance movement including Red Cloud, Sitting Bull, Black Elk and Big Foot. Both Sitting Bull and Big Foot became victims of the Ghost Dance retaliation. Sitting Bull was killed on December 15, 1890 by Indian police at Fort Yates on the Standing Rock Reservation in North Dakota. After his death, many of Sitting Bull's people fled the reservation to join Chief Big Foot at the Cheyenne River Reservation located in South Dakota.

Fearing a similar fate as Sitting Bull, Big Foot took his people and fled off the reservation heading to the sacred badlands to wait for the *return of the buffalo.* His party of 370 was intercepted on December 28, 1890 at Wounded Knee Creek on the Pine Ridge Reservation. The following morning a shot was fired while the soldiers were disarming the group. The soldiers panicked and opened up with their machine guns (Hotchkiss) killing 84 men and boys, 44 women and 18 children and wounding another 33, many who eventually died from these wounds. For all intents and purposes, the Wounded Knee massacre spelled the end of the Ghost Dance Movement and along with it any hopes of returning to the traditional ways (Brown, 1970; Neihardt, 1972; Utley, 1963; Standing Bear, 1975).

Traditional ways were severely suppressed for nearly a century for the Plains Indians. Reciprocal animosities between the Sioux and their white neighbors, mainly the descendants of those who violated the 1868 Treaty and subsequently benefitted from this action, continues to be intense--a factor counselors need to be aware of given the level of anger, especially among Sioux teens and young adult males. This level of hate and anger, coupled with non-traditional avenues of counting coup and dog soldiering (risk taking), accounts for the disproportionate number of Indians within our jails and prisons. Those of us working with traditonal American Indians need to keep in mind that according to traditional Siouan values, bravery and fortitude, the two traditional virtues addressed by counting coup and dog soldiering, are critical prerequisites for the higher virtues, generosity and wisdom.  In a recent issue of *The Criminologist*, Betsy Price stated:

> Indians are spending more time on the wrong side of the legal system than any other minority group.  The reality is, of minorities, Indians are the smallest group, but Indians have the largest percentage of their people in prison.  In fact, the percentage is so high that most Indian men living on reservations believe they will sometime in their life spend at least the night in jail. It is a given (Price, 1994: 1).

This is an important consideration for counselors and therapists because it is highly unlikely that anyone working with Indian clients can avoid these and other forensic issues.

## Clinical Treatment for the Contemporary Warrior

Wounded Knee II in 1973 began the new movement toward a renewed Indian traditionalism.  The U.S. again heard the angry voices of American Indians, and again the non-Indian public was frightened and even the U.S. Army was mustered to combat this new perceived "Indian" threat.  Now Leonard Peltier, Dennis Banks, Russell Means, George Mitchell and Vine Deloria, Jr. were the names that crossed the nation's lips like Sitting Bull, Crazy Horse, Red Cloud, Big Foot and Crow Dog had nearly a century earlier.

The interrelationship between risk taking, correctional treatment, and revised traditionalism is best illustrated by Charles LaPlante, the Director of the Santee Sioux Alcohol and Drug Prevention Program and first Director of the Aberdeen Area All-Indian Substance Abuse Certification Board.  Charlie spent his youth and young adult years in the Nebraska State Prison (sixteen years in all) attempting to count coup against the white society.  He witnessed the landmark legal decisions that provided for traditional customs and rituals for incarcerated Indian inmates. Charlie worked with NARF (Native American Rights Fund) in this effort and, once released, coordinated cultural, religious and treatment efforts through the Lincoln Indian Center. This process extended some twenty years from the mid-1970's, the time surrounding the turmoil at Wounded Knee II. These efforts culminated in the All-Indian Substance Abuse Certification process initiated in the early 1990s as well as the legitimatization of traditional religious customs, most notably, the Sun Dance.

The American Indian Movement (AIM) had a sizeable membership among the *contemporary warriors,* that generation of marginal Indians who were disenchanted with the paternalistic nature of reservation life. They saw the failure of the federal policy of forced accommodation and wanted a return to traditionalism. White Clay, a notorious border town just off the Pine Ridge Reservation, was, and continues to be, a death magnet with its bars (Pine Ridge and Rosebud are dry reservations). These border towns provide a substantial proportion of the Indian inmates in Nebraska. The others come from the Nebraskan Sioux tribes -- Omaha, Winnebago, Ponca and Santee Sioux. Alcohol is the prime factor in most of the crimes resulting in Indian incarceration. A less than sympathetic non-Indian criminal justice system completed the equation of discrimination that prevailed at the time of Wounded Knee II and the suit at the Nebraska Penal Complex. The Nebraska Penal Complex was run much like the old boarding schools where any act of Indianism (language, dress, tradition) was readily punished. Not only were Indian inmates punished for being and acting Indian, unlike their white, African American and Hispanic counterparts, they were denied any special recognition as a whole. They were even punished for seeking each other's company. They were expected to reject their Indianism and join the western-type organization that served white, African American and Hispanic inmate interests. This process of isolation and harassment led to the actions by the AIM faction in the early 1970s.

This process began in Nebraska in 1972 when Indian prisoners sought special protection of their religious and cultural rights. Toward this end, they filed a class action suit in U. S. District court: *Indian Inmates of the Nebraska Penitentiary v. Charles L. Wolff, Jr* (CV 72-L-156). The resolution of this suit preceded the 1978 American Indian Religious Freedom Act by four years and, most likely, influenced its passage. The Native American Rights Fund, out of Boulder, Colorado, aided the inmates in this action resulting in the 1974 consent decree: *Indian Inmates of the Nebraska Penitentiary v. Joseph Vitek.* Vitek, the Director of Correctional Services in Nebraska, inherited the litigation from Wolff. The Order-Judgment and Decree stipulated that: ...the defendants, their agents, servants, employees and their successors in office are hereby permanently enjoined and ordered to:

1. Permit the wearing of traditional Indian hairstyles, provided such hairstyles are kept clean at all times.

2. In order to meet the religious and spiritual needs of the plaintiff class, defendants shall allow inmates access to Indian medicine men and spiritual leaders and provide facilities for spiritual and religious services, including but not limited to the Native American Church. Further, defendants will set aside a percent of its budget (that reflects the percent of the Indian inmates in the Penal Complex) which at any given time is allocated for other clergy salaries and expenses attendant to providing services to members of other religious faiths, to payment of fees and expenses attendant to providing Indian religious services and ceremonies.

3. To take the necessary steps to instruct all employees that all benefits presently given to inmates for "religious participation" be extended to those members of the plaintiff class who participate in the aforementioned Indian religious services, ceremonies, or culture group meetings.

4. Extend official recognition to an Indian inmate spiritual culture club composed of members of the plaintiff class and take the necessary steps to ensure that:

(a) The same privileges presently extended to other inmate clubs ... are extended to the Indian Culture Club, and that

(b) Active membership in the Indian Culture Club be given the same recognition in terms of inmate pay raise points or other benefits presently given for active membership in other inmate self-betterment or religious groups.

5. The defendant and plaintiff's counsel shall formulate an affirmative action hiring plan designed to locate job applications and to secure employment and training by the defendant of qualified Indian personnel, recognizing the unique culture needs of Indian inmates. Said plan will be submitted to the Court for its approval by the parties within thirty days after the effective date of this Consent Judgment.

6. The Indian club will designate certain representatives to participate in advising the Athletic and Recreation Committee concerning the type of movies to be shown at the Complex.

7. The defendants will offer accredited courses in Indian studies at the Nebraska Penal and Correctional Complex within a reasonable time after the effective date of this Order. The plaintiffs will aid the defendant in obtaining personnel, materials, and financial resources, as well as aiding in the formulation of the course subject matter.

8. Plaintiffs waive counsel fees.

Charlie was a part of this movement within the Nebraska Correctional system along with a colleague -- Perry Wounded Shield, better known as the "Old Warrior." Together, they worked very closely with Walter Echo Hawk of the Native American Rights Fund (NARF), the organization that assisted in the suit and subsequent consent decree. Perry is an Oglala Sioux from Pine Ridge and Charlie is a Santee Sioux from the Santee Reservation. They were instrumental in the creation of the *Native American Spiritual and Cultural Awareness(NASCA) group.* Soon each facility within the Nebraska Penal Complex, including the county holding and serving jails and the Women's Prison in Hastings, had their chapter of NASCA. Its primary function was to coordinate Indian-specific religious and cultural events. These events included services by Emerson Jackson and the Native American Church and Leonard Crow Dog, Jr. and the Sioux Council of Medicine Men. Emerson Jackson came from Wisconsin for his services while Leonard Crow Dog, Jr. traveled down from the Rosebud (Brule) Reservation in South Dakota. Sweat lodges were erected at the various penal sites and purification sweats and the smoking of the sacred pipe were two of the first of the long abandoned traditional rituals reintroduced to the Contemporary Warriors (incarcerated American Indian males).  Soon other customs and rituals were added including traditional meals with buffalo meat and powwows with drumming, singing, dancing and hand games.  Both the University of Nebraska and Southeast Community College faculty and staff joined in assisting the implementation of the Consent Decree, much to the chagrin of the extremely conservative correctional personnel.  Elizabeth Grobsmith, a fellow faculty at the University of Nebraska, was one of these concerned individuals who later wrote a book on the legal aspect of this process (Grobsmith, 1994).

To counter their resistance, the Governor initiated the Nebraska Indian Commission comprised of Indian members.  Two of their major charges were substance abuse and criminal justice issues. Located in the capitol, Lincoln, along with the two largest complexes of the penal system, the Nebraska Indian Commission worked closely with the two Urban Indian Centers located in Omaha and Lincoln.  Urban Indian Centers are outgrowths of the Relocation movement of the 1950s and have a separate federal administration other than the Bureau of Indian Affairs, which administers Indian matters in Indian country (federally-recognized reservations).  ANA, Administration of Native Americans, is the BIA counterpart authorized to administer Urban Indian Centers. The Consent Decree placed the spot light on the Lincoln Indian Center (LIC).  Demands were soon placed upon the Lincoln Indian Center to coordinate the services provided by the Native American Church and the Council of Medicine Men.

I met Charlie in the fall of 1977 following my move from Western Carolina University to the Lincoln Campus of the  University of Nebraska. Charlie served his first sentence counting coup in the Adult Reformatory doing time from 1960, when he was fifteen, until 1967.  He again counted coup on a "cowboy" bar (Indians not welcomed), and subsequently beat his antagonists like before and this time entered the State Prison.  This sentence lasted from 1968 until his release on October 20, 1975. He got married in 1976 to a member of the Stabler clan, a traditional Omaha Sioux family (Rodney Grant, of *Dancing with Wolves* fame is one of her kin who is deeply involved in FAS in his new home in Sante Fe, New Mexico). Clarissa had three daughters from a previous marriage and they had a new-born daughter, Liz, when I met Charlie. Charlie was working for a sod company when I met him and had not yet given up drinking.

In my capacity as an advisor to the Nebraska Alcohol and Drug Certification Board, I was instrumental in encouraging Charlie to take the recently vacated Director of the Ex Offender Program at the Lincoln Indian Center. He held this position the three years I was a consultant to the Lincoln Indian Center and Nebraska Indian Commission. It was during this time that we developed and implemented our "Native American Correctional Program" -- a federally funded program. Once I left, support for the ex-offender program died, but Charlie carried on the mission as a counselor in the Alcohol Program at the Lincoln Indian Center. He also worked with the "Four Winds" in-patient program with the Omaha Indian Center and left in 1986 to serve his people on the Santee Sioux Reservation. He was first hired as a counselor in the Santee Sioux Alcohol and Drug Prevention Program and became its director in 1988 -- a position he still holds today. At this time I served on the Nebraska Indian Commission's Criminal Justice Advisory Committee as well as advisor to Charlie's program at the Lincoln Indian Center and as the Administrative Advisor and Special Consultant to the Executive Director (Marshall Prichard) of the Lincoln Indian Center. It was within this capacity that we developed the $250,000 federal grant entitled: "Native American Correctional Treatment Program."

We were influenced by the American Indian Survival School which was implemented at the Red School House, an alternative, combined primary and secondary, Indian school located in St. Paul, Minnesota. The Sioux and Objibwa Indians who ran the school and developed its curriculum realized that American Indians learn better from participatory methods rather than just verbal lessons. Many who work with Indians of at least 50 percent Indian blood sense there is a strong likelihood that these individuals utilize both hemispheres of their brain more so than do their non-Indian counterparts. This is why the experiential factor is so critical in traditional healing and learning methods. At the Red School House, both the children's *Indianism* and activities of daily living skills were stressed. The school curriculum combined American Indian heritage with an awareness of contemporary society and the problems this duality presents to the Indian youth as he or she learns to live in two worlds. The curriculum had a strong cultural spiritualism and used traditional ceremonies. Cooperation, and not competition, was stressed while the traditional circle arrangement was incorporated to eliminate class rank and artificial forms of class strata and stigma. This philosophy of pedagogy was an innovative approach within Indian country in 1978 (Banai, 1978). Today it is widely mimicked within schools throughout the nation, going by the name -- cooperative learning.

We applied this epistemological construct to our correctional treatment at the Nebraska Penal Complex. The targeted population was the incarcerated contemporary warriors, many who grew up on the Sioux reservations in Nebraska and the Dakotas. The 1974 Consent Decree opened the doors to our cultural intervention. The incarcerated contemporary warriors were aware of their traditional culture (such as language), to varying degrees, but were sufficiently marginal so not to have been adequately enculturated to enable them as to survive counting coup within the larger U. S. society. For the most part, these adult Sioux counted coup while under the influence of alcohol, and lost. Some of them participated in the 1973 Wounded Knee uprising and many were members of, or sympathetic to, the American Indian Movement (AIM). Charlie was their freed colleague who now served as their contact with the Native American Church and the Rosebud Association of Medicine Men. Perry Wounded Shield was our main contact inside the state prison.

In our experiment, we found that jails and prisons offer ideal therapeutic environments for the survival school method providing: (a) that the correctional system is receptive to cultural interventions, and (b) that American Indian clients have a reasonable chance for probation or early release back to Indian country. The new 1994, Major Crimes Act with its "three strikes and you're out" provision will make component b more difficult to implement.

The principles of the Red School House (active participation, developing one's Indianism, and the survival-skills component) were adapted to the adult incarcerated Indian population providing a model for minority correctional treatment nationwide.

We also added an American Indian Alcoholic Anonymous component. These American Indian AA sessions were conducted in both the correctional environments (jails, prisons, reformatories) and in the community. They were sponsored by both the Lincoln Indian Center and the Nebraska Indian Commission.

Our Native American Correctional Treatment Program reflected our adaptation of the Red School House philosophy in the following manner. The survival school concept is one whereby cultural minorities, here American Indians, are provided with traditional instruction which is intended to enhance their cultural awareness. There are two stages to this process. The first, and most significant, component is that which addresses the cultural issue. Here marginal American Indians (those caught up in the conflict of two contravening worlds without fully belonging to either) are taught about, and encouraged to participate in, their traditional heritage. The purpose of this component is to help develop a strong sense of self-worth. Essentially, this component of the Survival School program is designed specifically to enhance the client's *Indianism*. In order for this component to work, American Indian instructors, notably traditional Indians, must be used as well as the utilization of the informal, cooperative, group instructional approach.

The second phase involves learning the appropriate behaviors necessary to survive in a pluralistic society. Here, the focus is upon the basics of public interaction (as against specific class room instruction involving educational curricula) such as how to get and hold jobs, write and balance check books, obtain and retain a driver's license, correspond and speak in mixed public situations.... The primary requisite for instructors within this component is that they be aware of the various Indian cultures and cultural conflict which exists between the Indian traditional cultures and the dominant Western-based society (French & LaPlante, 1978).

Both components of the Survival School intensify when applied to incarcerated populations. The challenge is to take the status and/or stigma of being a "con" and process this within the traditional cultural milieu. If we fail in this effort, not only does the Indian client feel that he has lost in his effort to count coup, he often feels that he has shamed his people thereby intensifying his sense of total failure. This is counterindicated to the goals of the Survival School program. Spirituality (purification sweats, sacred pipe, Vision Quests) plays a significant role here as the incarcerated contemporary warrior comes to see the traditional goals of counting coup (bravery and fortitude) as means to larger ends -- that of traditional acceptance of self and the acquisition of generosity and wisdom. This process is similar to what Abraham Maslow (1968; 1970) detailed in his work on motivating and personality and the hierarchy of needs. In our Survival School concept, we look at culturally-specific deficit needs and the Jonah complex (alcohol abuse and criminal activity), growth needs (traditional goals), self-actualization (Indianism), and metamotivation and peak experiences (sweats, Vision Quests, Sun Dances).

For our program to work, we needed a strong support system, one that could sustain the incarcerated Indians between visits from Emerson Jackson and Leonard Crow Dog, Jr. Here, we followed the Cherokee Cultural Therapy model. At the Lincoln Indian Center the older women (*Grandmothers*) established sewing and cooking groups preparing shawls and ribbon shirts as well as traditional Sioux meals which were then shared with the inmates through functions of the NASCA --the Native American Spiritual and Cultural Awareness Group. Several grandmothers also taught the Lacota language on a regular basis. Powwows, singings, dances and hand-games kept the traditional spirit alive between sweats and visits from the Native American Church and the Medicine Men. When this program began nearly twenty years ago, word spread throughout Indian country and we received positive feedback. This made the contemporary warriors all the more receptive to the traditionalists within their tribes and on their home reservations. The positive recognition of the grandmothers also served to reinforce the elderly Sioux female's traditional status of *honored woman*.

The enthusiasm over the seeming success of our Native American Correctional Treatment Program led to a more ambitious effort -- that of establishing an all-Sioux prison designed to serve all the Siouan tribes. Swift Bird Correctional Facility would utilize a treatment, as against punitive, approach. The Native American Correctional Treatment Program was the model for this facility. The Swift Bird effort was initiated by the

Native American Rights Fund in conjunction with the National Congress of American Indians' National Indian Law Enforcement Association, the National Indian Youth Council, National Tribal Chairman's Association, the Institute for the Development of Indian Law, the National Institute of Corrections and the National Indian Education Association as well as the Nebraska Indian Commission, Legal Services Corporation and the Medicinemen's Association of Rosebud.

Perry Wounded Shield (still incarcerated at this time), Charlie and I assisted NARF in developing the plan. The "Swift Bird Correctional Treatment Project" proposal intended to converting a newly built, but never used, federal Job Corps facility, located on the Cheyenne River (South Dakota) Reservation, into a regional minimum-facility, Indian-run correctional unit serving the Aberdeen Area (North Dakota, South Dakota, Nebraska, Iowa) as well as Wyoming, Colorado, Montana, Minnesota, and Kansas. The Native American Rights Fund had the funding and agreements worked out so that all that was needed was for the respective State Departments of Corrections to relinquish their Indian inmates to the authority of the Swift Bird facility.

Our plan was to coordinate clinical and social services for Swift Bird and its catchment area. Specifically, we proposed providing critical clinical services, patterned after our successful Native American Correctional Treatment Project, to those Indian clients arrested, jailed, imprisoned and/or paroled within the Swift Bird area. The programs were slated to be administered from the Lincoln Indian Center which at that time held a record three error-free audits from ANA. The services rendered were to be interfaced with existing programs in the area (Colorado, North and South Dakota, Nebraska, Minnesota, Iowa, Montana, Kansas). In our proposal, we stated that the Lincoln Indian Center is noted as one of the leading urban Indian centers in the nation, stressing Indian self-reliance, sobriety and responsibility as well as the preservation of the native cultural heritage. Our proposed American Indian criminal justice program fits this philosophy, hence cultural-orientation as well as mainstream survival skills are integral aspects of our program philosophy. Here, both the Pan-Indian and, more specific, Siouan cultural-orientations will be integrated into all aspects of our program (French, LaPlante, Wounded Shield, 1979).

Unfortunately, no white-dominated Corrections Department wanted to relinquish its authority to "punish" their Indian inmates in the fashion that they saw fit so the Swift Bird project died on the drawing table as did our plan to coordinate clinical services. This notoriety made things worse for Perry in prison and in 1987 he had to file a suit to be able to attend the most significant spiritual events in a warrior's life -- the annual Vision Quest and Sun Dance. This was a reversal of previous practices allowed under the 1974 Consent Decree. Perry was eventually allowed to complete his required four Vision Quests and Sun Dances but the extent that he had to go to exercise these basic rights so hard fought for in the 1974 decree merely illustrates the degree of ethnocentrism prevalent within the criminal justice system (see Wounded Shield et al. v. Gunter, 1987 CV 85-L-459). This degree of intolerance toward American Indian inmates continues to the present, an issue counselors need to be aware of when working with these clients.

## American Indian Spirituality and Counseling: Its Use and Abuse.

Today, American Indian spirituality has gained in popularity not only among Indians themselves but among non-Indians as well. It is an integral component of the New Age Movement and contemporary "pop" psychology trends. Not surprisingly, these non-Indian uses of Indian spirituality upset many traditionalists within Indian country. Nonetheless, not all these applications constitute abuses of Indian spirituality. To best understand the appropriate clinical applications of Indian spirituality we must first look at the 1978 American Indian Religious Freedom Act along with its 1994 amendment.

President Grant's famous "Indian Peace Policy" of 1870 changed U.S. policy from one of physical genocide to one of cultural genocide. Instead of being hunted down like bounty animals, American Indians now were to be relegated to military-run reservations whose primary purpose was to concentrate the Indians into camps so as to free up the land to white settlers and to reeducate and indoctrinate these captives. Regarding the latter, the captives were to be taught the evils of their traditional (savage) ways and the merits of the Christian religions and the Protestant Ethic. Over a century later, and one hundred and ninety-one years after the Continental Congress guaranteed religious freedom to U.S. citizens, President Carter signed the American Indian Religious Freedom Act.

> Whereas; the freedom of religion for all people is an inherent right, fundamental to the democratic structure of the United States and is guaranteed by the First Amendment of the United States Constitution; Whereas the United States has traditionally rejected the concept of a government denying individuals the right to practice their religion and, as a result, has benefited from a rich variety of religious heritage in this country; Whereas; the religious practices of the American Indian (as well as Native Alaskan and Hawaiian) are an integral part of their culture, tradition and heritage, such practices forming the basis of Indian identity and value system; Whereas; the lack of a clear, comprehensive, and consistent Federal policy has often resulted in the abridgement of religious freedom for traditional American Indians; Whereas; such religious infringements result from the lack of knowledge or the insensitive and inflexible enforcement of Federal policies and regulations premised on a variety of laws; Whereas;such laws were designed for such worthwhile purpose as conservation and preservation of natural species and resources but were never intended to relate to Indian religious practices and, therefore, were passed withoutconsideration of their effect on traditional American Indian religions; Whereas such laws and policies often deny American Indians access to sacred sites required in their religions, including cemeteries; Whereas; such laws and policies often deny American Indians access to sacred sites required in their religions, including cemeteries; Whereas; traditional American Indian ceremonies

have been intruded upon, interfered with, and in a few instances banned:

Now, therefore be it Resolved by the Senate and House of Representatives of the United States of America in Congress assembled, That henceforth it shall be the policy of the United States to protect and preserve for American Indians their inherent right of freedom to believe, express, and exercise the traditional religions of the American Indian, Eskimo, Aleut, and Native Hawaiians, including but not limited to access to sites, use and possession of sacred objects, and the freedom to worship through ceremonials and traditional rites. The President shall direct the various Federal departments, agencies, and other instrumentalities responsible for administering such laws to evaluate their policies and procedures in consultation with native traditional leaders in order to determine and implement appropriate changes which may be necessary to protect and preserve Native American religious cultural rights and practices.

The first major test of the 1978 American Indian Religions Freedom Act came ten years later in a challenge to the Native American Church's use of peyote in their ceremonies. (Peyote was not allowed within the Nebraska Penal Complex despite the 1974 Consent Decree. Indeed, even the Medicine Men's pouches were searched to make certain that the sacred pipe tobacco mix did not contain marijuana.) In this situation, two substance abuse counselors at the Douglas County, Oregon Council of Alcohol and Drug Abuse Prevention and Treatment (ADAPT) Program were charged with taking peyote, ostensibly as part of the Native American Church ceremony. Since both were recovering substance abusers, as a condition of their employment as counselors, they were also required to abstain from using alcohol or any nonprescriptive mind-altering agents. Their use of peyote resulted in the loss of their jobs and denial of unemployment compensation. This case went to U.S. Supreme Court and lead to the congressional revision of the American Indian Religious Freedom Act. One reason that the peyote issue, as it relates to the Native American Church, was not addressed by the U.S. Supreme Court is because one of the defendants was non-Indian (Employment Division v. Smith, 1988; 1990). The 1994 revisions stipulate what a qualified Indian member, Medicine Man and spiritual leader is and under what circumstances traditional rituals may be performed, or at least be legally sanctioned by the U.S. government. Specifically, only enrolled Indians who are qualified by their tribe as spiritual leaders may possess peyote and perform certain traditional rituals. Public Law 103-344, American Indian Religious Freedom Act Amendments of 1994, states:

SEC. 3 (a) The Congress finds and declares that -

(1) for many Indian people, the traditional ceremonial use of the peyote cactus as a religious sacrament has for centuries been integral to a way of life, and significant in perpetuating Indian tribes and cultures;

(2) since 1965, this ceremonial use of peyote by Indians has been protected by Federal regulation;

(3) while at least 28 States have enacted laws which are similar to, or are in conformance with, the Federal regulation which protects the ceremonial use of peyote by Indian religious practitioners, 22 States have not done so, and this lack of uniformity has created hardship for Indian people who participate in such religious ceremonies;

(4) the Supreme Court of the United States, in the case of Employment Division v. Smith, 494 U.S. 872 (1990), held that the First Amendment does not protect Indian practitioners who use peyote in Indian religious ceremonies, and also raised uncertainty whether this religious practice would be protected under the compelling State interest standard; and

(5) the lack of adequate and clear legal protection for the religious use of peyote by Indians may serve to stigmatize and marginalize Indian tribes and cultures, and increase the risk that they will be exposed to discriminatory treatment.

(b)(1) Notwithstanding any other provision of law, the use, possession, or transportation of peyote by an Indian for bona fide traditional   ceremonial purposes in connection with the practice of a traditional Indian religion is lawful, and shall not be prohibited by the United States

or any State.  No Indian shall be penalized or
discriminated against on the basis of such use,
possession or transportation, including, but not  limited
to, denial of otherwise applicable benefits under public
assistance programs (P.L.103-344:1-2).
Traditional American Indians are very sensitive about unqualified
Indians and non-Indians alike performing sacred rituals such as
the Sun Dance, Vision Quest, Snake Dance, Kiva Ritual, et
cetera (DeAnngelia, 1994).

An article in the November 30, 1994 issue of the *Cherokee
One Feather* addressed the fake Medicine Man scam.  Here,
Searles states that:

> The mystique of pulsing drums and chanting singers, healing
> rituals depicted in movies such as 'Dances With Wolves,' is
> causing headaches among authentic American Indian medicine
> men (Searles, 1994: 1).

He goes on to claim that many non-Indians with terminal diseases
such as AIDS or cancer as well as a growing number of New
Agers seek out Medicine Men for cures and that a new group of
non-traditional Indians are cashing in on this phenomenon by
posing as Medicine Men.  Traditional Medicine Men and Tribal
Elders call these phonies "plastic" Medicine Men.

Certainly this is a problem for counselors.  We must be aware
of credentials before we make referrals.  The best method is to
check with the Indian client's tribe first.  They, not us, are the best
qualified individuals regarding these matters.  More tribes are
taking action themselves to end this type of exploitation.  The
Hopi recently put an end to the "Smoki Snake Dance" held from
1921 until 1991 every August in Prescott, Arizona.  This ritual
mimicked the sacred Hopi Snake Dance.  In 1991, Hopi
Chairman, Vernon Masayesva, called for an end to this sacrilege.
The Smokis' white leader, known only as "Chief Ponytail,"
ceased the imitation snake dance following the Hopi protest.
However, the non-Indian Smoki continue to dress as Indians and
take on fake "Indian" names such as "Chief Ponytail."  This
pseudo-Indian ceremony certainly predates Robert Bly's
"woodland outings" and Lynn V. Andrews' "Medicine Women"
by decades.  Again, the wisest action by those of us counseling

American Indians, whether we be Indian or not, is to consult with the client's tribe, or in the case of a Pan-Indian, with officials of the Native American Church.

A growth area within American Indian counseling is that of substance abuse counseling. This is primarily because alcohol and, to a lesser extent, other drugs, such as inhalants, are such high risk factors in Indian country, especially among marginal Indians. This concern was first openly recognized as a problem in 1977, culminating in the "First North American Native American Alcohol Conference," held at the University of California, Berkeley. I represented the Eastern Band of Cherokee Indians at this historical event.

As mentioned earlier, Indian-specific AA programs were part of the 1974 Consent Decree at the Nebraska Penal Complex. On November 10th-13th, 1994, the "First Native American Convention of Alcoholism Anonymous" was held at the Boundary Tree Hotel on the Qualla Boundary of the Eastern Band of Cherokee Indians (Welch, 1994). Other efforts toward integrating traditional Indian spirituality and rituals into clinical programs emerged in the late 1970s and early 1980s. One such vehicle was the National Association of Interdisciplinary Ethnic Studies and their annual meetings in LaCrosse, Wisconsin (1978, 1979) and Arcata, California (1980). Here, African Americans, Asian Americans, Hispanics and American Indians shared ideas about the problems within their populations. We were honored by the presence of such noted Indian elders as Ruth Hutchingson and Bea Medicine at these meetings. The 1980 meetings included the presence of the American Indian Historical Society -- clearly, the main vehicle for the dissemination of information within Indian country and within urban Indian communities (Wassaja, Wee Wish Tree, The Indian Historian plus a number of books written about Indians by Indians).

Oklahoma became the first state to have its own Indian alcohol and drug abuse counselors training and certification program doing so in the late 1980s. New Mexico was always sensitive to the needs of its large Hispanic and American Indian (21 separate tribes) populations, especially given their high risk toward alcohol and drug abuse. In 1991, the theme of the Twenty-Fifth Annual Alcohol and Drug Counselors Training Institute (held at Western New Mexico University) was "Honoring the Ethnic Diversity of

New Mexico." American Indian and Meistzo cultures dominated that conference and have become an integral component of subsequent institutes. Indeed, our cultural initiative was recognized by the National Association of Alcohol and Drug Abuse Counselors (NAADAC) which, in turn, has been instrumental in bringing cultural issues to the national level. In 1994, the New Mexico Alcohol and Drug Abuse Counselors Association had a full-blooded Indian as its President (Dennis Lorenso, an Acoma Pueblo) and the President of the State Alcohol and Drug Abuse Counselors Certification Board was Jane Goodluck, a Navajo.

In 1988, the Indian group with the highest fetal alcohol rate in the U.S., and one of the highest in the world -- the Sioux of the Aberdeen Area -- created its own cultural-specific alcohol and drug abuse counselors training and certification program. This is the "Northern Plains Native American Chemical Dependency Association" (NPNACDA) serving North Dakota, South Dakota, Nebraska and Iowa (IHS, Aberdeen Area). Charlie LaPlante serves as its first director. The NPNACDA's headquarters are located in Rapid City, South Dakota where its 28-bed in-service facility, "Sacred Hills," is also located. Their cultural-specific program philosophy is stressed in the following training goals.

I.  Five Greatest Obstacles to Chemical Dependency regarding Diagnosis, Treatment and Recovery.
1. Not Knowing - What to look for; The disease entity itself.
2. Not Knowing - How to find it; The symptoms.
3. Not Being Able - To get at it; Denial/defense system.
4. Inability To See Reality; Addictive delusion.
5. Drug Dominated Feelings and Drug Driven Behavior; Addictive compulsion.

II. A highly successful therapeutic intervention is for the therapist to share personal experiences (self-disclosure). It is significant in establishing a positive alliance (trust).

III. Counseling should be geared toward the Holsitic approach -- learning to live in balance. Personal  identity; physical health care, awareness of mental processes, control and appropriate expression of emotions,

responsible social behavior, and the development of a
personal spiritual belief system need to be addressed
during treatment.

IV.  Patients need to be assessed on a Heritage
Consistency Scale for their level of involvement in
their culture and their feelings about that.  Special
consideration needs to be given to the patients'
level of bi-culturalism and how it impacts their
life.

V.  Encourage patients to face reality and make
value judgment about their behavior from a
cultural as well as the addictive aspect.

VI.  Indian patients are often compliant which needs
to be recognized when addressing the denial system.
This complacency is often utilized as a primary
"defense mechanism."

VII.  In order to change behavior the patient needs to
understand how misconception of cultural beliefs
enable negative behavior and often precipitates
guilt/shame emanating from intra-personal (within) values
conflict.

VIII. Peer evaluations are effective in promoting
and increasing the level of self-awareness, trust and self-
disclosure (see attached evaluation).

IX.  Spontaneous disclosure by the patient occurs
only following a development of trust within the group
process and in individual sessions with the therapist.
Generally, it is an unrealistic expectation that patients will
disclose "shame based" issues.  These  issues are best
addressed in a  one-to-one setting (Incest, etc.).

X. Everyone, of course, has right and left
hemisphere capabilities and modes of
consciousness.  They work together in an extremely
coordinated way.  Both are needed for true learning to
take place.  The left brain organizes and  structures
information.  The right brain creates ideas.  Many
treatment centers have an overabundance of left-brain
methods, resulting in the handicapping of those with
right-brain or holistic strengths.

XI.  Patients need to be assessed to ascertain their

reading level and comprehension. This is essential in assigning tasks related to their Individualized Treatment Plan.

XII. Experiential groups are generally productive. Role plays facilitate expression of feelings in a spontaneous and dramatic way. However, it is essential to integrate the cognitive component with emotional work. The link between past emotional issues and options for change of current behavior must be conceptualized.

XIII. Psychological testing has become an integral part of the treatment process in identifying dual disordered patients and providing indicators that suggest therapeutic interventions that would be beneficial or counter productive. (Example--beating on the pillow when the psychological profile indicates an extreme hostility.)

XIV. Cultural activities such as Talking Circle, Cultural Awareness Group, Sweat Lodge Ceremony, Story Telling by Elders, etc., need to be blended in the program. An over-balance of the cultural aspect could diminish the essential/primary focus on the pathology (disease).

Charlie uses this orientation in his program at Santee. He completed his fourth Sun Dance at the annual Santee Sioux ceremony during the summer of 1994. On March 24, 1991, I was fortunate to join Charlie (as his guest) and eight other traditional males in the Tribal recognition of the 38 Santee Sioux executed on December 26, 1862 -- the largest official execution in the United States. These were desperate warriors who chose to fight rather than face the starvation and harassment being doled out by the U.S. government at that time. This was a very therapeutic ritual for all. I was deeply moved by the 38 stone sweat. It was my fiftieth birthday.

# Chapter 5

## The Navajo Beauty Way Perspective

**Laurence French**

### Introduction

The Navajo tribe represents the largest American Indian group in the United States with an enrolled population of 225,000. The Navajo Nation encompasses nearly 15 million acres and is located in three states: northwestern New Mexico, northeastern Arizona and southeastern Utah. According to the latest data from the Navajo Area Indian Health Service (1990), 174,000 Navajo live within the Navajo Nation (reservation) while another 25,000 reside near the Navajo Nation and the other 26,000 live elsewhere. The Navajo Nation is located near where four states share a common boundary; this is known as the Four Corners Area (southwest Colorado, northwest New Mexico, southeast Utah, and northeast Arizona). They share this area with their cousins, the Jicarilla Apache, as well as with the Ute Indians and numerous Pueblo groups (Hopi, Zuni, Acoma and Laguna tribes).

The Spanish called the Navajo *Apaches de Nabaju* -- Apaches of the Cultivated Fields. Apparently, the Spanish had one term for the Athapaskans regardless if they were Navajo or Apache. This distinction made in the 1500s attests to the adaptability of the Navajo illustrating their ability to adopt the horticultural lifestyle of their Pueblo neighbors long before the advent of non-Indians (the Spanish and their African entourage). Clearly, the Navajo represent a blend of Athapaskan and Pueblo phenotype much like the Cherokees represent a blend of Iroquoian, white and African phenotypes. Nonetheless, the single most significant distinguishing feature of the Navajo is their language, a cultural attribute that has remained to the present. Language provides a significant socio-cultural, and hence psychological, boundary allowing the Navajo to identify themselves as a separate Indian group -- the *Dine*. Like the Cherokee, the Navajo's term for themselves translates to *The People*. Many parallels exist between the Navajo and the second largest Indian group in the U. S., the Cherokee. Both shared: (1) a horticultural lifestyle augmented by hunting and gathering; (2) a majority presence among numerous smaller tribes during the pre-Columbian era; (3) a preference for baskets over pottery; and (4) Forced Removal at the hands of the U. S. Army. The major difference between these two groups, however, makes these similarities pale in comparison. The Navajo (Dine) mixed with and adopted lifestyles similar to their traditional Pueblo neighbors and thus have maintained a high degree of Indian blood (granted some of it was mixed with their Pueblo neighbors generations prior to white contact) as well as their language. The Cherokees, along with the other *Civilized Tribes*, have mixed with whites and African slaves. So, while most Navajo know their adopted traditional culture and language, most Cherokees do not practice their traditional culture and fewer speak their native language.

These differences in one's degree of *Indianism* surfaced in 1990 and in the most recent U. S. Census. Following the census, the Cherokee appeared to be the largest tribe in the United States. This was due mainly to 118,156 wanna-bes falsely claiming to be Cherokee on the census. Initially, the Cherokee accepted their status as the largest tribe but retracted their claim when the Navajo complained. Even then, when blood degree is taken into account, the Navajo far outnumber the Cherokee. And if blood degree itself was the criteria for claiming Indian status, the Sioux could perhaps lay claim to second place ahead of the Cherokees. The Western Cherokee (Cherokee Nation of Oklahoma) enrolls anyone who is a descendant of anyone listed on the final Roll (Dawes Rolls) compiled in 1899 - 1906. This included all Cherokee, regardless of blood degree as well as whites who bought membership on the rolls ("white Indians") and former slaves of the Cherokee Nation. The Eastern Band of Cherokees, in 1992, reduced their blood quantum from 1/16 to 1/32 while the Rosebud Sioux are contemplating reducing their blood quantum from 1/4 to 1/16.

The point here is that the Navajo represent the dwindling number of Indian groups in the U. S. who have preserved their traditional culture, know their language and have a high degree of blood quantum among their members. Many of these Indian tribes are located in the southwest and are being challenged by encroachment from non-Indian developers. The Navajo recognize this dilemma and have been preparing to preserve their culture through education. This section looks at the educational and clinical challenges involved in this endeavor to preserve the culture of the Dine.

## Navajo History and Culture

Little is known about the Navajo prior to European (Spanish) contact. It is generally recognized that the Navajo, or Dine (Dineh), along with their Apache cousins, came from western Canada centuries prior to white contact. There is even controversy over how the Dine, the term that Navajo traditionally used to call themselves, came to be called *Navajo* or *Navaho*. Some claim that this is a term that the Zuni called them, signifying *raiders of the fields*. The Navajo and Apache were late comers to the southwest, raiding their Pueblo neighbors. The Navajo eventually adopted the horticultural ways of the Pueblo as did some of the western Apache. The other claim is that Navajo (Nabaju) was a Pueblo term for these Athapaskans, but that the term signifies the original place of residence, or settlement of the Dine (Dinetah) raiders meaning *Apache (raiders) of Nabaju*. This place, Nabaju, was located in the Chama Valley and a portion of the San Juan Basin in what is now northwest New Mexico. The Spanish coined this term and provided the definition in 1626.

The Navajo/Dine actually represent a blend of Athapaskan and Pueblo cultures. This blending process occurred some 600 years prior to European influence. Perhaps the greatest influence came from the Hopi Pueblo which today is surrounded by the vast Navajo Nation. Pueblo refugees fled to the Navajo Nation following their defeat in the 1690 - 1692 war with the Spanish. Many stayed even after the Pueblo Indians soundly defeated and routed the Spanish in 1680. Today, following more than a thousand years of interaction, the Navajo/Dine tend to look more like their Pueblo neighbors than their cousins, the Apaches.

The Navajo had a long history of raiding whites and other Indian settlements resulting in a number of Spanish military expeditions during the early 1800s. Often the Ute and Navajo raided together. Most treaties were shortlived and in 1846, the U.S. inherited this conflict. The first U.S. treaty, the Treaty of Ojo del Oso in 1846, was necessary for the U.S. to get through Navajo country in order to raid the Mexican state of Chihuahua during the war with Mexico. Part of the problem was that the Navajo, like their Apache cousins in the region, lacked any form of centralized leadership. Hence, these treaties were never recognized by the entire tribe. Matters worsened once Fort Defiance was abondoned in 1861 at the beginning of the Civil War. The Navajos, Utes, Apaches, Zunis and other Pueblo Indian groups, along with Hispanics and Anglos, engaged in raids on each other during this lawless period. The Navajo became the target for revenge by the U.S. government leading to Colonel Kit Carson's punitive expeditions which began in June, 1863. Crops, herds and villages were destroyed and those Navajo who refused to be removed were systematically executed regardless of age and gender. On March 6, 1864, the first of the LongWalks began; a 300-mile trek to Fort Sumner in New Mexico. Only children and the handicapped were allowed to ride in the wagons. The rest walked and those who could not keep up were killed. Eventually some 8,000 Navajo were removed to Fort Sumner. Many more died at Fort Sumner and in 1868 it was realized by all that this was a failed program. The Navajo were now allowed to return to their ravaged home land (Bailey & Bailey, 1968; French, 1994; Kluckhorn & Leighton, 1946).

While the Navajo adapted to many of the Pueblo lifestyles,

they kept their distinctive living habitat -- the hogan. Like the sweat lodge of the Plains Indians, the door of the hogan always faces east -- the power path. Early hogans were constructed of wood frames and covered with branches, bush and mud. They later replaced the branches with adobe (mud/straw mix) blocks to fill in between the pole frame. Today, hogans are six or eight sided and are made of either adobe or wood. They still play a significant role in Navajo/Dine spirituality.

Both the Pueblo and Navajo horticultural lifestyle was augmented with the introduction of sheep from the Spanish. The Spanish provided the sheep and contracted with the Navajo/Dine to produce wool for export. The pastoral lifestyle also served to "tame" the Navajo, further demarking differences between them and their raiding cousins -- the Apache. The Navajo now had wool for weaving and food. The latter was needed since the sheep depleted the vegetation that previously sustained small game. Mutton stew and Navajo blankets are inseparable elements of the Navajo lifestyle.

The Pueblo Indian influence permeated all other aspects of Navajo life -- even their lineage. They adopted the Pueblo matrilineal clan structure, but kept their local group or band autonomy much like that of their Apache cousins. The Navajo matrilineal clan structure, in turn, influenced the western Apache who adopted a similar structure. The band structure, unlike the clan or village, is linked by language, rituals and kinships and is not restricted to any region. Both the Navajo and Apache have diffuse bands scattered throughout Indian country.

The matrilineal structure of the Navajo was, and continues to be, one that offers women a higher status than do other Athapaskan groups. Within this system, property passed through women who controlled lineage property, including the sheep. When she married, the wife was empowered since her husband had to move into a hogan near her mother (matrilocal arrangement). If they divorced, the man returned to his mother's hogan much like the aboriginal Cherokees. This also meant that the children were closer to their mother's relatives who lived close by. The social situation was made even more difficult for the husband in that he had to observe the *mother-in-law* taboo whereby he was forbidden to look at his wife's mother or to be in the same room as her. The Apache adopted this taboo as well.

The social organization of the Navajo, along with its Pueblo and Spanish influences, was one where the band provided the individual with his/her Indian identity or cultural persona. They lived in matrilineally related extended families known as outfits. These outfits were the farming and herding units much like the aboriginal Cherokee *gadugis* (horticultural units). And like in the Cherokee gadugis, males headed the Navajo outfits. The next level of social organization among the early Dine was the clan structure. To a certain extent, this structure is still in existence among the traditional Dine within the Navajo Nation (Bailey & Bailey, 1986; French, 1994; Garbarino, 1976; MacDonald, 1978; Underhill, 1956).

The Dine creation myth and accompanying ceremonies and rituals are still as well guarded as they are for the surrounding southwestern tribes. What is generally understood about the Navajo origin legend is that they have their corresponding deities for Father Sky and Mother Earth. Father Sky is *Bekotsidi* while Mother Earth is *Estsanatlehi.* Bekotsidi is the powerful Sun God but apparently started out as a mortal Dine (One of the People). Estsanatlehi, on the other hand, is The Woman Who Changes. She is highly revered because she is reborn each Spring with the planting of the crops, notably corn, and ages until the harvest is in and finally becomes an old woman during the winter. Each year, Mother Earth changes with the seasons. Estsanatlehi is represented on Earth by turquoise. She is the wife of Bekotsidi the Sun God and together with her sister, *Yolkai Estsan,* produce the sun, nourishment and water necessary for sustaining life for the Dine and all other creatures and objects in their environment. They provide the essence of the Harmony Ethos for the Navajo. Yolkai Estsan is a lesser god and is represented by white shells (heishi) which, in turn, is symbolic of water. Two other lesser, but significant dieties, are the twin sons of the two powerful gods, Bekotsidi and Estsanatlehi. The sons are named *Nayenezgani* (Slayer of Alien Gods) and *Tobadzistsini* (Child of Water). Together, their mission is to destroy alien gods, to assist warriors in battle and to aid those afflicted by witchcraft or who are ill. They play a major role in healing ceremonies, especially those involving the *Kethawans* (sticks and cigarettes sacrifice), Sand Altars and masked Shaman. A host of lesser gods (*Yei*), local gods and alien gods complement the Dine creation myth thereby providing meaning to their traditional ceremonies, customs and rituals.

Navajo ceremonies are somewhat unique from the Cherokee and Sioux but not from other southwestern tribes. Elements of these ceremonies, which have survived to the present, include the "corn pollen blessing," cigarettes (originally reeds filled with feathers and a local tobacco mix), sacrificial sticks, sand altars, and masked shaman. Kethawans are comprised of sacrificial sticks representing certain dieties and cigarettes (medium for communication with Father Sky) placed in a sacred basket and are used for special ceremonies. Kethawans are considered to be sacred sacrifices.

Sand, or dry, paintings represent sand altars and are used in all the great rites of the Dine. In this ceremony, sand is brought into the medicine lodge (hogan for lesser rites) and spread out to a depth of about three inches. Five pigments, white, red, yellow, black, and gray, are used in the ceremony. These paintings represent relevant abstract images of dieties deemed necessary for the healing process being addressed in the ceremony. When the picture is completed, a number of ceremonies are performed over it. The painting is usually blessed with corn pollen. The most popular use of the sand altar is for healing. Traditional shaman reproduce the sand paintings from memory without the benefit of drawings of pictures. Sand altars are dismantled following the ceremony. Masks are also used in Navajo ceremonies much like those used by the Hopi (Kachinas) and the aboriginal Iroquois and Cherokees. The masks represent the various dieties portrayed in the sand paintings. Male masks cover the entire head while female masks cover only the face. Once masked, the Navajo spiritual healer utters cries and not words (Bryde, 1971; Boyce, 1978; French, 1987; French, 1994; Matthews, 1897; Underhill, 1956).

The Navajo (Dine or Dineh) believe that they have passed through three previous worlds. The first world was black and comprised of four corners over which appeared four clouds which were black, white, blue and yellow. The black cloud represented Female Being or substance while the white cloud represented Male Being. Hence it was here that the first Dine were created. When the first world became crowded everyone climbed into the second or blue world. Other people already

lived in the second world and conflict between them and the
Dine resulted.  In order to escape the fighting and killing, the
Dine climbed into the third or yellow world.  This world had no sun
so eventually they climbed into the present world.  They
emerged through a lake surrounded by four sacred mountains.
The four sacred mountains define the current Navajo Nation with
Mt. Blanca *(Sisnaajini)* to the east repesenting the color white; Mt.
Taylor *(Tdoodzil)* to the south representing the color blue
(turquoise); the San Francisco Peak *(Dook's'oosliid)* to the west
representing the color yellow and the precious stones abalone
and coral; and Mt. Hesperus *(Dibe'nitsaa)* to the north
representing black and jet.  The Dine offer chants to these
mountains, a ritual known as *Dressing the Mountain.*  Corn pollen
is the medium for communication during these chants.
Traditional Navajo also adhere to the custom of marrying out of
their clan.  Indeed, when identifying themself to others they state
that they are the son or daughter of their parent's respective
clans (Bailey & Bailey, 1986; Mariano, 1994; Underhill, 1956).

## Marginality Issues

Navajo marginality has become a reality, especially among those
living on the fringe of Dine influence.  The dilemma is that some,
notably the federal and local (New Mexico, Arizona, Utah)
governments, feel that it is time to fully assimilate the Navajo into
the larger dominant society.  This effort, plus the advent of the
mass media (radio, television, movies and the popular press), has
had an eroding effect on some Navajos. This process to
*Christianize* and *Anglocize* the Navajo has been in effect for over
forty years and is evident in increased substance abuse, notably
alcohol and inhalant abuse, among Navajo residing near off-
reservation towns.   Thus, while the mass media is an
unintentional influence, the same cannot be said about the BIA,
missionaries, and non-Indian entrepreneurs (owners of bars,
liquor outlets, trading posts and *hock* shops, etc.) who target
marginal Navajos.  We mentioned earlier that the Navajo fetal
alcoholism rate, and even their overall alcoholism rate, is lower
than many other tribes, notably the Sioux.  Nonetheless, the
sheer number of Navajo makes substance abuse stand out as a

major problem, especially on the border areas where the Navajo Nation and non-Indian communities intersect.

To aid in understanding the nature and extent of this phenomenon, we will look at the process of marginality among the Navajo, keeping in mind that marginality begins in the formative years of childhood and adolescence. Next, we will address the substance abuse issue. The following section will address educational and clinical (treatment) issues relevant to substance abuse prevention, intervention and treatment as well as cultural-specific educational goals currently being devised by the Navajo Nation in an effort to reverse the marginality trend among its children and youth.

As the first President of the Navajo Nation (previous leaders held the title of *Tribal Chairman*), Peterson Zah recognized the fact that a significant number of Navajo were influenced not only by the non-Indian dominant society but by other Indian groups beyond the Pueblo Indians. This is evident in the number of Navajo who participate in Pan-Indian traditions, including the purification sweat and the peyote ritual. In his October 29, 1994 *Report to the Navajo People on the American Indian Religious Freedom Legislation*, he recognized and supported those Navajo involved in the Native American Church.

> Congratulation to all members of the Native American Church (NAC) and many other church leaders for the extraordinary work in the passage of H.R. 4230, the American Indian Religious Freedom Act Amendments of 1994, to protect the religious use of peyote by American Indians. President William Clinton signed H. R. 4230 into Public Law 103-344 on October 6, 1994. I take this opportunity to thank Pat Lefthand for his support as the other Co-Chair of the American Indian Religious Freedom Coalition.This is a great victory for members of the NAC and Indian Country. The passage of H. R. 4239 is a culmination of countless effort by you over several years. I highly commend you for your patience and dedication in the long struggle leading to the passage of H. R. 4230. We remember our relatives that played an important role in promoting the use of sacrament peyote who are not with us today or are now in hospitals....The passage of H. R. 4230 places a tremendous responsibility on our shoulders as members and practitioners of the Native American Church.

Much work is yet to be done to ensure the use of sacrament of peyote is protected and preserved. Also, the full religious freedom for American Indians including protection of sacred sites, prisoners' rights and access to eagle feathers, plants and animals is still yet to be resolved. I ask for your continued support and dedication to achieve this legislation in the next Congress.

It has been a long struggle for members of the Native American Church and it is my pleasure to have worked with many of you to achieve this important legislation. The protection of our religious practice is very important in our everyday life and for our children in the future generations. May the Great Spirit be with you (Zah, 1994:1).

Zah's statement represents the cultural-specific response to spiritual diversity within Indian country. This is a recent effort within Indian country mainly because it has been only within the past twenty years that tribal and spiritual leaders have been allowed to support traditional alternatives to strict Western style Christian orientations. And while these efforts pertain mainly to adult Indians, the non-Indian, Christianization and Anglolization efforts have been more devastating in the long run since they target Indian children and youth, in this case, the Navajo and other southwestern tribes.

Active efforts to assimilate through American-style education began during the Eisenhower administration in the 1950s. Perhaps the most significant educational endeavor at this time was that which Commissioner Glenn Emmons initiated for the Navajo. This program was designed to detraditionalize the nation's largest tribe and was officially known as the Navajo Emergency Education Program (NEEP) and more generally known as the Bordertown Program with borderline schools.

Emmons was an advocate of the termination policy and advocated assimilating Indians into the majority society theoretically eliminating Indian traditionalism within a couple of generations. The borderline schools were seen as a potential means for the assimilation process. The NEEP program was comprised of a federally subsidized public school system targeted to accommodate thousands of Navajo youth. These schools were built off the reservation in borderline towns, like Gallup, and were incorporated into the existing state education

system.  NEEP schools even provided dormitories making them
Indian public boarding schools.  However, while these were
considered to be public schools, the Indian students were
subsidized by the federal government and had a special mandate
- - that of detraditionalizing Indian children and youth.
Interestingly, this program met with considerable approval from
the Navajo tribe, the Bureau of Indian Affairs, and the State of
New Mexico.  Even then, some questioned the commissioner's
motives especially since he was also a Gallup banker.

Seeing an opportunity for the revival of the old missionary
church influence in Christianizing and detraditionalizing Indians,
American Indian children and youth, the Mormons (Latter Day
Saints-LDS) initiated their LDS Placement Program.  This
program  coincided  with  the  federal  policies  of
termination/relocation in general and the federal NEEP school
program, in particular.  Here, the Mormons place Indian children
and youth (Navajo, Ute, Pueblos) with white Mormon families
during the nine-month school year, subjecting them to the
unique Mormon socio-religious perspective.  For these programs
to operate with the latitude that they have clearly indicates federal
and state (notably Utah) support of the Mormon Church's efforts.
In addition to robbing them of their traditionalism, American Indian
traditionalists are concerned about the secretive nature of this
program.  Apparently no records are available.  Of equal concern
is the proximity of the *Mormon State*-- Utah-- to the largest
American Indian tribe in the United States.

The magnitude of the outcry from the American Indian
community is due to the negative status the Mormon Church has
for them.  Within the Mormon doctrine, American Indians are
known as *Lamenites.*  The Mormons believe that American
Indians represent one of the lost tribes of Israel and that their
color and aboriginal/traditional culture reflect God's wrath for their
greed and evilness.  According to Mormon doctrine, two of the
lost Israeli tribes survived and were living on the American
continent during the pre-Columbian era.  Both tribes were white
and were quite successful as is evident in the artifacts now
attributed to South and Central American Indians.  One tribe
became greedy and killed off the other.  God punished the bad
tribe by making them American Indians.  The spirit of the lone
survivor of the *good* white tribe later came to Joseph Smith in a

vision in the early 1800s, hence the beginning of the Mormon Church.

Navajo feel that being Navajo and Mormon is a contradiction. Navajo leaders have voiced concern that the Mormon Placement Program not only *brainwashes* Indian youth during their formative years but has a more sinister, latent function of placing these *Navajo Mormons* back among their people as agents of change. Navajo Mormon males are even sent among other tribes as *missionaries.* They usually travel in pairs, while in their late teens, with the specific purpose of converting other Indians to the Mormon religion. I knew one such individual who was sent among the Plains Indians to do his *missionary* duty. Today, he is a *Jack Navajo Mormon* tribal police officer, one who is not only marginal but who has a serious drinking problem as well  Many Indian youth who experience this resocialization process end up with the same result, that of cultural genocide through the process of marginality.

Collectively, the LDS Placement Program and the NEEP borderline schools are two of the most significant contributing factors to Navajo marginality -- a problem which has manifested itself within the past forty years. Ironically, the *two generation cultural genocide* plan did not eliminate the Navajo traditional culture, it merely created a noticeable *marginal* subculture and created negative diversity among the Navajo. Add to this the lifting of the one hundred and twenty-one years (1832 - 1953) federal ban against the selling of alcohol to American Indians and we can see how the contemporary "Indian problem" began. The nature and extent of the marginality problem, as it is manifested through substance abuse, is addressed next.

The late Reuben Snake, a Winnebago-Sioux who provided assistance to our Siouan correctional treatment project, served as the chair of Task Force Eleven: Alcohol and Drug Abuse. In the Final Report to the American Indian Policy Review Commission, Reuben made the following statement about forcing Western-style education and religious conversion upon American Indians nineteen years ago.

> The steamrolling effect of the "civilized society" upon the Indian people has wreaked a havoc which extends far beyond that of loss of material possessions. The American Indian and

Alaskan Native are caught in a world wherein they are trying to find out who they are and where they are, and where they fit in. The land which was once their "mother," giving them food and clothing, was taken. Their spiritual strengths were decried as pagan, and familial ties were broken. Their own forms of education, i.e., that of legends, how to live, how to respect themselves and others, were torn asunder by the "white society's" reading, writing, and arithmetic. No culture could, or can be, expected to be trust into a world different from its own and adapt without problems of cultural shock. Also, the Indian people were not even given citizenship until 1924. An 1832 federal Indian law prohibiting the sale of liquor to Indian people remained in effect until 1953 and could have been instrumental in the formation of the "hidden group," "drink until it's gone," and "quick" drinking patterns that Native American people exhibit. The Indian people of today are proud of their heritage and are fighting to maximize its influence upon their lives in a dominant white world. Many have succeeded. Many have not (Snake, 1976: 13).

Today, inhalant abuse has emerged as a critical problem among American Indian youth. Gasoline sniffing has become the *cheap high* on the reservation, especially on remote reservations like the Navajo Nation where the sale of alcohol is prohibited. A 1985 study of four large samples of American Indian youth indicates that when compared with non-Indian youth, Indian young people have shown much higher rates of inhalant use. The study noted that inhalant use is not only an increasing phenomenon, but that it begins at a very early age (pre-teens). Inhalant abuse, notably gasoline, can cause rapid, and irreversible, physiological damage in addition to leading to psychopathological conditions (Beauvais, Oetting & Edwards, 1985; Bloom, 1988; May, 1982). In the early 1990s, I conducted a study on the *Adolescent Assessment/Referral System*. The AARS is a substance abuse screening instrument for youth (ages 12-19) devised by the National Institute on Mental Health and recommended for use in the Indian Health Service, Regional Youth Treatment Centers. In my study, I was interested in providing rural, minority norms for the AARS's assessment component -- the POSIT (Problem Oriented Screening Instrument). This 139-item questionnaire is designed to measure ten domains, each with a cutting score

indicating at-risk significance for the adolescent taking the test.
     Substance Use/Abuse
     Physical Health Status
     Mental Health Status
     Family Relations
     Peer Relations
     Educational Status
     Vocational Status
     Social Skills
     Leisure and Recreation
     Aggressive Behavior and Delinquency
     The research was conducted from 1992-1994 and included the following rural populations: Anglos (New Mexico), Mexicans (Palomas, Mexico), Mexican Americans (New Mexico), African Americans (Mississippi), Navajo (Ramah, New Mexico), and Choctaw (Mississippi). The total sample size was 656 subjects (340 males; 316 females) with an average age of 16. The results show that the Choctaw and Navajo males had the highest rates of substance abuse (Choctaw = 9.0/Navajo = 5.0). A score of 1.0 indicates significance. The next highest scores were registered by the Navajo females (4.4), African-American males (3.5) and Choctaw females (3.0). The Choctaw males had the highest scores for mental health (11.3), followed by Navajo females (10.9), African-American females (8.7), and Chotaw females (8.0). A score of 4.0 indicates a risk of psychopathology. Similar patterns existed for education (school problems) and aggressive behavior and delinquency. The Ramah Navajo, while part of the Navajo Nation, are physically separated from the main reservation and are surrounded by white and Pueblo (Zuni & Acoma) neighbors. They best qualify as *borderline* Navajo. This level of pathology would not likely be the case in the interior of the Navajo Nation where these American Indian children and youth have access to their traditional culture and language and are removed from the exploitation of off-reservation bars and alcohol sales. Even the influence of Western-style education is minimized by the traditional environment and Navajo teacher's aides. The Mississippi Choctaw, on the other hand, have long been removed from their traditional culture and many have mixed with African-Americans and whites. They truly fit the marginal Indian prototype.

The *borderline Navajo*, however, has caught America's attention with the expose about Gallup, New Mexico -- *Drunk City, U.S.A.* A report from the Robert Wood Johnson Foundation stressed the significance of the alcohol problem among the Navajo in the Gallup area. Northwest New Mexico is unique. What distinguishes this region from other parts of the country is the impact which residents of the *dry* (Navajo Nation) have on the border towns where alcohol is legal. This is particularly true of Gallup, which has received a national reputation as *Drunk Town*. Gallup and the surrounding region are faced with an epidemic of alcohol abuse which has received national exposure after the *Albuquerque Tribune* did a six-part expose (October 26-November 1, 1988). The broadcast media followed up on the story, and segments on Gallup have since been aired on NBC's 'Today Show,' ABC's '20/20,' PBS's *On Assignment*, and the syndicated *Inside Edition*.

Gallup is the major border town of the region and is the most heavily impacted by alcohol abuse. Gallup's population on weekends expands from its 21,000 residents to well over 100,000 people. Gallup has 61 liquor outlets, which exceeds New Mexico's quota system by 50. The roads are filled with Navajo and Zuni going to get drunk. Individuals who become intoxicated are picked up by the police to protect them from injury and death, such as might result from staggering onto the highway or freezing to death. More than 30,000 people are taken into *Protective Custody* (incarcerating the individual without criminal offense for up to 12 hours) each year in Gallup. More than one-third of these individuals are Arizona residents (most are American Indians, either Navajo or Pueblo Indians).

The National Institute on Alcoholism and Alcohol Abuse, *U.S. Alcohol Epidemiologial County Problem Indicators,* found McKinley County (Gallup is the County Seat) had the highest composite index of alcohol-related problems of all 3,107 counties in the United States (for the 1975-1980 time period). Death rates from cirrhosis of the liver in McKinley County were three times higher than thenational average, alcohol-related traffic accidents were seven times higher, chronic alcoholism rates were 19 times higher, and deaths from all alcohol-related causes were four times higher.

Ellis noted that in one year (1988), 164 deaths, which

represents 40% of all deaths in McKinley and San Juan counties (the two New Mexico border counties) were alcohol-related. The carnage includes deaths from exposure, pedestrians run over by trucks and trains, acute alcohol poisoning, child abuse, automobile collisions, drownings, suicides and homicides (1994 :1-2).

The problem in Gallup began with the interventions by the BIA and Mormons during the "termination/Relocation" era of the Eisenhower Administration, including the lifting of the ban of selling alcohol to American Indians. The situation in Gallup and other border towns near the Navajo Nation are so bad that Mother Theresa, the Nobel Peace Prize laureate, includes Gallup on her list of blighted and forsaken places in the world. Government attempts to deal with this problem include the 1990 effort to drop off drunk Indians at the city limits following their twelve hours of protective custody in the drunk tank. This practice drew protests from the Navajo Nation as well as from the McKinley County Sheriff's Office (since they would still likely be within the jurisdiction of the county once out of the city limits). Both parties contended that Indians released from protective custody are safer in the city rather than on the isolated, rural, and often dangerous roads heading to and from the Navajo Nation and the Zuni Pueblo.

Perhaps the most bizarre strategy was proposed in April, 1990 by six Gallup city officials. They wanted to build a "combat zone" in Gibson Canyon, north of the city. In their plan, all Indian bars would be moved to Gibson Canyon thereby creating "an attractive environment" for Indian drunks. Along with bars and liquor stores, the combat zone would have soup kitchens, plasma center, adult bookstores, restaurants, motels, and ground transportation. The architects of this plan compared the Gibson Canyon Plan with that of Six Flags over Texas and Disneyland -- entertainment centers away from any center proper. The stated reason for the Gibson Canyon Plan is "to make Gallup a better place," and I would add one that does not take away the high profit made on Indian alcoholism. The Chief of Police, City Attorney, and Directors of Planning, Community Development, and General Services all supported the Gibson Canyon Plan.

# Clinical and Educational Programs for Navajo Children and Youth

It should be evident that marginality reflects a serious flaw in the socialization and enculturation process of infants, children and youth. It is during these critical formative years that the seeds of identity, language and culture are planted and nourished. Deliberate attempts at cultural genocide, such as those just described (borderline schooling, Mormon Placement, Westernization of Indian education, exposure to alcohol and other substances), do not just, "kill the Indian in the child", as they are intended; these efforts kill the spirit of the Indian as well.

A major consideration when looking at American Indian versus Western learning styles is that of the role neurophysiology plays within these diverse, and often contravening, epistemological methodologies. Any viable substance abuse prevention and clinical treatment approaches with American Indians needs to take into consideration these differences. And any interventive and preventive efforts needs to effect American Indians as early as possible in the socialization process. The argument of avoiding ethnocentrism in either education or counseling is made clear by Erich Goode.

All civilizations set rules concerning what is real and what is not, what is true and what is false. All societies select out of the data before them a world, one world, the world taken for granted, and declare that the real world. Each one of these artificially constructed worlds is to some degree idiosyncratic, unique. No individual views reality directly, in the raw, so to speak. Our perceptions are narrowly channeled through concepts and interpretations. What is commonly thought of as reality, that which exists, or simply is, is a set of suppositions, rationalizations, justifications, defensed, all generally collectively agreed-upon, which guide and channel each individual's perception in a specific and distinct direction. The specific rules governing the perception of the universe which man inhabits are more or less arbitrary, a matter of convention. Every society establishes a kind of epistemological methodology (Goode, 1969: 84).

These relative constructs of reality do, in fact, leave indelible marks on our identity, language and personality. A shared language and cultural view provides the roots of our identity, doing so at an early age. Language not only gives us an accent, but research now indicates that the way we are socialized to speak and think actually affects the neuropathways of the brain. The brain's plasticity and capacity to compensate during the critical formative (neuro-developmental) years creates neurophysiological patterns for individuals sharing a similar socialization process. Usually these changes occur within the biological parameters determined by neurophysiological development according to gender. While our sex is determined at conception, differences are not noticed until the ninth week when males (XX chromosome configuration) begin to develop testes. This change alone is credited with much of the average attributes associated with human males and females. When looking at infant and toddler development, regardless of culture, males appear to be more aggressive at an early age and have more acute visual-spatial abilities, while females, on the other hand, appear to be more verbally fluent (Bloom & Lazerson, 1988).

There are even instances where socialization overrules biological laws. Western cultures appear to use the left hemisphere heavily at the expense of right hemisphere development. Non-Western cultures, including traditional American Indian cultures, indicate a more balanced use of both hemispheres. This is often reflected in their language development which is perhaps the best indicator of their enculturalization. Studies of traditional Japanese illustrate the dual hemisphere development for language and culture. By using two forms of communication, *kana* and *kanji,* the traditional Japanese utilizes both hemispheres of the brain. This dual development indicates a significantly smaller rate of dyslexia and a greater rate of recovery from strokes. I contend that American Indians socialized within their traditional Harmony Ethos share a similar neurophysiolgical developmental process. Western cultures emphasize "logical" thinking stressing Aristotelian logic whereby everything is reduced to premises and conclusions. The end result here is finding "the bottom line." This process, initiated at an early age, utilizes left hemisphere brain activity.

Traditional American Indian socialization, in contrast, uses "stories" much like Socrates and Plato did in presenting their arguments. The Harmony Ethos, along with its descriptive, "circle arguments," better fits the Socratic, than the Aristotelian method. This approach tends to utilize both hemispheres rather than one at the expense of the other. The Navajo and Pueblo Indian "story tellers" illustrate this traditional process.

As both Erickson and Maslow postulated, the strength of our identity and personality is directly related to the strength of our socialization. We also know that by weakening a child's sense of belonging, by deliberately or inadvertingly creating duality or chaos in their lives during the critical formative years, we can produce psychologically marginal individuals. This is where the clinical/educational dilemma for the Navajo child rests today.

The Navajo situation a generation later, in 1973, consisted of 21 Mission Schools, 53 Federal Bureau of Indian Affairs Schools (including boarding schools), 30 Public Schools (borderline schools), four Community Controlled (Contact) Schools (Borrego Pass, Rough Rock, Rock Point and Ramah), as well as 102 Headstart School sites on the Navajo Nation. There were also two Homestart schools located at the Tuba City Agency and at the Eastern Agency. Of the 58,029 students enrolled in these schools, 1,000 were enrolled in Mission Schools, 24,248 within the Federal-BIA schools, 29,404 within the Public (borderline schools), 946 in the Community Controlled schools, and 2,431 in tribal (Headstart and Homestart) schools. Of these, 414 Navajo students were enrolled in special education. At this time, the Navajo Community College also began offering Associate Degrees. These figures do not reflect the students taken off the reservation by the Mormons.

1973 marked the eleventh educational program of the Navajo comprehensive educational plan, the plan that reflected the full influence of the Borderline School Program, the Mormon Placement Program and the legalization of sales to Navajo by whites off the reservation. In line with the BIA goals of assimilation, or the more realistic concept of *cultural genocide*, the manifest purpose of "Program 11" was the creation of a youth development and employment program.

Program 11 will be attempting to reach approximately 70,000 to 80,000 Navajo, youths and young adults; as the Program matures, some of its components, e.g., recreation and adult education, will also appeal to some 20,000 to 40,000 other adults.

There has never been a well planned comprehensive youth and young adult program in operation on the Navajo Nation. During the non-school hours there are few planned activities available to occupy, much less develop, these young people. Hence, many of them use their time to drift around, few making any significant contributions toward self-development or Tribal improvement.

There is little doubt in the minds of the Navajos on the NDOE staff that the lack of a well planned youth program is a major contributor to the many serious social problems currently engulfing the younger generation, e.g., dropping out of school, consuming excessive amounts of alcoholic beverages, committing crimes against property and people, and failing to develop career skills and knowledge. The degree to which these problems retard the socioeconomic conditions of the Tribe will never be fully known, but it is obvious that they are of serious proportions. Other problems have also "turned off" Navajo youths. A classic example is the constant clash of the Navajo and white cultures with the young people caught in the middle. This has created many unique and difficult problems for the young people of today. Situations developing from this problem have brought disrespect and embarrassment to the Navajo people (Tonigan & Platero, 1973: 66).

While proposing "more of the same", this description of the "Indian problem" a generation later clearly attests to the devastating effects of the programs initiated in the 1950s. This (cultural genocide) was the intended purpose of *Termination* and *Relocation*. The ethnocentric bias is clearly evident. Condemn traditional Navajo culture thereby creating "marginality" and then measuring success and failure using Western concepts -- those dictated by the Protestant Ethic. The research two generations later, the late 1980s and early 1990s, indicates a continuation of marginality among Navajo children and youth.

The contemporary dropout rate for Navajo is reported to be nearly one-third -- rates significantly higher than any other minority group in the U. S. (Brandt, 1992). Research indicates that the main reason for this dismal failure is the negative effects of forty years of "cultural genocide" directed toward Navajo children and youth.  Boyce and Boyce (1983) found that Navajo children coming from families pulled between two cultures (marginality) had greater health problems including mental health problems.  Tempest (1987) saw another effect on Navajo children, not being able to conceptualize auditorily in either English or Navajo.  This inability to conceptualize was because the Western-style educational system in the borderline schools and the contrasting cultural demands on these children restricted language mastery in either culture.  This finding was reinforced by research by Deyhle (1991), who found that the imposition of Western-style education resulted in miscommunication as well as prejudice toward Navajo children and youth.  Not only did this affect the children but served to alienate the Navajo parents as well.  Rhodes (1989), on the other hand, addressed the issue of using Western-style measurements (which are predominately left-hemisphere dominant) in order to measure "academic success."  We need to keep in mind that "success" here is defined within the Protestant Ethic and not necessarily within the Harmony Ethos.  Rhodes noted that Navajo students living on the reservation and attending public schools scored lower on achievement tests than did Navajo students living off the reservation and attending public schools.  Depending upon the perspective, these findings could spell either success or failure.  According to the goals of "Termination/Relocation," this spells success for the borderline schools in that the process of cultural genocide seems to be working.  From the traditional Navajo perspective, this process spells failure.

The issue of intelligence, especially in light of the controversial surrounding this topic today, is another issue that needs to be looked at from a cultural-specific (Harmony Ethos), and not ethnocentric (Protestant Ethic), perspective.  This issue has been argued in the courts since 1972 with the *Larry P. v. Riles* case (1972; 1974; 1979; 1984).  Briefly stated, this California case claimed that minority students were being disproportionately being labelled as "EMR" (Educable Mentally Retarded -- those without any specific genetic or identifiable etiologies).  The cause of this discrimination was stated to be the Western-style IQ tests which primarily measure the general ability of white middle-class Americans.  Tempest and Skipper (1988) noted these differences when employing the most widely used intelligence measure for children in the U. S. -- the Weschler Intelligence Test for Children. They used the WISC-R and not the most recent WISC-III version in their study. They found significant differences in how Navajo students and non-Navajo students respond to certain of the sub-tests. When looking for a culturally-free measure of IQ, MacAvoy, Orr and Sidles (1993) found that the Raven Coloured Progressive Matrices (RCPM) worked well up to grade 2 and the Raven Standard Progressive Matrices (RSPM) from grades 3 through 9 for Navajo children. In my own work, I have found the Lieter International Scale (LIS) to work well with American Indian children and youth.

The Navajo leadership has long been aware of, and opposed to, the cultural genocide plan initiated during the 1950s. However, they were unable to do much about the situation until1989 with the passage of the current federal policy toward American Indians -- that of the *New Federalism*. Here, Indian country is supposed to be able to have greater control over day-to-day tribal operations, including education. The Eastern Band of Cherokee Indians quickly took advantage of this effort by taking control of the reservation schools. The Navajo have a similar plan. With the assistance of a Ford Foundation grant, the Navajo Nation Teacher Education Consortia was developed for the purpose of preparing 4,000 new Navajo teachers to take over all teaching positions in Navajo schools. The consortia explained the situation and their plan in the following fashion.

> The Navajo Nation has a great need to have more qualified Navajo teachers to teach its children. Currently the 242 schools (K-12) on or near the Reservation are staffed primarily by non-Navajo teachers. Teachers employed by the Navajo Nation schools typically are not Indians and when they are, they are not from the Reservation. These teachers are generally unprepared to work with children from a culture different from their own. Over 6,000 teachers make up the teaching force on the Navajo Nation with responsibility for the education of 70,000 Navajo children. Only approximately 8% of the teachers are Navajo, though virtually all of the teacher aides in the schools are Navajo.
> It is well documented in the literature that different cultures produce different learning styles. Cultural influences not only

affect learning style, but the subtler aspects of perception and cognitive behavior as well. For example, in comparing non-western to western cultural groupings, non-western cultures (Native American, Mexican American, etc.) emphasize group cooperation, value harmony with nature, approach time as relative, accept affective expression, and engage in holistic thinking. Western cultures, on the other hand, emphasize individual competition, achievement for the individual, master and control of nature, adhere to a rigid time schedule, limit affective expression, and promote dualistic thinking (NNTEC, 1991: 2, 4).

Another objective of this project is the establishment of a Navajo State Department of Education. This would take the authority of teacher certification/licensure away from Arizona, New Mexico and Utah and give it to the tribe so that they could determine the criteria for teacher certification for all teachers employed in Navajo schools. Two endorsement areas would be required under this plan: (1) Navajo language, and (2) Navajo culture. As it stands now, teachers within Navajo schools do not have to have these skills. Instead, they rely on Navajo teacher aides. The borderline schools do not even have to pretend to care about Navajo issues at all. And those Navajo children and youth stolen away from the reservation and placed in Mormon families attend Mormon-oriented schools where the LDS world-view and values, not Navajo culture, are stressed. This is the beginning of a long journey -- but certainly a worthwhile and necessary journey. Remember that it took over twenty years for our Cherokee cultural-education plan to materialize to the point where the tribe now has control over its own schools.

While the educational plan is designed to provide Navajo children and youth with a positive traditional self-image reinforcing their *Indianism,* clinical interventions are needed more than ever to undo the damage afflicted upon those children and youth socialized as *marginal* Indians. Unfortunately, they are now parenting another generation of *marginal* Navajos with the potential for substance abuse and mental and physical health problems. Contemporary efforts designed to curb this negative influence include the use of the *Talking Circle* with Navajo students, Robert Wood Johnson efforts in Gallup (Taking the Long View), and a consorted effort by Indian Health Services to articulate a treatment network for Indian substance abuse in the area.

The Navajo Talking Circle is a common traditional custom involving a blessing using a feather fan and smoke from tobacco, sweet grass, sage or cedar. These elements from Mother Earth are burned in an abalone shell and the smoke is fanned over the individuals sitting in the sacred circle beginning from the east and going clockwise just like in the Siouan purification sweat. The smoke blessing is performed head to feet with the fan touching first the right shoulder and then the left. Recipients usually use their hands in facilitating the smoke over their body. This ritual represents communication between the human being, Mother Earth and Father Sky. The feathers in the fan represent the birds who are a medium between earth and sky. The shell represents not only earth but the source of life, water. The herbs, tobacco, and plants burned represent the growth of plants sustained by Mother Earth with the aid of water. At the end of the blessing, the members share thoughts and small token *give away* items. A hand-rolled Navajo cigarette/cigar is usually shared among the participants at its conclusion. The circle itself represents the balance between Mother Earth and Father Sky, the Harmony Ethos.

We developed a *Talking Circle* prevention curriculum for at-risk Navajo students. The goal of this model is to reduce the effect or eliminate the risk factor for alcohol and substance abuse that affects the Navajo youth. Substance use and abuse by the child, family, and friends coupled with a history of cultural and personal marginality are the main factors which, in turn, manifest themselves in poor development -- culturally, physically, socially, and educationally. According to the architect of this model, Terrill Piechowski, the *Navajo Talking Circle* has the following goals:

1. To offer a comprehensive and unified program that is based upon sound behavioral counseling theory and is specifically designed to reduce the effects of, or eliminate, high risk factors for Navajo youth.

2. To offer a program that is culturally sensitive to, and meets, the needs of the Navajo child (culturally specific Individual Educational Plan).

3. To offer a program that makes effective use of the Navajo bilingual/bicultural counselor, teacher,and

paraprofessionals, working in conjunction with non-Navajo professionals in order to treat a large number of high-risk Navajo children.

4. To offer an extension activity (Talking Circle) that can be supported by the entire school staff, parents, and community.

5. To offer a model that can, and will, be evaluated.

6. To implement a model that can be continued by existing school staff.

7. To offer a model that can be duplicated by other schools.

8. To offer training to counselors, teachers, and paraprofessionals in the use of this model, including the advanced training of the project staff and staff working in the target schools.

A major component of this model is the *Beauty Way curriculum.* The Beauty Way curriculum is a Navajo-specific substance abuse prevention curriculum which was developed during the late 1980s by the Navajo Nation Division of Education. The Beauty Way curriculum was originally developed for grades K-8. It now covers grades 9-12 as well. The primary goal of the Beauty Way curriculum is to present drug and alcohol related information that can be utilized by educators working on or near the Navajo Nation. Ideas and concepts presented in the curriculum are drawn from Indian culture and tradition. The *Beauty Way of Life* itself represents the ideal traditional life prescribed for Navajo as prescribed by the Dine Holy People. In regards to substance abuse prevention among Navajo children and youth, the Beauty Way curriculum is designed for culturally-specific support groups (those fashioned in the Talking Circle format). The support group component of the Talking Circle is based upon the goals of the Unity/Youth 2000, United National Indian Tribal Youth, Incorporated. This is the affiliate of Unity Network, a network of American Indians and Alaska Native youth groups and offers the Navajo students a connection with the larger Pan-Indian network. The link between this program and the popularity of the UNITY Regional Youth Treatment Center in Cherokee, North Carolina becomes clearer.

In the early 1990s, the Robert Wood Johnson Foundation provided a more culturally sensitive alternative to the Gibson

Canyon "combat zone" Plan. The vehicle for conducting this alternative was a Regional Task Force called "Northwest New Mexico Fighting Back." The Task Force is comprised of political leaders, health professionals, judges, recovering persons, prevention and treatment experts, members of the clergy, justice and law enforcement professionals, school officials, leaders of business and industry, and members of parent groups and service clubs. Their goal was to select the indicators representative of the "Indian problem" in these borderline communities. On September 28, 1994, the Task Force provided a report of their progress. This report is entitled *Taking the Long View: A Review of Substance Abuse-related Social Indicators in McKinley County, New Mexico.* One of the findings was the claim that from 1986 to 1993, McKinley County twelfth graders reduced their self-reported frequent alcohol use and significantly reduced both yearly and frequent marijuana use. During the same time period, twelfth graders statewide showed no improvement or increased their alcohol and marijuana use. Another improvement claimed from 1989 to 1993 was that property-related crimes reported and alcohol-related arrests by the Gallup Police Department declined significantly. However, violent crime reports increased during the same time period. The problem with the Task Force's results is that it does not discern between Indians and non-Indians. The Task Force concluded:

> This social indicators report brings to the Mckinley County community much good news. There is strong, consistent and convincing evidenced of a downturn in substance abuse-related problems for this county. It is hoped that this report provides support for the proposition that communities can change when it comes to substance abuse, even those communities like McKinley County on which the consequences of this social problem have weighted most heavily over the past two decades (Ellis,, Jr., 1994: 39).

The American Indian community, notably the Navajo and Zuni, would certainly challenge the optimistic perspective of the Task Force. Jayne T. Goodluck, a prominent Navajo professional and former President of the New Mexico Alcohol and Drug Counselor's Certification Board, in her role with the

Navajo Area Indian Health Services, Alcohol & Substance Abuse Program composed a network of culturally-sensitive services available for Navajo and other American Indians within this area. The work, co-edited with Janet L. Phillips, is entitled *Navajo Nation & Regional Areas Resource Directory.* Listed below are counseling providers which address American Indians within the Four Corner Area.

Albuquerque Indian Center
7717 Zuni SE, Albuquerque, NM 87108
Outpatient counseling and referrals.

Alliance Hospital
100 Laura Court, Santa Teresa, NM 88008
Individual and group counseling, ropes course,
Sweat Lodges, horse-care to help younger patients.

Ama Doo Alchini Bighan, Inc. (ADABI)
P.O. Box 1279, Chinle, AZ 86503
Crisis counseling, domestic violence.

American Indian Eagle Lodge
824 Atlantic Avenue, Long Beach, CA 90813
12 step, Sweat Lodge, domestic violence, aftercare,
sexual issues.

Behavioral Health Services
P.O. Box 328, Acoma, NM 87034
Holistic approach & 12-step modality.

Child Haven
3705 E. Main, Farmington, NM 87402
Individual & group counseling.
Children in Need of Services (C.H.I.N.S.)
309 W. Arrington, Farmington, NM 87401
Eclectic, behavior modification.

Chinle IHS - Mental Health
P.O. Box PH, Chinle, AZ 86503
Varied therapies.

Colorado Psychological Services
925 South Broadway, Cortez, CO 81321
Eclectic therapies.

Crownpoint Girls Youth Home
P.O. Box 1090, Crownpoint, NM 87313
Mental health therapies.

Department of Behavioral Health Services - Chinle
Agency
P.O. Box 777, Chinle, AZ 86503
Medicine Wheel approach in the areas of physical,
mental, spiritual and cultural.

Department of Behavioral Health Services -
Crownpoint Agency
P.O. Box 878, Crownpoint, NM 87313
AA and Counseling.

Department of Behavioral Health Services -
Shiprock Agency
P.O. Box 389, Shiprock, NM 87420
Outpatient counseling services.

Department of Youth and Community Services -
Police Family Liaison Program, Chinle Agency
P.O. Box 847, Chinle, AZ 86503
Court ordered and voluntary outpatient counseling
services.

Department of Youth and Community Services -
Tuba City Community    Center
P.O. Box 1690, Tuba City, AZ 86045
Wholistic community development.

Eagle Lodge, Inc.
1264 Race Street, Denver, CO 80206
Cognitive with emphasis on Native American
spirituality.

Family Focus
P.O. Box F, Window Rock, AZ 86515
Family, individual & group therapies.

Family Services Unit - Child Protective Services:
Navajo DSS
P.O. Box 3289, Shiprock, NM 87402
Eclectic approach.

Farmington Inter-Tribal Indian Organization
P.O. Box 2322, Farmington, NM 87499
Social services.

Four Corners Regional Adolescent Treatment Center
P.O. Box 567, Shiprock, NM 87420
Navajo 12-step.

Friendship House Association of American Indians,
Inc.
80 Julian Avenue, San Francisco, CA 94103
Native American 12-step.

Gallup Indian Medical Center - Substance Abuse
Program
P.O. Box 1337, Gallup, NM 87305
Native American 12-step.

Gila River Alcohol & Substance Abuse Program
P.O. Box 7, Sacaton, AZ 85247
Traditional & non-traditional.

Indian Rehabilitation, Inc.
650 North 2nd Avenue, Phoenix, AZ 85003
Cultural and spiritual therapies, Sweat Lodge.

Medical Social Services, Shiprock PHS Hospital
P.O. Box 160, Shiprock, NM 87420.

Na'nizhoozhi Center
2205 East Boyd, Dr., Gallup, NM 87301
Pre-detoxification, referral.

NACA Family Health Center - Mental Health
Services
1355 N. Beaver, Suite 160, Flagstaff, AZ 86004
Preventive therapy.

National Indian Youth Council, Inc. Employment &
Training Project
100 W. Elm St., P.O. Box 2322, Farmington, NM
87401
Traditional therapy in career counseling.

Native American for Community Action (N.A.C.A.)
2717 N. Steves Blvd., Suite 11, Flagstaff, AZ
86004
Child & family counseling, youth programs,
substance abuse.

Navajo DWI School
P.O. Box 1592, Window Rock, AZ 86515
Bilingual covering cultural & traditional values.

Navajo Nation Department of Youth Community
Services
P.O. Box 3257, Shiprock, NM 87420
Youth incentive program, teen life center,
temporary youth shelter and treatment center.

New Directions - USA, Inc.
P.O. Box 4109, Cave Creek, AZ 85331
Traditional Native American groups.

New Ways - New Hope Program
P.O. Box 712, Navajo, NM 87328
Substance abuse counseling, domestic violence,
temporary shelter, women's groups, men's groups.

Path of Renewal, Inc.
P.O. Box 105, Rehoboth, NM 87322
Native American AA.

Peaceful Spirit
P.O. Box 429, Ignacio, CO 81137
Inpatient (40 day) substance abuse & mental health
treatment for American Indians.

Santa Clara Rehab
P.O. Box QQ, Espanola, NM 87532
Substance abuse treatment for any Native American
from New Mexico, Arizona, Utah or Colorado.

Shiprock Alcoholic Counseling Center
P.O. Box 1772, Shiprock, NM 87420
Individual, group & family therapy for American
Indians.

Shiprock Youth Center, Inc.
P.O. Box 2129, Shiprock, NM 87420
Individual, family, group & homebase treatment for
substance abuse & crisis intervention.

Shiprock - IHS Mental Health Program
P.O. Box 160, Shiprock, NM 87420
Multi-disciplinary & multimodelity treatment of
substance abuse and mental health problems.

Southern Ute Alcohol Recovery Center (Peaceful
Spirit)
P.O. Box 429, Ignacio, CO 81137
Sweat Lodge, individual, group & family counseling

Torreon Counseling Services, Inc.
P.O. Box 1989, Cuba, NM 87013
Individual, group & family counseling for the five
Eastern Navajo Reservation Chapters: Torreio, Ojo
Encino, Pueblo Pintado, Whitehorse Lake and
Counselor, New Mexico.

ommunity Mental Health Program
ealth Center, Towaoc, CO 81334
l services.

ɪ ouɪɪ & ɪ amily Intervention Center
P.O. Box 848, Crownpoint, NM 87313
Substance abuse counseling for American Indian
boys.

## Summary

The challenge for anyone counseling American Indians, youth or adults is to make certain that we hold our own values in check while, at the same time, attempt to provide viable cultural-specific services to our clients. The following set of guidelines should help in this endeavor.

Theresa LaFramboise, a Miami Indian and noted Indian psychologist, was my mentor at the University of Nebraska. Now at Stanford University, Dr. LaFramboise spelled out a number of steps for counselors when working with American Indian clients:

1. Provide a supportive, open atmosphere for discussing spiritual issues.
2. Use the right helping style (remember most clinical approaches are Western oriented).
3. Relax standards of goal attainment (remember that traditional Indians are community, not individually, oriented).
4. Structure therapy with Native American values in mind.
5. Keep the termination process open-ended (remember that "termination" reflects the "bottom line" Western concept) (DeAngelis, 1994: 36).

Lastly, my colleagues in Gallup, New Mexico, Phyllis Tempest and Elaine Jordon, developed a protocol for testing borderline school Navajo students:

1. Conduct a comprehensive interview in order to determine the degree of enculturation of the child.
2. Take all steps to avoid testing bias.
3. Analyze the learning style of the Indian child

(most Navajo children demonstrate a preference for a
visual spatial, holistic mode of learning).
4. Determine the appropriate counseling
intervention models when working with Navajo children
(family issues and degree of traditionalism are important
issues).
5. Apply the RULES.
R= Respect for the person(s) involved in the problem - as
opposed to misdirecting energy toward anger and
blaming.
U= Understand the problem.
L= List the possible solutions.
E= Elect a solution you are willing to try (and
are capable of administering).
S= If the problem has not been solved, "share" the
situation (seek guidance from a traditional Navajo healer).

A reminder which works for me is to remember that I am not a
"missionary." As a clinician I need to keep my personal beliefs to
myself and respect and tolerate those of my clients. Then, and
only then, can spirituality be a viable therapeutic component.

# Chapter 6

## The Mestizo's Ways: Herbal Healing and Spiritual Rituals of the Cuanderismo

### Introduction

In this section, Patsy Ybarra presents the herbal healing and spiritual rites performed by the *Cuanderismo* -- an Indian, or mixed Indian/Hispanic healer using a mix of traditional Native American and early Mexican folk cures. These practices have survived to the present in the rural southwest. Folk Catholism of the Spanish during the 1500s coupled with the aboriginal ways of the traditional Pueblo tribes mixed and survived among Mestizo in the rural southwest. Today these methods of folk healing are prevalent among the mixed Mexican/Indians (Mestizo) as well as among the dozens of Pueblo tribes located in New Mexico and Arizona. Patsy Ybarra is a Cuanderismo of Yaqui/Mexican descent. She has over twenty years experience as a professional mental health and substance abuse counselor. She draws on her aboriginal roots and training in many aspects of her practice. Ms. Ybarra is also widely sought out as a consultant regarding her knowledge of the rural Mestizo client. The following is Ms. Ybarra's sharing of the Mestizo's ways.

# Curandismo

Curandismo is a distinct, Hispanic mode of health care with its roots in two cultures -- American Indian and Spanish. Curandismo is based on what is now called Holistic Medicine where the mind, body and the spirit are considered as one and are treated together. Yet while it is called "Holistic Medicine" today, the concept is old and universal in both the aboriginal Indian and folk Spanish cultures. Curandismo integrates herbs, massage, rituals, and prayers into the healing process.

Indian medicine, as represented in the Aztec culture for example, was highly advanced. The Aztecs divided their health workers into well defined specialties, basing their knowledge on the spiritual belief that the Gods were responsible for specific components of human health. One of these specialists was the Teixtomani, the elite charged with the mandate of therapy.

Spanish medicine, which came to the new world in the 1500s, was a combination of rational and spiritual ideas. The rational component, much like that of the rest of Europe at that time, was based on Arab and Greek sources and was mainly for the benefit of the upper classes and nobility. The spiritual, or folk, component represented the lay practice administered by and for the peasant masses. A major component of the latter was the belief that one's health was in the hands of God. Physical and mental illnesses, according the this belief system, is due to an alienation of the body, mind and spirit. A believer in this folk metaphysics is known as an *enbrujardo,* hence the similarities between the American Indian beliefs and that of the folk Spanish culture of the 1500s.

## The  Curandera

The person who has been born with the *don*  or gift, to be a Curandera (female) or Curandero (male) must be born with certain distinct attributes.

    1. A thin covering of skin over the face of an infant at
    birth is one indicator. In the Mexican belief, this veil is
    removed and put in a red pouch made of silk or satin. No
    one is to mention the birth or the veil until the child is

seven   years old.
2. The other indicator is that the fetus will cry in the
mother's womb in her seventh month.  This also must
never be spoken of until the child is seven years
old.

The child with the *don* will usually be very strong willed and independent.  These children spend a lot of time day dreaming and often state that they talk to angels.  Many Curanderas have had experiences, as children, where they have experienced the sensation of having seen or spoken to saints and Jesus.  They also have a way of calming others and being able to foresee the future.  In becoming a full Curandera, the child needs to be well versed in the rituals associated with this profession.  This is usually done by an older relative or close friend of the family.

Once trained the Curandera must be able to recognize the ills of the person requiring help.  This involves knowing and understanding the culture, the physical conditions, the emotional state of the client, and, most importantly, she has to know  they believe that they are enbrujado.  Confirmation of the client's status as an enbrujado is the first step in the Curandera's therapeutic plan.  The overall treatment plan includes the following:

1. An examination and discussion of the problem(s):
when did it start and how long have you had this
problem? (onset, course and duration).
2. Culture-specific spirituality (tribaltraditional
ways/Hispanic sub-cultural ways).
3. The Curandera must then determine the
appropriate ritual for the illness or curse.
4. The main focus of the healing process is to give the
client confidence and improved mental and physical
health.

## Patsy Yberra's Story

My grandmother was a Curandera.  She was born in Mexico near the city of Aquas Calientes and was a full blooded Yaqui Indian.  My grandmother survived the slaughter of her people.  She attributes her survival to her gift in healing.  It is told that she saved the life of a man in Aquas Calientes and his family, in return, raised her in their Mexican household.

Despite her survival, her memories of this life were not happy. She would tell me of her many struggles, but most of all she constantly warned me never to marry any man from Zacatecas. She spoke of her arranged marriage to a humorless and cruel man from Zacatecas and how she became free only after his sudden death following a heart attack. She then traveled to Juarez and renewed her acquaintance with Clotilde, her friend who was married to an Irish railroad engineer. She became her maid and was happy for the first time. She would relate how she was able to earn a living and also help people with her gift of Curandismo. In 1914, her friend's family were transferred by the railroad to a small town in the United States, Santa Rita, New Mexico. My grandmother decided to stay in El Paso, but one year later she was summoned by her friend's husband to please come and help his ailing wife. Soon afterwards Clotilde died from the flu. My grandmother then married Clotilde's husband and this is where my story begins.

The gift of Curandismo, according to Yaqui tradition, is handed down every other generation. The child who was blessed with the gift of healing would have a *don* or a special talent. The child's birth date and birth time were very important for verification of the *don* as well as were other indicators such as being born with a veil of her face or crying during the seventh month of pregnancy. In my mother's seventh month of pregnancy, my grandmother, my mother, and my grandmother's comadre all heard me cry. Moreover, I was born of the seventh day, Sunday at 7:00 am on the 14th of March, and I was born with the veil on my face. Subsequently, I was raised by my grandmother and taught and guided by her.

As a child I saw people with hats all the time. The hats were always with colors and the colors would change. My grandmother would always tell me not to mention this to anyone since she knew that others would not believe me. A more important reason for not disclosing the nature of my gifts is that by doing so I would lose them. The reason for not disclosing the nature of my term and birth as well as my unusual auras was not disclosed to me until I underwent my first ritual at age seven.

Growing up, I would describe myself as very independent, very stubborn, and very rebellious. I used to be very frightened by things that I saw and could not tell others about. Also, I found out that I could tell death by the auras. I was nine years old when my grandmother died. I knew about her death before anyone told me. Her death sent me into a deep depression. Till this day I am not sure of what happened, but eventually I came out of my depression and I know that my grandmother is still with me and has always been with me.

During my adolescent years I fought with myself. I could tell things were going to happen but, at the same time, would be frightened and not say anything. During this time I also suffered a lot from anxiety. My mother knew of my gift and she would try to get me to tell her what I saw and what I felt. She would not scold me but I could tell that she was frightened as well. I stopped telling anyone what I saw or felt for a long time.

In this section I will share what Cuandismo is. I will describe what Curandismo does and I will share *Cuentos, Remedios* and *Rituals.*

## Mestizo Traditional Remedios (Herbal Cures)

**Terms:**

*Analgesic:*Something that takes pain away but does not cause loss of consciousness. An analgesic may be swallowed or rubbed on the skin.

*Anaphrodisiac:* An herb that lessens sexual desire.

*Anesthetic:* A substance which causes loss of consciousness. It could also refer to one that does not lead to a loss of consciousness such as oil of cloves which merely kills sensation.

*Anodyne:* This refers to a pain killer or merely to something that soothes.

*Anthelmintic:* A herb that eliminates worms.

*Antidote:* A substance which counteracts the effects of a poison.

*Antiemetic:* Stops vomiting and nausea.

*Antihydrotic:* The opposite of a diaphoretic. It refers to a substance which dries up bodily fluids.

*Antipyretics:* An herb that reduces fever.

*Antipasmodic:* Stops muscle spasms and cramps.

*Aphrodisiac:* Something that increases sexual desire.

*Astringent:* Something applied to make spores smaller.
*Antiflataulent:* An anti-gas agent.
*Cathartic:* A laxative.
*Coagulant:* Makes the blood clot.
*Demulcent:* Soothes an inflamed area.
*Diaphoretic:* Increases sweating.
*Diuretic:* Increases the flow of urine.
*Emollient:* Softens and soothes the skin.
*Expectorant:* An agent used to expel mucous.
*Restorative:* A herb taken to increase energy.
*Soporific:* An agent taken to induce sleep.
*Styptic:* An astringent applied to stop bleeding.
*Tranquilizer:* An agent which calms the nerves.

## Remedies (Remedios):

*Aloe Vera:* Aloe Vera can be used for arthritis, rheumatism and stomach disorders. The Aloe Vera is mixed with water and must be taken three times a day. The dosage is about three ounces. Aloe Vera is also used for cuts, burns, rashes, insect bites, acne and as a wrinkle preventative.

*Anis:* For colic, boil anise seeds in milk and add virgin honey. For coughs, boil anise seeds in water and drink as needed. For use as an eye wash, boil anise seeds in water and apply directly to the eye. For stomach gas, chew anise seeds.

*Ash:* Ash, or fresno, is used as a remedy for snakebites, gout, rheumatism and to reduce fever. Here a tea is made of the leaves. The leaves should be boiled with water and then left overnight. The tea can be sweetened with virgin honey. It needs to be taken three times daily to be effective. Moreover, the leaves of the tea can be put directly on snake bites. This draws out the poison.

*Basil/Albahaca:* Basil can be used for sore throats or to heal sores in the mouth and insect stings. A tea is made of either fresh or dried basil. Both the leaves and flowers of the herb can be used in making the tea. A mixture of basil, honey and nutmeg is good for a mother immediately following childbirth to aid in expelling the afterbirth.

*Bay Laurel:* The bay leaves are used in making a tea for colic or diarrhea. The oil from the berries can be applied externally to sore muscles and for rheumatism.

*Bayberry/Arbol de la Cera:* The berries can be chewed and are good for coughing as well as dysentery. A tea made from the root or the bark will also stop coughing and dysentery. Making a powder of the bark will cure nasal congestion while mixing the powder with water makes a good mouthwash. It also cures sore and bleeding gums and other mouth infections.

*Birthwort/Moja de Guaco:* When the leaves are soaked in alcohol and strained, this makes an effective remedy for insect bites especially from poisonous insects.

*Borage/Borraja:* A tea made from this plant increases sweating and urination. It is also used to decrease fevers, especially fever associated with measles. It is also used to treat bladder infections.

*Camphor/Alcanfor:* The oil from the leaves of this plant is used to treat ear aches. It is also used for rheumatic pain and for headaches.

*Century Plant/Mescal Maguey Agave:* The leaves of this plant are cut and applied to cuts. They can also be heated and placed on abscesses to drain the pus.

*Chamomile/Manzanilla:* A tea made from this plant is used for calming nerves and also to reduce fevers. It is also a good eye wash. Moreover, the steam from boiling chamomile is useful in clearing nasal congestion.

*Citron Flowers/Flor de Azahar:* The flowers are made into a tea which is used to treat insomnia.

*Cloves/Clavo:* For a toothache, place a clove on the infected tooth in order to relieve pain. For earache, wrap a mashed clove in cotton and place it in the infected ear. The oil of the cloves are also used to stop vomiting.

*Comfrey/Consuelda:* Boil the leaves and use the leaves as a compress to heal a cut or to stop bleeding. Comfrey tea can also be used to stop internal bleeding.

*Coriander/Cilantro:* A tea made from the dried seeds is good for nausea and diarrhea.

*Cornsilk Barbas/de Elote:* The cornsilk strands are boiled and made into a tea. This tea is good for treating kidney and bladder infections. The tea is also used for children who are bedwetters as well as for painful urination associated with prostate problems.

*Delphinium (larkspur):* The flowers and seeds of the Espuela de Caballero (dolphinium) plant are ground and soaked in either alcohol or vinegar and made into a curative mixture. The mixture is left overnight and then it can be used externally to the body of lice, including pubic lice. This mixture should be applied after a hot bath for a week, daily. This mixture can also be used on pets.

*Evening Primrose/Flor de San Juan:* Extract the oil from the flowers and use it nightly for problems associated with the menstrual cycle. The usual dose is two drops per glass of water.

*Elm/Olmo:* The bark should be dried and then soaked for 48 hours in cold water. The mixture should then be boiled for a least 30 minutes and then strained. This tea is used to relieve swelling due to water retention. It is also used to clear up the complexion. Externally, compresses can be applied to any skin eruptions.

*Elder/Sauco:* A tea made from the bark is used as a diuretic and as a laxative. It can also be used to relieve water retention. Poultices made from the flowers are used as a skin conditioner. Crushed elder leaves, mixed with olive oil, will relieve hemorrhoids.

*Eucalyptus/Eucalipto:* When the leaves are boiled and made into a tea this is used for aiding digestion. It is also used to relieve congestion and coughs. The dried leaves are smoked to relieve asthma.

*Fennel/Hinojo:* A tea is made from the leaves, seeds, stems and roots of this plant. This tea is used to increase appetite as well as being used as a diuretic. The dried seeds can be cooked in a cup of milk and drank hot to eliminate bloating and gas. This mixture is also good for flu symptoms. Boiling the seeds and inhaling the steam will soothe the pain of migraine headaches.

*Goldenrod/Mariquilla:* To make a tea, dry and grind the leaves into a powder. This tea is used to relieve arthritis. It is also used for diabetes, to reduce water retention and to break up kidney stones.

*Jimson weed/Toloache:* This plant should never be used internally since it can lead to convulsions, coma, and even death. The leaves are burned and the smoke from the burning leaves are inhaled to relieve and control the spasms associated with asthma. The same method can be used for relief of sinusitis. The plant can also be made into a poultice and applied to painful joints.

*Juniper/Enebro Tascate:* A tea made from the berries is effective as a means of birth control. A tea made from both the leaves and the berries is good for reducing water retention. For treatment of cystitises and urethritises, crush the berries and soak in a covered container of water for 24 hours. Apply as needed.

*Lettuce/Lechuga:* For constipation and for nervousness, boil the lettuce leaves and take at bedtime. The tea will also induce sleep. Lettuce tea is also used to decrease sexual drive. Wild lettuce can also be dried and smoked to relieve anxiety.

*Lilly of the Valley/Lirio de Los Valles:* The flower and the root are made into a tea which is effective in treating heart problems. It is also effective as a tonic.

*Linden Flower/Flor de Tila:* The flower is boiled and made into a tea. This tea is an effective tranquilizer. It should be taken in small doses and only at bedtime.

*Nutmeg:* The nuts are ground into a powder and boiled to produce a tea which is good for indigestion and to eliminate gas. Large amounts of nutmeg can cause nausea, vomiting and even stupor.

*Nettle/Origa Mayor:* The juice from the plant is extracted and this juice can be used to control nose bleeding. It can also be used internally in order to control excessive menstrual bleeding and even for internal bleeding associated with ulcers. Nettle tea is also used to stop bed wetting.

*Olive:* The oil from crushed olives is used to treat coughs. It is mixed with egg whites to make a soothing ointment that is applied to the neck and chest. It can also be taken orally. A spoonful of olive oil is used to protect against intoxication.

*Onion:* Raw onion is eaten to treat anemia, exhaustion, bronchial problems and gas. Onion that is chopped, and cooked in oil, is also used to prevent scarlet fever and diphtheria. Onion that is crushed, and mixed with honey, is good for coughs or a sore throat. The onion can also be used as a poultice for burns, bites, wounds or even over joints which are troubled by arthritic pain. A roasted onion has great drawing power and can be applied to boils. Mixed with hot vinegar, onions are applied to the chest to provide relief for pneumonia.

*Oregano:* The leaves and heads of the flowers are dried and used to brew a tea taken to regulate menstruation, relieve premenstrual pain and cramps. This tea will also loosen phlegm and soothe a sore throat.

*Prickly Pear Cactus/Nopal:* Extract the juice, mix it with egg yokes and honey, and create a paste to treat burns. The juice mixed with Maguey and drunk is seen as a cure for Hepatitis. The fruit of nopal can be sliced in half, heated and placed on abscesses in order to draw out infection.

*Parsley:* Regular consumption of parsley tea is used to cure alcoholism. It will also dissolve gallstones when taken daily. The tea will also relieve indigestion and menstrual cramps. Making a tea of the crushed seeds will aid in drying up a mother's breast milk. Mashed parsley leaves applied to cuts, bleeding wounds or insect bites will stop the bleeding and the itch. It is also believed that parsley eaten each day will prevent cancer.

*Potato:* The raw juice can be taken for relief from stomach ache, diarrhea and fluid retention. Slices of raw potato can be placed on the temples in order to relieve headaches. Grated potato is applied as a poultice to puffy eyelids, cracked skin, sunburn and insect bites.

*Rue/Ruda:* Rue tea, taken in small amounts, will stimulate menstruation. The same tea, in small dose, is used for relief from congestion, headache nausea, fainting spells, difficult breathing and stomach cramps. Externally this can be used as a wash to kill body lice. A stem of ruda wrapped in cotton and placed in the ear will cure an earache.

*Valerian/Raiz de Valeriana:* Only the roots of this plant are used. They can be used to induce abortion. A tea made of the root and taken once a week is said to cure alcoholism. The tea, in small amounts, can be used as a sedative. The root can also be taken for nervous conditions but only as needed since regular use can cause depression.

## Cuentos (Stories)

In the Meistzo culture stories of good, bad, and advice giving are very important. These stories are usually told to the children by the elders in the family. The stories are also used as a means to console, or to advise, someone who is in emotional pain. One such story is used to teach that abortion and being promiscuous is a sin. This story is widely known in the southwest. The name of the story is *La Llorona.*

Many years ago, there lived a very beautiful woman. It was said that she lived in sin. She had many love affairs and aborted every time she got pregnant. She was said to be evil and had no respect for the Catholic church. She even defied God. She never asked forgiveness, and when she died, she died alone and without any family. The women of the village attended her in death. They dressed her body and had the velorio (wake) in the home of one of the families. They had her body in the center of the room surrounded by holy candles. The people from the village came to pray for her soul, and as the velorio continued, the women noticed that strangers had been coming to pay their respects. The first stranger who came in was very handsome, well dressed, and appeared to be a very important man. He walked up to the body, nodded his head and proceeded to leave. One of the women asked him, "Who are you?" He responded, "My name would have been Jorge, and I would have been an attorney." The next stranger was a woman. She did the same thing, and when asked the same question, she replied,"My name would have been Elena, and I would have been a teacher." The story goes on to say that many more strangers came and they all stated that their names would have been and what they would have been. These were the souls of her aborted children. God punished her and punishment was that for all eternity her soul was to search for the bodies of her aborted children and to have them buried in blessed ground. It is said that on nights, you can hear the cries of the Llorona who is weeping and searching. Many of the Meistzo today will tell you that they have heard her cries.

*The story of the Grieving Mother*
Dona Ofekuas' only son had been killed in an accident. He was only 18 years old and the youngest of all her seven children. She had taken the death very hard and for the year of luto (mourning) her family and friends had been very supportive. However, she did not improve and her grieving continued even after the year of mourning passed. She would no longer do any household chores. She did not attend church. She did not even want her family around. Her family was very concerned because she was crying all the time and becoming ill. On the night of the Feast of Santa Rita every one was at the church and she stayed home as she had done since the death of her son. This night, her

commadre, stayed with her. The night was full of stars with a beautiful full moon. Her house was located half way down the hill and the women had a good view of the top of the street as well as a view of the church at the bottom of the hill. Dona Ofelias and her commadre were talking and remembering other fiestas before the death of Dona Ofelias' son. They decided to sit outside and get some fresh air, and as they were sitting outside they noticed a figure of a person who was stooped down. The figure appeared to be carrying something very heavy and was walking down the hill very slowly. They continued to watch, and as the figure got closer, they could tell it was a man with a large gunny sack over his shoulder. As the figure got closer, the women were wondering who could it be since everyone was at the fiesta. As the figure got to the gate of Dona Ofelias' house he stopped. The women asked him what he wanted but he did not respond. They decided to go down to the gate and find out who he was. As they approached him, he lifted his head and they saw that it was Dona Ofelias' deceased son. She was so happy, and not at all frightened, but very concerned since he looked so tired. She asked him, "Son, why are you so tired? Why are you carrying such a heavy load?" He answered, "Madre, I am carrying all of your tears and I can not rest until you allow me to." This story is often told to people who extend their mourning period past the year of Luto.

## Traditions

*Luto*

Luto is the mourning process. This is a time of mourning which lasts one year. It is traditional for women to wear black for a year. During this year the family does not attend any festive occasions such as dancing, parties, or joyful outings. They pray and show respect and give masses for the deceased family member.

*Descansos*

This is the tradition of placing a cross at the place where someone has died. The tradition goes back to when the Meistzos and Mexican people would carry the coffin from the church to the graveyard and where the carriers would stop to rest, and say the rosary for the deceased. This is also called a *recuerdo* the place where a person died and where his soul rested for the last time. Recuerdo means a memorial.

### Lent

During the 40 days of lent, the person should make sacrifices such as giving up something enjoyable. Many Meistzo, who are chronic alcoholics, will give up alcohol for 40 days. They will not go through withdrawals or suffer the symptoms of withdrawals which they would under different circumstances.

### Pregnant Women

If there is an eclipse of the moon or the sun, the pregnant woman is to wear a key around her stomach until the eclipse is over. It is believed that the metal of the keys will protect the unborn child. If the woman does not wear the keys, the unborn child could have parts of his/her body eaten by the effects of the eclipse such as cleft palate, etc.

## Rituals

A Curandera uses symbolic objects because she feels that her powers come from God. The symbols are those which are shared by many religious people such as pictures of saints, votive candles and such. The Curandera also uses everyday materials: olive oil, water, and most commonly a fresh egg. The religious articles most important are holy water and the rosary.

### Evil Eye/Mal Ojo

The symptoms are similar to colic: irritability, drooping eyes, fever, headache and vomiting. It is said that if a person admires a child and does not touch the child then the effect is mal ojo. The ritual for the cure of the curse of mal ojo is as follows:

Mal ojo is treated by having the child lie down and sweeping him three times with an egg. The sweeping is done by forming crosses with the egg on the child's body, starting at the head and going to the feet. While sweeping, the Curandera recites the Apostles' Creed three times, making sure that she sweeps both the front and back. The egg is cracked and dropped into a glass filled with water. The glass then is placed on the child's head and another creed is recited. Then the egg is placed on the child's chest. If the child has mal ojo, an eye will appear in the yoke of the egg. The Curandera will then pray and make the sign of the cross over the child. If the cure is successful, the yoke of the egg will break. The child is then rubbed all over and washed with holy water. Now the cure is completed. It is also believed that if the ritual does not work, then the parents must find the person who admired the child and make him/her touch the child.

## Susto

Susto is a loss of spirit or even the loss of the soul itself. Receiving bad news can cause susto as can a bad scare or anything that is traumatizing. It is believed that a trauma can temporarily drive the person's soul from the body. Susto has to be treated immediately or it will lead to a much more serious version called susto pasado or susto meco. An old susto is more difficult to treat and can even lead to death.

The symptoms of susto are weakness, feeling wobbly, chills, shakes, drowsiness, headaches, nausea, loss of interest, insomnia and loss of appetite.

The ritual for curing susto involves a broom. The person lies down and is completely covered with a sheet. The Curandera sweeps the patient with the broom saying the Apostle's Creed three times. At the end of each creed, the Curandera whispers in the client's ear: "Come, don't stay there." The sick person must perspire and is given some tea of yerba anis to drink. The Curandera then places a cross of holy palm on the client's head and prays to God to restore the patient's spiritual strength. The cure for susto involves having the following ritual conducted on three consecutive nights with the last day being the most effective. The client lies on the bed with arms extended in the form of a cross while his entire body is cleaned with alum or a whole egg and he/she is swept with a bundle of herbs. This bundle should contain horehound, rosemary, pepertree, redbrush or naked seed weed, all tied together with a red ribbon. The ritual involves an invocation to the client's soul to return. When the soul responds indicating that it is back, the ritual is completed.

*Empacho*

Empacho is an aliment  reflects the need for balance of food. It is thought to be caused by improperly mixing hot with cold foods, or eating such foods in improper sequence.  Eating too quickly and not chewing the food completely is another cause for empacho.

The symptoms associated with empacho are constipation, stomach pain, nausea and fever.

The ritual for treating empacho involves rubbing the client's stomach with an egg.  Where the egg bursts indicates the location of the empacho on the body.  The Curandera then rubs the egg all over the stomach.  This is followed with a rub with olive oil.  The healer then massages them from the waist down to the ankles.  As she massages the Curandera pulls the skin to where the skin pops.  The snapping noise of the skin is said to loosen the trapped food particles.  A tea is then given to treat the damaged stomach.  The client then should experience a complete bowel movement within one hour of finishing his/her tea.

*Mal Puesto*

This is a curse put on another person.  It is done for various reasons but mostly that associated with hate and revenge.  A mal puesto is brought about by a *Bruja*, a person that engages in black magic and evil.  The ritual depends on what the mal puesto is. These rituals and cures are sacred and therefore can not be shared with those not trained as Curandera.

# Religious  Beliefs

The Meistzo have great faith in the saints, and many  times when they have problems *mandas* are promised.  A manda is a promise to a saint for a special favor.  These promises can be having a mass dedicated to the saint, conducting a pilgrimage on their knees as a means of giving thanks, or by saying a novena to the specific saint.  The following are saints and their special powers.

*San Jude*

San Jude is the patron of desperate and impossible cases.  In many homes the statue of San Jude is present with candles lit in his honor. San Jude is seen as being very miraculous and is believed to grant considerable favors.

### San Lorenzo

San Lorenzo is the patron saint of the poor. It is believed that when people ask a favor of San Lorenzo, and the favor is granted but the granteesdo not keep their promises of thanks, they will receive small burns of their body. In Mimbres, New Mexico, where the San Lorenzo church is located, every August 10th, on his birthday, people from the southwest make a pilgrimage in his honor. Some will walk the eighteen-mile pilgrimage route barefooted while others will make the trek on their knees. Many families make the pilgrimage together. It is a lifelong event for the Meistzo family.

### San Anonio de Padua

San Antonio is the patron saint of the poor and will find lost items. It is believed that if a woman wants to find a husband she will ask San Antonio's assistance addressing her prayers away from Jesus Christ and directing them instead to San Antonio until she is married.

### Our Lady of Guadalupe

Our Lady of Guadalupe is the Virgin Mother of Mexican, Mestizo, and Pueblo Indians. The shrine of Our Lady of Guadalupe, located near Mexico City, is one of the most celebrated places of pilgrimage in North America. According to this belief, on December 9, 1531, the Blessed Virgin Mary appeared to an Indian convert, Juan Diego, and left him with a picture of herself impressed upon his cloak.

Cuandismo is based on the belief that the Curandera is working with the help of all the saints and God. However, the Curandera relies heavily on Our Lady of Guadalupe for her own strength. Curanderas often keep candles lit in her honor. It is a request for assistance in the Curandera's practice. Curanderas commonly recommend that their clients, notably the female clients, keep candles lit in honor of Our Lady of Guadalupe.

Lastly, it is important to realize that the Cuandera never accepts any money for her services. Moreover, she must never refuse help to anyone who requests her help.  More significantly, the Cuandera must never use her power to do evil.  If she does, then her powers will be gone forever.

# Bibliography

Adear, V. (1990). *Child Protection Reference Book.*
Washington, DC: U.S. Department of the Interior, Bureau of
Indian Affairs.

APA (1980). *Diagnostic and Statistical Manual of Mental
Disorders (Third Edition).* Washington, DC: American
Psychiatric Association Press.

APA (1994). *Diagnostic and Statistical Manual of Mental
Disorders (Fourth Edition).* Washington, DC: American
Psychiatric Association Press.

Bailey, G., & Bailey, R. G. (1986). *A History of the Navajos.*
Sante Fe, NM: School of American Indian Research Press.

Banai, E. (1978). *We, Yesterday, Today, Tomorrow.* St. Paul,
MN: Red School House Publication.

Baurer, F. B. (1970). *Law of the North Carolina Cherokees.*
Brevard, NC: George E. Buchanan Press.

Beauvais, F., Oetting, E. R., & Edwards, R. W. (1985). Trends in
the use of inhalants among American Indian adolescents.
*White Cloud Journal,* 3, 3-11.

Bedford, D. R. (1972). *Tsali.* San Francisco, CA: The Indian
     Historian Press.

Bellack, L. & Bellack, S. S. (1989). *Children's Apperception
     Test.* Larchmont, NY: C. P. S., Inc.

Berlin, I. (1987). Suicide among American Indian adolescent.
     *Suicide and Life-Threatening Behavior,* 17, 218-232.

Bloom, F. E., & Lazerson, A. (1988). Life-span development of
     the brain. *Brain, Mind and Behavior.* New York, NY: W. H.
     Freeman and Company, 54-85.

Blum, R., et al. (1992). American Indian-Alaska native youth
     health. *JAMA,* 267, 1637-1644.

Boyce, G. A. (1978). *When Navajo Had Too Many Sheep.* San
     Francisco, CA: Indian Historian Press.

Boyce, W. T., & Boyce, L. (1983). Acculturation and change in
     health among Navajo boarding school students. *Social
     Science Medicine,* 19, 219-226.

Brandt, E. (1992). The Navajo area student dropout study.
     *Journal of American Indian Education,* 332, 48-63.

Brown, D. (1970). *Bury My Heart at Wounded Knee.* New York,
     NY: Holt, Rinehart and Winston

Brown, E. B. (1953). *The Sacred Pipe.* Norman, OK:
     University of Oklahoma Press.

Bryde, J. F. (1971). *Modern Indian Psychology-Revised Edition.*
     Vermillion, SD: Institute of Indian Studies, University of
     South Dakota.

Coleman, M. (1988). *Bibliotherapy with Stepchildren.*
     Springfield, IL: Charles C. Thomas Publisher.

Collier, P. (1973). *When Shall They Rest.* New York, NY: Holt, Rinehart & Winston.

Costo, R. & Henry, J. (1977). *Indian Treaties: Two Centuries of Dishonor.* San Francisco, CA: Indian Historian Press, 208-227.

DeAngelis, T. (1994). History, culture affect treatment for Indians. *APA Monitor,* 27, 36.

Deyhle, D. (1991). Empowerment and cultural conflict. *Qualitative Studies in Education,* 4, 277-297.

Dorris, R. A. (1989). *The Broken Cord.* New York, NY: Harper & Row.

Ellis, B. H., Jr. (1994). *Taking the Long View.* Gallup, NM: Northwest New Mexico Fighting Back Report, 1-40.

Employment Division v. Smith (1988/1990). *Employment Division, Department of Human Resources of the State of Oregon, et al. v. Smith,* No. 86-946 U.S. Supreme Court (April 27, 1988) 660-79/U.S. 872 (1990).

Erikson, E. H. (1975). *Life History and the Historical Movement.* New York, NY: Norton.

Finkelstein, N. (1990). The changing needs of today's addicted woman. *The Counselor,* 8, 21-23.

Fleischmann, G. (1971). *The Cherokee Removal, 1838.* New York, NY: Franklin Watts, Inc.

Forrest, W. (1956). *Trail of Tears.* New York, NY: Crown.

French, L. A., & Crowe, R. (Eds.) (1976). *The Wee Wish Tree: The Qualla Cherokees of North Carolina* (Special Issue), 5, 1-1-48.

French, L. A., & Hornbuckle, J. (1977). Cultural clash in our educational system. *Indian Historian,* 10, 33-39.

French, L. A., & Hornbuckle, J. (Eds.) (1981). *The Cherokee Perspective.* Boone, NC: Appalachian Consortium Press.

French, L. A. (1987). *Psychocultural Change and the American Indian.* New York, NY: Garland.

French, L. A. (1990). Substance abuse treatment among American Indian Children. *Alcoholism Treatment Quarterly,* 7, 63-76.

French, L. A. (1993). Adapting projective tests for minority children, *Psychological Reports,* 72:, 15-18.

French, L. A. (1994). *The Winds of Injustice.* New York, NY: Garland.

Furst, P. T. (1974). *Flesh of the Gods.* New York, NY: Praeger Publishing, Inc.

Garbarino, M. S. (1976). *Native American Heritage.* Boston, MA: Little, Brown & company.

Gearing, F. (1962). *Priests and Warriors.* Mesasha, WI: American Anthropological Association.

Goode, E. (1969). Marijuana and the politics of reality. *Journal of Health and Social Behavior,* 10, 83-94.

Goodluck, J. T., & Phillips, J. L. (1993). *Navajo Nation & Regional Areas Resource Directory.* Gallup, NM: Navajo Area Indian Health Services Report, 1-168.

Grobsmith, E. S. (1994) *Indians in Prison.* Lincoln, NE: University of Nebraska Press.

Grossman, H. J. (1983). *Classifications in Mental Retardation.* Washington, DC: American Association on Mental Deficiency, 137, 173.

Gulick, J. (1960). *Cherokees at the Crossroads.* Chapel Hill, NC: University of North Carolina Press.

Harris, D. B. (1963). *Goodenough-Harris Drawing Test Manual.* New York, NY: Harcourt Brace Jovanovich.

Hassrick, R. (1967). *The Sioux.* Norman, OK: University of Oklahoma Press.

Holder, P. (1970). *The Catawba Nation.* Athens, GA: University of Georgia Press.

Kluckhohn, C., & Leighton, D. (1946). *The Navajo.* Cambridge, MA: Harvard University Press.

*Larry P. v. Riles* (1972). 343 F. Supp 1306 (N.D. Cal). Preliminary Injunction.

*Larry P. v. Riles* (1984). No. 80-4027, (9th Cir., Jan. 23).

MacAvoy, J., Orr, S., & Sidles, C. (1993). The Raven Matrices and Navajo children. *Journal of American Indian Education, 33*, 32-44.

Mac Donald, P. (1978). *Navajo Tribal Code (Vols. 1-4).* Oxford, NH: Equity Publishing Corporation.

Mails, T. (1972). *Dog Soldiers, Bear Men and Buffalo Women.* Englewoods Cliffs, NJ: Prentice-Hall.

Malone, H. (1956). *Cherokees of the Old South.* Athens, GA: University of Georgia Press.

Mariano, L. J. (1994). Walk in Beauty of the Holistic View of the Navajo Nation Clan Systems within the Four Sacred Mountains. Paper presented at the *WNMU Indian Studies Seminar* (May 5th).

Maslow, A. H. (1968). *Toward a Psychology of Being (2nd Ed.)*. New York, NY: Van Nostrand Reinhold.

Maslow, A. H. (1970). *Motivation and Personality (2nd Ed.)*. New York, NY: Harper & Row.

Matthews, W. (1897). *Navajo Legends.* Boston, MA: Houghton Mifflin.

May, P. (1982). Substance abuse and American Indians. *International Journal of Addictions,* 17, 1185-1209.

Medicine, B. (1982). New roads to coping-Siouan sobriety. *New Directions in Prevention among American Indians and Alaska Native communities* (Manson, S. M., Ed.). Bestheda, MD: National Institute of Mental Health, 189-213.

Mooney, J. (1972). *Myths of the Cherokee and Sacred Formulas of the Cherokees.* Nashville, TN: Charles Elder Reprints.

Murray, H. A. (1971). *Thematic Apperception Test Manual.* Boston, MA: Harvard University Press.

Neihardt, J. G. (1961). *Black Elk Speaks.* New York, NY: Pocket Books.

NNTEC (1991). Statement of need, cultural barriers. *Navajo Nation Teacher Education Consortia Manual.* Window Rock, AZ: Ford Foundation & Navajo Nation.

Price, B. (1994). The criminologist and the Indian. *The Criminologist,* 19, 1, 4-5, 24.

Prucha, E. P. (1990) *Documents of United States Indian Policy.* Lincoln, NE: University of Nebraska Press.

Public Law 99-570 (1986). *Indian Alcohol and Substance Abuse Prevention and Treatment Act of 1986* (H.R. 5484) (October 27) 100 STAT 3207-0-133 (21 USC 801).

Public Law 101-630 (1990). *Indian Child Protection and Family Violence Prevention Act, Title IV* (25 USC 3210) (November 28).

Public Law 103-344. (1994). *American Indian Religious Freedom Act - Amendments of 1994.* H. R. 4230, 1-3.

Reid, J. P. (1970). *A Law of Blood.* New York, NY: New York University Press.

Reid, J. P. (1976). *A Better Kind of Hatchet.* University Park, PA: Pennsylvania State University Press.

Rhodes, R. (1989). Native American learning styles. *Journal of Navajo Education,* 7, 33-41.

Rights, D. (1974). *The American Indians of North Carolina.* Durham, NC: Duke University Press.

Rivers, P. C. (1994). *Alcohol and Human Behavior.* Englewood Cliffs, NJ: Prentice-Hall, Inc.

Schultz, D. (1990), *Theories of Personality.* Pacific Grove, CA: Brooks/Cole, 249-252.

Searles, D. M. (1994). Fake medicineman' scam the dying. *Cherokee One Feather,* 28, 1.

Sheehan, B. W. (1974). *Seeds of Extinction.* New York, NY: W. W. Norton.

Snake, R. (1976). Report on alcohol and drug abuse. *Task Force Eleven: Alcohol and Drug Abuse.* Washington, DC: U.S. Government Printing Office (77-466), 1-97.

S. Prt 101-60 (1989). *A New Federalism for American Indians* (101st Congress, 1st Session).

Standing Bear, L. (1975). *My People the Sioux.* Lincoln, NE: University of Nebraska Press.

Tempest, P. (1987). The physical, environmental and intellectual profile of fifth grade Navajo. *Journal of American Indian Education,* 27, 29-40.

Tempest, P., & Skipper, B. (1988). Norms for the Weschler Intelligence Scale for Children-Revised for Navajo Indians. *Diagnostique,* 13, 123-129.

Thomas, R. K. (1958). *Eastern Cahrokee Acculturation* (Master's Thesis). Chapel, NC: University of North Carolina.

Tonigan, R. F., & Platero, D. (1973). *11 Programs for strengthening Navajo Education.* Albuquerque, NM: Case-Modern Printing company.

U.S. Statutes at Large (1802). *Trade and Intercourse Act* (March 30) 2, 139-146.

U.S. Statutes at Large (1834). *Trade and Intercourse Act* (June 30), 4, 729-735.

U. S. Statutes at Large (1887). *General Allotment Act (Dawes Act).* (February 8), 24, 388-391.

U.S. Statutes at Large (1891). *Amendment to the Dawes Act* (February 28), 26, 794-796.

U.S. Statutes at Large (1893). *Commission to the Five Civilized Tribes (Dawes Commission).* (March 3), 27, 645-646.

U.S. Statutes at Large   (1898).   *Curtis Act.*   (June 28), 30, 497-498.

U.S. Statutes at Large   (1934a).   *Johnson-O'Malley Act.*   (April 16), 48, 596.

U.S. Statutes at Large   (1934b).   *Wheeler-Howard Act (Indian Reorganization Act).*   (June 18), 48, 984-988.

U.S. Statutes at Large   (1953a).   *House Concurrent Resolution 108.* (August 1), 67, B132.

U.S. Statutes at Large   (1953b).   *Public Law 280* (August 15), 67, 588-590.

U.S. Statutes at Large   (1977).   *Menominee Restoration Act* (December 22), 384 Federal Supplement 343, 406-407.
U.S. Statutes at Large   (1978).   *American Indian Religious Freedom Act* (August 11), 92 STAT. 3069-3078, 469-70.

Underhill, R.   (1956).   *The Navajos.*   Norman, OK:   University of Oklahoma Press.

Uterly, R. M.   (1963).   *The Last Days of the Sioux Nation.*   New Haven, CT:   Yale University Press.

Wax, M., & Wax, R.   (1972).   The enemies of the people. *Native Americans Today* (Bahr, H., et al., Eds.).   New York, NY:   Harper & Row.

Weiner, L., Morse, B., & Garrido, P.   (1989).   FAS/FAE: focusing prevention on women at risk.   *International Journal of Addictions,* 24, 385-395.

Welch, R.   (1994).   Cherokee AA convention.   *The Cherokee One Feather,* 28, 1-2.

Wood, B.   (1979).   The Mormons and Indian child placement -- is native culture being destroyed?   *Wassaja,* 7, 7-9.

Woodward, G. S. (1963). *The Cherokees.* Norman, OK:
    University of Oklahoma Press.

Young, T. J. (1988). Substance use and abuse among Native
    Americans. *Clinical Psychology Review,* 8, 125-135.

Zah, P. (1994). *President Peterson Zah Report to the Navajo
    People on the American Indian Religious Freedom
    Legislation* (October 29). Window Rock, AZ: Official Navajo
    Nation Publication, 1-8.

# Index